TAKEN BY THE WIND

TAKEN BY THE WIND

Memoir of a Sailor's
Voyage in a Bygone Era

MIKE JACKER

TALKING BIRD PRESS

Taken by the Wind: Memoir of a
Sailor's Voyage in a Bygone Era

Mike Jacker

Second edition, 2021

For rights and permissions, please contact:
Michael Jacker, Michael.Howard.Jacker@gmail.com

ISBN: 978-1-7360161-1-4

Interior design by Euan Monaghan
Map art by Beth Shadur

Photo of Dr. Frances Wright: CC BY-SA 4.0
Harvard University Archives

Contents

Author's Note vii

Prologue 1

1. Wanderlust 3
2. Louis 8
3. The Plan 13
4. Clark 19
5. List of Lists 21
6. Rhiannon 28
7. To the Gulf Coast 32
8. First Passage 43
9. Mexico 61
10. A Change of Plans 79
11. St. George's Caye Day 89
12. Gracias a Dios 102
13. In the Zone 110
14. Depression 136
15. Las Islas Encantadas 145
16. The Southeast Trades 170
17. The Marquesas 186
18. A Green Cloud 214
19. The Stowaway 224
20. Tahiti 229
21. The Cook Islands 252
22. Facing Reality 266
23. The Longest Passage 271

Epilogue 283

Glossary 287

Appendix 1: How Cruising Has Changed in the 21st Century 297
Appendix 2: Ignorance is Bliss (or the Importance of Good Luck) 300
Appendix 3: The Cal 2-30 302
Appendix 4: Checklists 304
Appendix 5: A Unique Celestial Fix 309
Appendix 6: Stowage Key 310

Author's Note

I WROTE THIS book as a personal memoir recounting the saga of a voyage to the South Pacific aboard a 30-foot sailboat named *Rhiannon* that took place in a bygone era. Long distance communication was slow and often impossible. Satellite navigation and offshore weather forecasting, as well as much of the other technology that permits safe and comfortable ocean passages today, simply did not exist. (See Appendix 1.)

It is the story of a lifelong friendship, of coming of age, and of the delicate balance between adventure, cautious preparation, and luck. Four and a half decades have now passed, granting me the perspective of time and experience. I have continued to own boats and sail throughout my life. A few years ago, in 2015, I once again sailed to the Marquesas with the advantage of 21st century technology. Looking back now, in 2020, affords me a greater appreciation of my journey in another age.

I reconstituted this narrative based upon my memories of past events. I attempted to tell my story truthfully, using both the clear details and the foggy impressions that remain in my mind. Photos and written records that still exist helped me to recall my experiences and feelings. I tried faithfully not to embellish or exaggerate; however, other people might recall some events differently. I intentionally changed a few names but kept the vast majority real. Inclusions and omissions in this book are purely the result of the limitations of my memory.

I wrote *Taken by the Wind* for readers from diverse backgrounds, including both seasoned sailors and those unfamiliar with sailboats and sailing. Rather than interrupt the story to explain technical details and terminology, I have included several appendices, as well as an extensive glossary of terms to assist the reader. The defined words and phrases are linked directly to their glossary entries in some eBook formats. Photographs and maps complement the text throughout the book.

Upon the advice of more experienced writers, I have tried to avoid using passive voice. The most conspicuous exception is the book's title. I specifically chose the words "taken by" because of their ambiguity. The reader may interpret these words to mean "conveyed by," "captured by," "attracted to or charmed by," or "cheated by." ... Perhaps they all apply.

I hope you enjoy reading my story.

Mike Jacker, November 2020

Prologue

Life is a dance. We listen to the music around us. We respond to the movements of our partners with complementary advances and retreats, leaps and turns. Sometimes we lead, sometimes we follow. When the music is unfamiliar, we improvise. We synthesize each new move based upon experience, intuition, and imagination. As the rhythm changes, we must adapt. But we must always keep moving, expanding our repertoire and redefining our goals.

Life is an adventure. Human nature drives us to pursue the unknown. That which is different may seem exotic and wondrous, or unpleasant and abhorrent. We are drawn toward new experiences, continuously seeking the balance between our internal demons and fears, and the innate desire to explore new horizons. The Schlitz beer commercial famously said, "You only go around once in life, so you've got to grab for all the gusto you can."

Life is determined by opportunity and fate. Some of us are fortunate to be born of privilege with a world of opportunities. Others are born in destitution with meager resources to face the world. All that anyone can do is maximize the possibilities of one's own circumstance. The choices we make for ourselves set our course as we each navigate the vicissitudes of life.

CHAPTER 1

Wanderlust

November 14, 1976 — I am cold, clammy, and nauseated. Rhiannon's once immaculate cabin has transformed overnight into a leaky den of black mold, dripping with condensation. The tiller is broken. Immense waves crash out of the darkness, relentlessly pounding the hull. In this gale we are hove to, drifting with unknown currents, unable to fix our position beneath the overcast sky. I dare not remove my homemade safety harness even as I lie exhausted in my berth trying desperately to fall asleep. How did I get here? And why?

THE ANSWERS BEGIN with my family.

From my father, Norbert Jacker, I inherited the "gene" for travel to remote and exotic places. While in the Army during World War II, my father was stationed in Morocco, as well as the Gold Coast (Ghana.) He spent considerable time off base exploring remote areas, frequently befriending locals. These experiences afflicted him with the bug for travelling off the beaten path. Growing up, I was exposed to my father's collection of old books pertaining to African exploration, National Geographic magazines, and foreign dinner guests arranged through the International Hospitality Society.

My father Norbert in North Africa in 1944

My mother, Lisette Jacker, grew up in France. As an orphaned Holocaust survivor who spent much of World War II in hiding, she always exhibited great courage and strength. Despite being uprooted from her family, she successfully forged a productive new life for herself in the United States. From my mother I learned that life can be precarious and how important it is to seize fleeting opportunities as they arise. Her balanced worldly perspective contributed immensely to my openness to new people and places.

My mother Lisette at age 14 in France with her younger sisters

Additionally, from the time I was quite young, my parents, my sister Anne, and I regularly attended the Saturday morning Edward Ayre lecture series at the Field Museum of Natural History in Chicago. These were travelogues, usually including slideshows or films. In the early 1960s, similar documentary programming was not yet available on television. (And, of course, there was no internet.) Several times, I watched with rapt fascination as Irving Johnson related incredible stories of adventure in places such as Pitcairn Island and the Sepik River in New Guinea, where he had sailed aboard *Yankee* during serial circumnavigations with his wife Exy and a crew of young men and women. I remember his dramatic film of vine diving, a male rite of passage on Pentecost Island in the New Hebrides (Vanuatu). On one occasion, Captain Johnson threw out to audience members some strange hand-carved toys collected on a remote Pacific Island. I caught one and have saved it over the years.

Another favorite speaker was William Albert Robinson. I credit him as being one of the most inspirational figures in my life. (Although I was always intrigued by his accomplishments, I must note that I have no respect for his prejudices or flagrant mistreatment of his wives and mistresses.) In 1931, Robinson completed a circumnavigation aboard *Svaap*, a 32-foot sloop. His voyage was documented in a bestselling book, *10,000 Leagues Over the Sea* (also known as *Deep Water and Shoal*). Later, after World War II, he settled in Tahiti and wrote several other books chronicling his Pacific Ocean journeys in *Svaap* and later passages aboard *Varua,* his schooner designed by W. Starling Burgess & L. Francis Herreshoff.

These Field Museum lectures exposed me to an amazing world of possibilities. The romance, adventure, and glimpses of a disappearing paradise left an indelible impression.

Through the 1960s, my father, a corporate attorney, was also the Assistant Secretary of Chicago Helicopter Airways, a company that flew a small fleet of Sikorsky S-55 and S-58 passenger helicopters between Midway Airport, O'Hare Field, and Meigs Field. As an airline officer in those days, he was able to obtain free tickets for our family on many carriers, including several international airlines. He was always somewhat concerned that these privileges might be lost if the word ever got out, so my sister and I were always sworn to secrecy about this lucrative benefit. However, my family did take advantage of it. As international airfares at that time were normally expensive, some people perceived us to be quite wealthy. At times we traveled in order to save money by visiting areas where food and lodging were cheap relative to our routine expenses at home. In 1959, when I was five years old and my sister was six, my family traveled through Europe and Israel. In 1962, we traveled through Southeast Asia and Japan.

In 1963, we experienced a more unique journey for that era when we traveled to Tahiti and Mo'orea in French Polynesia. To get there, we first flew to Honolulu. Once there, we boarded one of two Lockheed Super Constellations owned by South Pacific Air Lines, on its once-weekly 11-hour flight to Papeete, Tahiti. While in Tahiti, we stayed in a well-appointed thatched-roof bungalow at the Hotel Bel Air, right on the shore of the lagoon in Puna'auia, just outside of Papeete. The abandoned longboat used in the then-recent filming of the Marlon Brando version of *Mutiny on the Bounty* was on the beach immediately outside our bungalow. We bought fresh baguettes at the Chinese grocery store near our hotel. I remember very well the quay in downtown Papeete with a few weathered sailboats and small trading schooners moored along the peaceful tree-lined Boulevard Pomare. I watched as motor scooters driven by women with flowing black hair, wearing brightly colored pareus, motored past. The French nuclear testing in the Tuamotus had not yet even begun. Motu Uta was a small palm-fringed islet on the reef across from downtown. A few years later this would become a busy container ship port and cruise ship dock.

One evening, my parents went into Papeete to check out Quinn's Bar and the Whiskey A-Go-Go, while my sister and I stayed behind in the bungalow. As a curious Midwestern boy unfamiliar with coconuts, I tried to cut one open with a pocketknife, which, not surprisingly, closed on my pinky finger, creating a significant gash. I was more afraid of being reprimanded for playing with the knife than worried about the bleeding wound. I never ended up needing sutures, but I still have the scar to remind me of that mildly traumatic day.

My parents and sister Anne with me in Mo'orea in 1963

Visiting a vanilla plantation on Mo'orea and gliding over the magnificent colorful reef in a glass bottom boat proved magical for me at age nine. One day in Tahiti, touring in our rental car, my father decided to look up William Albert Robinson, who was living there. We had a chance to meet him at his home, together with his Tahitian daughters. I left Tahiti knowing that French Polynesia was rapidly changing. But I hoped that someday I might return.

On that same vacation, back in Hawaii, I wandered with my father through the Ala Wai Boat Harbor in Honolulu. At that age I was not yet a sailor, but I enjoyed walking along the docks looking at the boats. We came across a wooden trimaran with a very suntanned, sandy-bearded man working on the deck. My father began speaking with him, and we quickly learned that he had sailed from Tonga and Samoa and just recently arrived in Hawaii. He brought out two magnificent 8-by-12-foot handmade tapa cloths from Tonga, which my father offered to buy for $50. This sailor regaled us with stories of his ocean voyage in the small trimaran. He happily parted with the tapa cloths. Through the years, I have always used one of these tapas to decorate my bedroom, serving as an ever-present reminder of the South Pacific. In all our family journeys, my mother came along as a white-knuckle flyer and sometimes-reluctant participant in the more daring exploits.

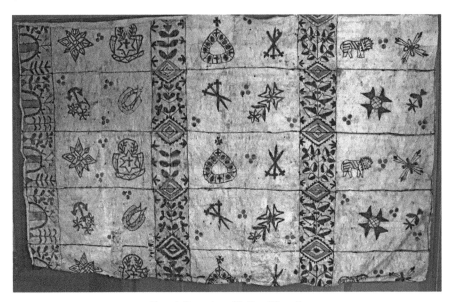

Tapa cloth purchased in Hawaii in 1963

I was no stranger to overland travel in the style of my father. Having this upbringing made backpacking through Europe while still in high school and other trips during college seem natural for me. My mother's siblings, my aunts and uncles who resided in France and Israel, provided comfortable supportive home bases for me as I traveled. At a relatively young age, I became well-versed in the exigencies of international travel.

I am aware that through the mere good fortune of my birth I was raised in the sheltered environment of a privileged white, upper middle-class American family. My upbringing prepared me to explore the world at large. Clearly, when an opportunity arose, I was primed to seize the opportunity. The stage had been set for something bigger.

CHAPTER 2

Louis

I FIRST MET Louis Gordon as a classmate in sixth grade when we were both 11 years old. I had just moved across town with my family and was new to Elm Place School in Highland Park, Illinois. As I recall, we were somewhat different in temperament. Louis, though usually very quiet, could be more volatile than me, occasionally losing his temper. I was only slightly more outgoing than Louis at that time. We quickly became friends and began sharing activities after school.

Most of the time, Louis would come over to my house. My family lived in an enormous old house for that first year of our friendship, between 1965 and 1966. The house was in disrepair and at times infested with rats. The ancient steam heating system never worked well. My father was attracted to the sprawling house. But my mother, being quite practical, convinced my father that we should move out after less than a year there. Louis and I always enjoyed playing in the house. Together, we scaled the ledges and lattices along the east side of the massive house in order to crawl in through an attic window with a faulty latch. We would time ourselves with a watch to see who could be fastest.

Camping with Louis and my father in 1966

8

We often rode our bicycles and explored our neighborhood and beyond. Once, we rode through the gates of Fort Sheridan, which at the time was the Fifth Army headquarters. No one stopped us so, we continued to the now defunct airstrip at the north end of the base. We rode our bicycles out onto the runway and looked around, just to see what was there. Without being noticed, we quickly pedaled off the base. Always pushing one another's curiosity, together we ventured where neither of us would have gone alone. We never got into trouble. Or perhaps I should say, we were never caught. Occasionally, something would strike both of us as funny, eliciting paralyzing fits of infectious laughter. This is something that has continued throughout our friendship.

Louis obligingly, though somewhat reluctantly, assisted me in the care of some of my pet reptiles, which included three caimans in a bathtub and a nine-foot boa constrictor named Longfellow. The snake ate live animals and sometimes required forced feeding necessitating two people. I, in turn, was introduced to sailing through Louis's father, Jim Gordon. Jim had been a sailor on Lake Michigan, participating in many Chicago to Mackinac Island races before World War II and owning his own keel boats into the 1950s. At the time I met him, he was not sailing on larger boats but had bought a 15-foot Albacore-class centerboard sloop to sail on Lake Michigan with Louis.

In the summer of 1967, Louis and I had many free afternoons during which we taught ourselves to sail. The two of us would go out onto Lake Michigan in the Albacore and experiment with all things possible on a sailboat. We sometimes removed the rudder to see if we could sail around a racecourse by balancing our weight, trimming the sails, and manipulating the centerboard. Sometimes we intentionally sailed backwards. On calmer days, we looked through the murky lake water in search of shipwrecks and lost treasure. Naturally, we ventured farther and farther from our home beach, as curiosity drove us to the limits of prudence. On Sundays, we raced at the local North Shore Yacht Club, Louis with his father and I as a pickup crew on other boats. The club was competitive, and we learned to sail well. We were among the very few local sailors to launch an Albacore into the surf of a Lake Michigan northeaster, to catch the face of a wave and fly back to shore at the knife edge of control. Knowing that the Albacore was designed by Uffa Fox to be sailed in the rough waters of the Solent, off the coast of England, we sensed that this boat would be capable of the 70 nautical mile (NM) sail across Lake Michigan. Despite our confidence, we also had enough sense never to try it. Neither of us had ever sailed offshore.

While in high school, Louis and I remained close friends. When I reached my 16th birthday, I got my driver's license, permitting me to tow a boat trailer. I was then able to buy an Albacore of my own along with another friend, Marty Thaler, as a partner. I had saved just enough money at that point from odd jobs and Bar Mitzvah gifts. My parents helped me out, as well. We bought a new boat at the minimum class weight limit, built by McGruer and Clark in Ontario. Louis and his father Jim quickly bought a new Albacore of their own, simply to remain competitive in our Sunday races. As competitors, Louis and I both finished at the top of our local club fleet. Jim stopped racing with Louis after an unpleasant capsize into the cold lake during a windy regatta. Louis continued racing with another crew. Encouraged by our local success, we decided to attend the Albacore Midwest championships, the Nationals, and once even the North Americans. As teenagers, Louis would trail his boat and I would trail mine to regattas in Chicago, Michigan, and Ontario. The trip to the Buffalo Canoe Club in Ridgeway, Ontario, for the Albacore North Americans was a weeklong caravan adventure with two cars, two boats, and a tent. At the regatta, we encountered 100 boats on the starting line. We each drove our boats forward utilizing our most aggressive strategic starts. Nonetheless, when the dust settled, we found ourselves near one another well toward the back of the pack.

During the winters, Louis and I played ping-pong in my basement a few afternoons a week, providing many hours for fanciful discussion. Our conversations would range from our own theories of psychology and affect, to questions of physics and engineering, solved through our debates. Today, of course, we would have jumped to the Internet for quick answers to our questions rather than struggling with hypotheticals and mental gymnastics to support our respective arguments. Nonetheless, our discussions led us down many fascinating paths as we refined our own unique practical approach to problem-solving.

One day, in the boating section of the second-floor stacks at the Highland Park Public Library, we came across the book *The 40-Knot Sailboat* by Bernard Smith. In 1969, sailing speed records of close to 30 knots were being set by C class catamarans. However, achieving 40 knots in a sailboat was pure science fiction. This book discussed the history of hydrofoil sailing and proposed designs for much faster sailboats with novel hydrofoil configurations. Of course, Louis and I were very intrigued. As had always been typical, we began to push one another toward something that neither of us would undertake on our own.

We conceived the notion of building a practical hydrofoil sailboat that perhaps could break a speed record, but more importantly, could become a racing class of sailboats that we might produce ourselves. When we spoke these words, we would burst into laughter. It seemed that this notion, though theoretically possible, was about as realistic for us as building a rocket to Mars. The challenge immediately sparked our enthusiasm. This is the subject for another book. Suffice it to say that we joined the Amateur Yacht Research Society in England and wrote away for their manuscripts relating to hydrofoil experimentation. We built a hydrofoil testing tank in the basement. We gained access to the nearly antique wind tunnel in a dusty, little-used Northwestern University engineering lab. And we pooled our $100 budget along with donated materials from friends to actually build a hydrofoil sailboat from scratch, over the course of two summers. Louis, Marty, and I cannibalized a rig from one of the Albacores and successfully foiled on Lake Michigan five years before the very first hydrofoil Moth was built in England by Frank Raison.

With Louis assembling hydrofoil laminates in 1971

With the inverted bow of our hydrofoil sailboat in 1971

Through college, I remained sporadically in touch with Louis. I studied biology at Harvard, while Louis majored in mathematics and swam competitively at Knox College in Galesburg, Illinois. I raced dinghies with the sailing team throughout college. Occasionally, Louis and I would get together during vacations, and our conversation would frequently turn to sailing. We both enjoyed reading magazines and books pertaining to sailing and were much attuned to news about long-distance sailing races and remarkable ocean passages. We had both read books of circumnavigations under sail by Chichester, Moitessier, Robinson, and others. We remained friends, always discussing and debating the workings of the world, able to pick up right where we had left off, even after months apart.

CHAPTER 3

The Plan

THE SUMMER OF 1975 was a time for decision. The peaceful country landscape of Lincoln, Massachusetts, not far from Walden Pond, provided the backdrop for my summer job as a research assistant for Professor Charlie Walcott. My work involved releasing and tracking homing pigeons in an ongoing quest to unlock the secrets of bird navigation. That summer, as I drove throughout the New England countryside to the pigeon release sites, I had ample time to contemplate my goals and direction in life. On my days off, I frequently drove to Salem, New Hampshire, where I learned to pilot a Schweitzer 2-33 sailplane. It would be an understatement to say that I was NOT eager to return to my final year of college and the unknown future that lay beyond. My course in life had been well plotted out up until that point, and it seemed that I was approaching a precipice, fearful of a wild fall. I had reached a crossroads.

Although I had considered becoming a research biologist when I entered college, my subsequent experiences in academic research had led me to reject this as a suitable career path. I enjoyed working with people and had decided to apply to medical school as an alternative. However, medical school also held little appeal during that summer, as alluring fantasies of travel and adventure were foremost in my thoughts. The Vietnam War had ended. Although I had registered with my local draft board on my eighteenth birthday, as required by law, I was never called to serve due to the high number my birth date had drawn in the draft lottery. And voluntary military service never enticed me.

At that time, I owned few material possessions and remained free of personal commitments or obligations. There were few obstacles to embarking upon an adventure immediately following graduation. I continued to read engaging stories of ocean passages under sail. Ramon Carlin had won the first Whitbread Round the World Race in a Swan 65 the previous year. As an avid small-boat sailor, long intrigued by tales of ocean journeys, I resolved that whatever effort it took, I would find a way to go to sea myself, within a year. In theory, this sounded great as a goal. The prospect of setting out to sea was less frightening than the option of attending graduate school.

Most people who know me have always assumed that I love to swim and play in the water. That could not be farther from the truth. At age four, I ran a high fever with the mumps. As instructed by our pediatrician, my mother repeatedly immersed me in a cold bath to bring down my fever. My fever broke. But I developed a particular aversion to cold water, and ever since then, I have hated swimming. When attending overnight camp in northern Wisconsin, I did everything possible to avoid swimming classes in the frigid lake, although I enjoyed the rowboats immensely. Being *on* the water for me was always separate from being *in* the water. I eventually learned to swim, out of necessity, as a requirement to graduate high school. However, I never have enjoyed the sensation of swimming in cool or cold water. And I have never been a strong swimmer.

In early September of 1975, I returned to Chicago, where I was visiting my parents before returning to college for my final year. While there, I met up with Louis, who also was unsure of his plans after college. He, too, had independently been toying with the notion of voyaging under sail. Our conspiring for adventure began in earnest once again. Following our old pattern, no project seemed impossible when the two of us made plans together. Although we had extensive experience racing sailing dinghies, neither of us had sailed offshore, dealt with currents, performed navigation, lived on a boat, or knew our propensities toward seasickness. As a reasonable goal, we aimed to set sail the following summer, in 1976. The plan was to pool our resources to make it happen. Many basic questions needed answering. Where would we get our boat? What kind of boat should we obtain? Where would we go? How much would the trip cost? For how long could we sail?

Following some quick calculations, we determined that we would need to have a boat by early spring to fully prepare her by summer. We discussed potential destinations before commencing our research. Quickly, we settled on making an Atlantic crossing our provisional goal, as the Atlantic Ocean would be most accessible to us. And intuitively the Atlantic felt less daunting than the Pacific.

At age 21, neither Louis nor I felt the need to run our nascent plan past our respective parents just yet. Our families always had granted us at least tacit approval and support for whatever projects we had undertaken in the past. Although they were not uniformly encouraging of all our activities, they generally allowed us to learn our own lessons through our independent pursuits. We selfishly reasoned that if our plans appeared thorough, we could spin the sailing trip to them in an advantageous way by minimizing the true hazards involved. As our fathers began to hear of the plan, they immediately became vicariously interested in the journey. After all, Jim Gordon was a lifelong sailor who had never sailed the oceans. And adventures that involve exotic travel had always captivated my father. Our mothers represented a different story. Naturally, they were fearful of losing their sons through unnecessary risks. Consequently, we resolved to make safety a priority and present our final plans in the most favorable light. We knew from experience that in the end, if we could put the trip together, we would eventually receive our mothers' blessings, as well.

So, we looked at each other and almost in unison said, "Let's find a boat!" We picked up the Yellow Pages and found the nearest boat yard in Chicago. Immediately, within minutes of concocting our plan, we headed off to see what boats were available. We had a limited budget. With only a few thousand dollars between us saved primarily from summer employment, we would need to procure a boat, modify or refurbish this boat as needed for an ocean crossing, obtain all the charts and gear necessary, and pay for all of our expenses. We figured that any seaworthy boat of sufficient size that we could purchase for under $5000 would most likely be a "project boat." In those days, the cheapest used boats were all wooden. A quick walk through a boat yard on the North Branch of the Chicago River informed us that a suitable boat would be extremely hard to find.

As our plan did not require actual possession of a boat until the spring, we remained undeterred. We focused our initial planning on all the other details involved in preparing for an extended voyage. After returning to our respective colleges, Louis and I communicated mostly by mail. We also sprung for the cost of occasional long-distance phone calls, which we kept affordably brief. (Long-distance calls were expensive, with charges accruing for each minute of a call.) In 1975, there were no guidelines or templates readily available for an endeavor such as we were planning. Neither Louis nor I personally knew anyone who had made a long voyage under sail who could serve as a consultant. In truth, we never sought out any individuals with personal experience because we feared possible discouragement that might derail our ambitious plan.

Only a few books about cruising voyages with any discussion of preparations existed at that time. Simply finding and procuring such books proved time-consuming. Additionally, the reliability of any single source was questionable. Therefore, we resorted to common sense, careful analysis, and thoughtful deliberations to cover any possible eventualities we could imagine. Years later, Secretary of Defense Donald Rumsfeld famously brought public attention to the concept of "known knowns, known unknowns, and unknown unknowns." We already knew many essential things from our reading. We also knew of many specific subjects that still required our study and mastery. But we both harbored unspoken fears, having descended deeply into the realm of "unknown unknowns."

With no complete model to study as an example for our plans, this lurking apprehension gnawed insidiously at our outward confidence. Never having cruised before, I continually felt that I might overlook one essential aspect of the preparation which might become blatantly obvious at some critical moment … when it would be too late. Perhaps we would be shipwrecked, lost overboard, or even thrown into a forsaken Third World prison due to an oversight in preparation. I could only continue forward by believing that safe and enjoyable cruising would be the eventual product of good sense, a level temperament, and thorough planning.

We soon investigated the weather patterns in the Atlantic and were disappointed to learn that the hurricane season corresponded with our earliest possible departure date. Equally foreboding were the cold Atlantic waters and Mediterranean gales in autumn. Without a boat, without a destination, and without the slightest oceangoing experience or knowledge of navigation, our proposed journey would have appeared outlandish even to hard-core daydreamers. As time passed that fall, Louis and I were becoming increasingly discouraged with each new revelation from our research. Nonetheless, we separately devoted our spare time to preparations, on paper, for what was still merely a fantasy.

In addition to seeking a boat, we divided up our initial roles to avoid redundancy. Louis compiled stowage lists from appendices in books and sailing journals. He learned about provisioning without refrigeration, critical spare parts, and anchoring. I was tasked with learning the essentials of navigation, weather, and safety equipment. At this time, some opportune good fortune finally appeared. Shortly after I had mailed an order to a maritime book club for a series of instructional books covering celestial navigation and coastal piloting, it became time for me to register for my fall courses at Harvard. Lo and behold, in the hidden depths of the ponderous course catalog, I stumbled upon a limited-enrollment seminar course, for credit, covering celestial and coastwise navigation. These were both essential skills to master. Before the advent of electronic navigation equipment, celestial navigation and traditional paper chart-based piloting represented the only means of determining one's position at sea. Naturally, I enrolled immediately in what proved to be the most essential and practical course that I have ever taken in school ... as well as the most memorable.

Dr. Frances Wright at that time was in her late 70s. She worked as an instructor and researcher at the Radcliffe Smithsonian Observatory. Teaching celestial navigation was her life's passion. Always a single woman, with no children of her own, Dr. Wright's students comprised her family. During World War II she had taught navigation to naval officers and ROTC students. She had written books on celestial navigation, as well as coastal piloting. Her course met at night in a cozy room on the top floor of the observatory, with easy access to the roof for sighting the stars and planets using sextants. Most evenings, she would bake fresh cookies for the handful of students in her class. A cheerful woman of short stature with an infectious cackling laugh, Dr. Wright enthusiastically read letters that she had received from her former students who were involved in expeditions to far-off places, including the Arctic North and tropical New Guinea. Needless to say, I studied every concept and applied myself intensely to all of the coursework, as if my life depended on it ... for I knew that someday soon, it might.

Frances Wright at Harvard University Observatory

Meanwhile, Louis traveled to the East Coast that fall in search of a boat to fulfill our needs. He and I both looked through Sunday newspaper classified ads and contacted boat yards. Louis visited yards around the Chesapeake Bay and together we investigated some boats in Rhode Island and Massachusetts. He rode a bus to Massachusetts where, together, we were shown all sorts of derelict and bizarre vessels close to our price range. These even included an old wooden boat that had once belonged to Burl Ives. She more closely resembled a miniature Noah's Ark than a sailboat capable of beating to windward at sea. Having met no success, Louis soon returned to the Midwest.

One cold Sunday morning in December of 1975, I found a new listing in the *Boston Globe* for a "30-foot steel ketch, fully equipped for ocean crossing, $8000." We thought our boat had finally appeared! I quickly made a phone call confirming that the boat had not yet been sold. I called Louis to relay the news and to decide what we should offer. I immediately made my way to the harbor south of Boston. When I arrived, I was greeted by the friendly well-weathered German gentleman who had skippered the stout little vessel on three transatlantic crossings. Unfortunately, I learned that moments earlier he had shaken hands with a man from California who claimed to have combed the entire West Coast before flying east to purchase this ketch. It was heartbreaking. Our time was running short to find a boat.

By January 1976, I had purchased and reviewed pilot charts of the world. These publications display the average wind direction, the average wind strength, and the likelihood of gales in each sector of the world's oceans for every month of the year. With this information alone, it was plain to see that a westbound Pacific crossing in the trade winds would be far more sensible than an eastbound crossing of the Atlantic during hurricane season. Accounts about sailing to the South Pacific that I had read, as well as memories of my visit to Tahiti as a child, made this route the obvious choice. Now, when people asked what I was planning to do after graduation, I could tell them nonchalantly that I was going to "sail to the South Pacific."

Most of my classmates had plans to attend law school or medical school, or to find work in finance or business. For me, continuing to graduate school and settling down in a profession at this juncture represented both a lost opportunity and total surrender to the inertia of blind conformity. My own plan was far more appealing. I knew this because of the reactions that I received whenever I related my unconventional intentions to people. Acquaintances older and wiser than I advised me that this sort of opportunity presents itself only "once in a lifetime." Most of my friends also thought that it was a great idea. Who would not want to do it? Nonetheless, as a backup plan, I did apply to medical schools with the intention of deferring my admission.

With no satisfactory, inexpensive boats to be found, Louis and I decided to change our strategy. We would invite a third partner to join in our adventure, which would allow us to consider buying a slightly more expensive boat. We reasoned that with a destination in the tropical Pacific and perhaps beyond, finding a third person to share expenses and round out our crew should be easy. I approached everyone I knew who might be able to pitch in financially and had a personality to complement Louis's and mine. Among my graduating classmates, several I approached were very intrigued. I listened carefully to the endless questions and unsolicited advice of friends who were variously appalled or envious. Whether they considered us crazy or brilliant, foolhardy or brave, everyone who caught wind of our plan was curious. "What will you eat? How much water will you bring? Will you carry guns? Does your boat have a motor? Do you have a radio? What will you do about sharks or aggressive whales? How will you navigate? How will you survive a storm? What can you do for appendicitis?" Unfortunately, as excited as some prospective crewmembers appeared to be, the requisite commitment generally proved too great. Thankfully, there was one classmate, Clark Pellett, who became more seriously interested. I said, "Clark, do you have any plans yet for next year? How would you like to sail to Tahiti?"

"Sure", he immediately replied. "That sounds great!"

The plan was on!

CHAPTER 4

Clark

CLARK GREW UP in Atlantic, Iowa, a rural totally landlocked community in southwestern Iowa. Back home he had been an academic and athletic star from a large, well-known, influential family in town. He had grown up in a farmhouse. His father, Paul Pellett, was an entrepreneur and among other things, owned a large regional liquid petroleum gas distribution business. Clark was physically much bigger than Louis or me. At 6'4" with a large frame, he played football for a while when he first arrived at Harvard. However, his major activity in college was organizing and managing the Model United Nations for high school students. This was a significant nationwide program that had consumed considerable amounts of his time.

In January 1976, given his enormous commitment to the Model UN and a rush to accumulate the course credits needed to graduate in the spring, Clark had not yet made definitive plans for the year following college. He was considering law school but was inclined to put that off a bit. He was thinking of travelling around the world. Clark was generally a calm and all-around good-natured, even-tempered guy, who got along well with almost everyone. He loved to laugh, which made him a pleasure to be around. He was a clear thinker and particularly good at solving practical problems. He was a natural leader when it came to dealing with other people, and he knew how to get things done. He was a member of a group of my friends living in Mather House, our dormitory during the last three years of college.

During college, Clark readily volunteered to lend a hand at political rallies and causes of importance to his friends. He was an asset as a non-Jewish advocate for Israel in support of his Jewish roommates. Once in Boston's North End, he got up to make a rousing public speech in support of Israel. But, most notably, Clark was a private person, generally reticent to voice his deepest personal feelings or inclinations. He attentively listened to the issues and problems of his friends, but none of us really knew Clark's inner thoughts. He was an enigma to many people. Although I was not among his closest friends during college, I had never heard anyone speak badly of Clark. He was physically strong and a quick study when it came to learning new skills. Based upon what I knew, Clark seemed like a great choice to round out our crew.

When I invited him to join in our emerging plan, Clark still had many over-whelming obligations before graduation. He saw this opportunity as a welcome light at the end of the tunnel and a perfect way to fill the void, putting off law school application or job-hunting. Although game for this adventure, Clark had never been aboard a sailboat, except perhaps once on his sister's fiancé's 27-foot Tumlaren in Chicago. Given his lack of sailing experience, I considered Clark to be the bravest among us. He could not have known what a sailing voyage might entail. Louis fully approved of my invitation to Clark. Our preparations could now begin in earnest.

CHAPTER 5

List of Lists

MY DREAM WAS now a reality. I would be on the "Louis and Clark Expedition" to the tropical South Pacific. Knowing that I would be the navigator, I felt a bit like an inexperienced reincarnation of Sacagawea, the Lemhi Shoshone guide of the historical Lewis and Clark Expedition. But how could we get to the South Pacific? Where was our boat?

By early spring, Louis raised the possibility of buying a six-year-old Cal 2-30 sailboat from his father, who was contemplating acquiring something different for himself. Transporting that boat from Chicago to the ocean would complicate our plan. Nonetheless, we decided that it would have to suffice as no boat had turned up on the East Coast. (See Appendix 3.) The Cal 2-30 is a stock 30-foot fiberglass sloop. It was designed for racing with a fin keel and spade rudder, rather than the full keel and protected rudder found on ocean cruising sailboats of that era. Crew accommodations and stowage space for cruising is adequate. The 2-30 has a reputation for being fairly stiff, handling heavy winds relatively comfortably for a responsive light displacement boat of its size. Being aware of the adage "A fast passage is a safe passage," Louis, Clark, and I agreed that she would be acceptable. Anyway, our time for finding a different vessel had nearly expired. We agreed on a price. Although we were unable to pay the full amount, Louis's father was incredibly supportive of our voyage plan and offered to allow us to pay the balance in the future when we had more money or eventually sold the boat.

We also rationalized that taking the boat down the Illinois and Mississippi rivers would itself be an epic adventure. The Tennessee-Tombigbee Waterway bypassing the final stretch of the Mississippi River en route to the Gulf of Mexico was still under construction; therefore, the entire trip from Chicago to New Orleans would need to be by river. The prospect of traveling down the Mississippi to the Gulf from our native Midwest evoked images of Huck Finn and paddle-wheeled steamboats. The notion of this extra dimension in our journey rekindled our enthusiasm for the arduous planning that lay ahead.

At this stage, none of us had answers to most of the questions we were being asked. I was not even sure how to find many of the answers. As questions arose, long "to-do" lists evolved. We compiled lists based on information that Louis and I had read about in books and formulated many more lists of our own.

These lists included essential modifications to the boat and her gear, additional subjects to be studied or researched prior to departure, items to be purchased, individuals and agencies to be contacted, and procedural checklists to keep aboard. Very soon, we had accumulated dozens of lists. Our tentative stowage roster alone, excluding food items, filled several typewritten pages. By late spring, we had even created a "list of lists" including emergency procedures, storm preparations, medical supplies, gear stowage, provisions, watch duties, maintenance checklists, expenses, books, navigational equipment and tables, addresses, etc. Some of the lists were finalized, typed, photocopied, and safely sealed in plastic to be taken to sea. (See Appendix 4.)

We even drew a diagram of all the compartments, drawers, and dead spaces aboard the boat with a coded key. We then began to create an alphabetized, comprehensive, cross-referenced list of almost all the individual items stowed, identifying their exact locations on the boat. (See Appendix 6.) I readily admit that we were a bit obsessive. The final stowage list contained 328 entries and resembled the merchandise index of a Sears, Roebuck & Co. catalog, despite our boat having no more space than a VW microbus. I am sure the meticulous organization served in large measure to reduce our anxieties. Nonetheless, we felt that the completeness was worth the effort.

One checklist that we created for "Port Entering Procedures" apparently unnecessarily warned us, in all capital letters, "REMEMBER TO GET DRESSED!" But we had no real notion of what our mental state would be upon reaching land after a long passage. We did not want to omit anything that might someday be important. I had vague recollections of reading about Joshua Slocum aboard *Spray,* and Robert Manry aboard *Tinkerbelle* hallucinating at sea. There were also speculative reports of Donald Crowhurst's suicidal insanity after falsifying his position aboard the trimaran, *Teignmouth Electron,* during the first single-handed round-the-world race. We simply did not want to take any chances. (See Appendix 4.)

With the assistance of four doctors, we listed precautions to be taken before departure, as well as schedules for taking the antimalarial drug, Chloroquine, while in endemic malarial regions. Clark took charge of provisioning our medicine chest. Most first-aid texts are based upon the assumption that professional medical help is nearby. For the sailor who is weeks from land, having prescription medications, including antibiotics and narcotic analgesics, with explicit instructions for proper use is indispensable. One essential book that we planned to take with us was *Advanced First Aid Afloat* by Peter Eastman, M.D., a surgeon, who lived aboard his Cal Cruising 46. (One year later we learned that Dr. Eastman unfortunately had run aground on the reef at Huahine in French Polynesia, not far from where we were at that time.) Shortly after his book arrived by mail in my dormitory, I read through it carefully. I took a bit of perverse pleasure in showing my dorm mates the chapter that included a graphic, step-by-step description of how to perform a limb amputation at sea ... using a hacksaw. It never bothered me much because I always imagined that if it ever came to an amputation, I would be the one holding the saw, not the one with the gangrenous leg.

Our research occasionally led us on some fun excursions. Given our land-locked Midwestern upbringing, none of us had a true understanding of the natural hazards of the deep. Coho salmon and lake trout were about all that Lake Michigan had to offer, though crayfish and tadpoles were more in line with our own first-hand experiences. So, on one rainy spring morning, Clark and I hopped on the MTA at Harvard Square and headed to the New England Aquarium in Boston. We slipped through a stairwell fire door leading behind the exhibition tanks and found the aquarium library. We searched the literature on poisonous and dangerous marine fauna and spoke with several of the curators. Predictably, the aquarium staff seemed more concerned with their ongoing Loch Ness Monster project than with our basic briefing on ocean life. We ended up watching some sand sharks circling in a tank of artificial coral, alongside a serene grinning sea turtle. Eventually, we left feeling at least a little more prepared to meet any menacing creatures potentially lurking beneath the salty blue waves.

Visas and cruising permits also required consideration far in advance of our voyage. By late spring, my mailman suspected that I was starting a smuggling network through a variety of obscure tropical countries. Eventually, by mail, I received information concerning official regulations and requirements to travel in Fiji, Tonga, the Cook Islands, French Polynesia, Ecuador, the Solomon Islands, Australia, and New Zealand. As a student of evolutionary biology, I was naturally fascinated by the Galapagos Islands. In general, private yachts were not permitted to enter the Galapagos Islands in the 1970s. I knew that very few exceptions were being made at that time. In March, I carefully followed the instructions from the Ecuadorian consulate in New York and applied directly, in Spanish, to the Commander General of the Ecuadorian Navy in Quito, Ecuador, for an entry permit. I never received a response. Accordingly, I devised several alternate plans to gain entry to the Galapagos. Scientific research was sometimes sanctioned. Therefore, I armed myself with an official-looking letter from a Harvard professor at the Museum of Comparative Zoology, in the hopes that this request to make certain specific ecological observations might later help us gain legal entry into one of the world's most spectacular biological refuges. This was the best I could do at the time.

Since all preparations required correspondence through the mail, considerably more time for preparation was needed in 1975 and 1976 than today. I ordered safety equipment, selected an assortment of gear to outfit the boat, and began procuring charts. Navigational charts were quite complex to obtain, as no comprehensive catalog of international charts existed. Before acquiring charts, we first had to decide which regions to include. Of necessity, without a definitive cruising plan, we needed to cover waters of the Gulf of Mexico, the Caribbean, Central America, the Galapagos Islands, French Polynesia, and the Pacific islands to the west. This even included Micronesia and Melanesia. Small-scale charts of large areas and detailed local charts would both be required. We anticipated that additional charts might be available later, in places such as New Orleans and Panama. The charts we requested and located were primarily British Admiralty charts, French charts, and United States government-issued charts. I was quite excited when I first examined nautical charts of remote islands with exotic names. Upon perusal of Pacific island charts, I noted with concern that many were based on Admiralty surveys completed in the 1700s. They occasionally included notations warning that the positions of certain islands might be inaccurate by as much as five nautical miles! Even more concerning, some charts highlighted areas far from land where "breaking waves with possible shoals" had been sighted from the deck of a ship decades earlier. Satellite-based surveys and Google Earth photographs were simply unimaginable fantasies in 1976.

One example of the bureaucracy we faced while still completing our senior year in college was our quest for a Panama Canal Tonnage Certificate. We learned that obtaining this certificate, necessary to transit the Panama Canal, would first require U.S. Coast Guard documentation of our vessel. After hiring an experienced professional for $50 to track down the title papers of previous owners and pay all the necessary government fees, we were placed on the mandatory three-month waiting list to receive our documentation. Following another four letters, two phone calls, and a trip to the Chicago Coast Guard office, we received an official registration number, but still no document. We were hoping to have our boat measured for the Panama Canal Tonnage Certificate while still in the United States. In theory, the policy stated that boats arriving at the Canal Zone with a Tonnage Certificate in hand would be exempt from the fee normally charged for being measured in Panama. Measurement by the Coast Guard in the United States was reportedly free of charge. However, the official admeasurer, who had sole authority to issue the Panama Canal Tonnage Certificate, needed to see the original registration document itself. Three long distance calls to the Coast Guard regional headquarters in St. Louis and one call to New Orleans confirmed this for us. We concluded that we would have to wait until we arrived in New Orleans to complete this process.

Louis and Clark tasked me with the navigational preparations. One balmy spring afternoon, I visited Robert E. White Instruments, Inc., at that time located on the Commercial Wharf in Boston. Browsing through this small traditional shop felt like visiting a museum of nautical history. The variety of polished brass chronometers, sextants, and taffrail logs neatly displayed in fine wooden cases was an impressive sight. The proprietor was a distinguished looking middle-aged man with graying hair. I was a kid with an unkempt Afro hairdo, wearing an old T-shirt. At first, Mr. White looked at me rather askance, but when I told him that I was there to purchase a sextant, he readily took interest. I had done my homework and knew the most reputable sextants by name. I received a thorough introduction from Mr. White to all the instruments necessary for the most precise navigation possible at that time.

I ended up buying a brand-new, all-brass, Heath 'Hezzanith" sextant, along with an assortment of single-handed dividers, navigational protractor triangles, a 1976 nautical almanac, and H.O. 249 reduction tables. This sextant, costing me $372.75, was one of the biggest purchases in my life. I had considered buying a taffrail log to stream behind the boat for measuring distance traveled through the water. However, I had read that the fish-like metal spinners of these taffrail logs were often grabbed by hungry sharks and lost. I resolved instead to install a mechanical sumlog attached through the hull of the boat. As for timekeeping, I learned that Louis's father had planned to give him a quartz chronometer in a wooden case, as a bon voyage gift. … With my mission accomplished, one more item could be checked off the list.

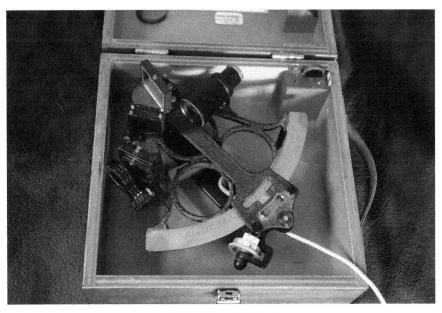

My Heath Hezzanith Sextant

Louis, Clark, and I were busy completing our respective final semesters in college. Due to our inadequate resources, we were forced to base many decisions upon insufficient information. We possessed a limited knowledge of electronics, and the boat's cabin was likely to be wet. Therefore, we elected not to invest in a shortwave radio transmitter. We did buy a portable Sony 10-band radio receiver, a first-generation 121.5 MHz emergency position indicating radio beacon (EPIRB), and some new crystals for the five-channel, crystal-tuned VHF/FM radio set already aboard the boat. A few "ham radio" friends from the college radio club tried to convince me to purchase some portable single-sideband gear for safety reasons. But I reasoned that in the event of an emergency, the electronics in our small, damp vessel likely would already be out of commission.

Some other concerned friends were astonished that we did not intend to carry firearms. A rifle could prove useful for hunting wild goats or for killing pirates at sea. But none of us had actual experience with guns, so we shied away from them, fearing potential accidents or quarrels, as well as stringent foreign entry regulations. I had lived in cities with some of the highest crime rates in the world without a gun and had never felt the need for one. I did understand that there were no police officers at sea. We would just plan to deal with pirates in some other manner. Louis and I concluded that Clark, at six foot four and quite husky, would prove better protection than any gun. As a final resort, we toyed with the notion of using our flare pistol to launch 16-gauge parachute flares into the belly of any would be Captain Kidd. Unfortunately, real-world piracy was a serious issue, not to be brushed off lightly. In 1975, near the coast of Columbia, several sailboats had gone missing with all crew lost. Speculation revolved around drug-trafficking outlaws who likely intercepted the boats offshore and commandeered them for illegal smuggling after summarily killing everyone aboard.

But all these decisions remained hypothetical. No single deliberation weighed too heavily upon me, for even then, I truly had not convinced myself that we would succeed in putting to sea. The preparations seemed more like a game, an exercise in virtual logistics. I was participating in a scheme so grandiose that the possibility of its realization sometimes frightened me more than the likelihood of its failure. I waited for some insurmountable obstacle to impede fulfillment of the dream. As the weeks passed, I paradoxically began to fear that our voyage might actually happen. It seemed illogical, improbable at best, that three total novices could have arrived so easily at this stage of preparation. Something was bound to fail. At some level I hoped it would. College commencement ceremonies that spring were replete with predictable speakers counseling various approaches to the challenges of life. I tried to envision how my plans might correlate with their advice. I saw clearly that this was the ideal time to earnestly embark upon a new path, far from academics. Following graduation, my commitment to the voyage became full-time. "All systems were GO."

By early summer, Louis, Clark, and I had determined that navigating down the hazard-filled Mississippi River for three weeks under auxiliary power presented the greatest potential impediment to our true goal of sailing to the South Pacific. To hasten our departure, we chose to transport the boat, located at Larsen Marine in Waukegan, Illinois, to Louisiana by truck. Through his father's business, Clark obtained access to a semi-trailer tractor and driver in Iowa. The truck had a "high-lowboy trailer" not designed for boat transport, and the driver had never moved a boat. The bed was one to two feet more elevated than that of a true lowboy flat-bed rig more suited to boat hauling. Following a few measurements and calculations, we concluded that it would work. The decision to forgo the river journey relieved us of considerable time pressure. The Atlantic hurricane season loomed ominously ahead, reaching full swing by August. Our naïve hope was to beat the storm season across the Gulf of Mexico. College was barely behind us ... And already we were far behind schedule.

CHAPTER 6

Rhiannon

AS I NOTED earlier, our boat was a seven-year-old Cal 2-30, built at the New Jersey factory of Jensen Marine in 1969. (See Appendix 3.) She had always been a freshwater vessel, sailed in Lake Michigan. The 2-30 is a little sister to the legendary Cal 40, which was a popular, fast racer that had achieved a great reputation on the West Coast as a "downwind sled" in the biennial Trans-Pacific Yacht Race (Transpac) from San Pedro, California, to Diamond Head, off Honolulu. The Cal 2-30, in contrast, is just over 30 feet in overall length with a draft of five feet. She has a low-aspect fin keel and a spade rudder with no skeg. Due to the extreme reverse transom, this boat looks fast, even while at anchor. The white hull with dark green trim was built with a heavy layup of solid fiberglass, as was typical in the 1960s. Unlike the California-built Cal 2-30s, our East Coast version included an encapsulated keel. This means that lead was poured into the forward three quarters of her hollow fiberglass keel, with a deep empty bilge sump occupying the after portion of the keel.

Her mast was aluminum with a 15/16 fractional head rig. Halyard winches were mast mounted and foresails were all hanked on. She was gasoline powered by a four-cylinder, 30 HP Universal Atomic 4 inboard engine. Our boat sported a two-blade Martec folding propeller. Though less than ideal for cruising, we could not afford a replacement prop. She came equipped with many sails including a mainsail, a 175% deck-sweeping Genoa jib, a 110% working jib, and a traditional light-air nylon spinnaker. Carrying a varied inventory of hanked-on jibs was essential. Without roller furling gear, changes in wind strength demanded sail changes to match the conditions. The main sheet led to a traveler across the stern rail. She was steered by a well-varnished, laminated wooden tiller. The side benches in the aft cockpit were long enough to accommodate sleeping on deck. Two commodious lazarettes for storage were accessible from the cockpit or the aft ends of the quarter berth. The cabin was arranged with two single quarter berth aft, a galley with a gimbaled two-burner pressurized-alcohol stove/oven along the starboard side of the cabin, and a C-shaped settee to port. A small marine head and hanging locker were located just forward of the main cabin. A V-berth occupied the forward cabin all the way to the forepeak. There was no anchor chain locker or windlass.

With the approval of Louis and Clark, I named her *Rhiannon*, the lyrical name of a notorious witch in Welsh mythology. Rhiannon, who was the wife of Pwyll and subsequently of Manawyddan, is said to have had three small birds whose song could revive the dead or kill the living. *Rhiannon* was also the name of one of my favorite Fleetwood Mac songs released the previous year. Unlike the three mythical birds, neither Louis, Clark, nor I could sing well, but I was always intrigued by the ambiguous yet somehow applicable lyrics of that song.

Throughout the month of June 1976, Clark was breaking his ties with land back in Iowa, while Louis and I readied the boat in Illinois. The Atlantic Ocean hurricane season lurked ominously ahead. To-do lists shortened rapidly, and items we had ordered by mail accumulated steadily until our departure date was in sight. The boat yard at Larsen Marine became deserted. The Lake Michigan sailors who store their boats in the yard for the winter had all launched their boats for the summer. *Rhiannon* sat conspicuously in her wooden cradle, high and dry, out of her element, while everyone else was taking advantage of the short Great Lakes sailing season. People often passed us in the boat yard as we worked away, wondering why we were waiting so long to launch our boat. One man cried up to us: "Hey! It looks like you boys are scared to put her into the lake. It seems that you've been working with that boat of yours hauled out all summer!" When we were brave, we would explain that we were preparing to bring our boat to New Orleans. If we were pressed, we sheepishly admitted to plans of sailing in the Caribbean. But the disbelieving chuckles rendered us totally incapable of confessing our audacious aspirations of reaching Tahiti.

We prioritized work that we deemed essential for offshore sailing. In a metal shop, I fabricated some enlarged cockpit drains, which we securely installed. We fashioned removable oak barricades for the companionway hatch, to be used in case of a storm. I drilled a hole through the rudder near its trailing edge, to accommodate a 3/8-inch rope that could be used for emergency steering. We painted the boat's bottom with a highly concentrated copper anti-fouling paint. Offshore, the marine toilet would be directly discharged into the ocean. Therefore, the unnecessary effluent holding tank came out, and a new Vetus collapsible-bladder drinking water tank made in Holland went into its place. With long passages of up to forty days anticipated and no equipment to desalinate seawater, we assiduously endeavored to maximize our potable water tankage.

We installed a VDO mechanical sumlog and even stowed a spare flexible cable for it. I painted *Rhiannon's* name on the transom. We packed away a collection of cable clamps and cables for emergency rigging repair. We installed spare halyards on the mast. Thus, if a halyard fouled or parted while at sea, we would not be forced to climb the mast amid the ocean waves. We fabricated mounts for the antique kerosene running lights given to us by Louis' father. From half-inch nylon rope and automotive seatbelt strapping we made three safety harnesses to secure ourselves to the boat. Louis and I devised a reel system in the V-berth for the large wooden spool of half-inch nylon to be used as anchor rode and Panama Canal transit dock lines. Unfortunately, none of the sleeping berths were long enough for Clark. We sawed an opening hatch into a nonstructural bulkhead to accommodate his feet. Knowing that we would be entirely self-sufficient with no possibility of outside assistance or supplies, we gradually accumulated spare parts and tools for all critical systems, cataloguing items as we stowed them. I completed the previously mentioned schematic diagram of every compartment, shelf, drawer and locker aboard *Rhiannon* and finalized the already growing stowage key, assigning a location to every catalogued item. That key would enable us to quickly find any of the hundreds of miscellaneous things tucked into every nook and cranny of the boat. (See Appendix 6.)

For several days, we sorted navigational charts of Pacific islands with unpronounceable names. Charts sprawled across the living room floor at Louis's parents' house. We pointed to remote islands, while enthusiastically discussing hypothetical sailing routes, as if the true distances were no greater than the dimensions of the charts themselves. We inspected our complete set of new international signal flags to be used to communicate with nearby vessels. One night, we tested our antique brass kerosene running lights in the garage. We then dipped 2000 blue-tipped matches individually into melted candle wax to protect them from moisture. To prevent cockroach infestation and loose paper floating in the bilge, we removed labels from hundreds of food cans and labeled them with a black marker. Eventually, we stowed the cans in any odd remaining nooks and bilge areas not already filled by gear. Even though our planned sailing date was at least a couple of weeks off, we visited a farm to get fresh, never-refrigerated chicken eggs, which we coated with Vaseline for longevity.

When it came time to consider a tender for ferrying ourselves ashore while at anchor, we realized that we no longer had any money in our budget. The only reputable dinghies at that time were made by Avon or Zodiac. Even their least expensive models were far beyond our price range. With little choice, we purchased two identical Sevylor inflatables, possibly more suited for use as toys in a swimming pool than as landing craft on rocky shores. We reasoned that if one inflatable failed, we would always have a second one to use while we patched the first.

Despite this frugality in dinghy purchasing, we spared no expense when it came to a life raft. We had specifically set aside money for this critical purchase. In our research we had discovered that only one company, Lloyd's of London, was underwriting cruising boat insurance policies. The price of a cruising policy was greater than the entire cost of our boat. But this was moot because many particulars of our circumstances rendered us completely ineligible for insurance. The life raft was our only insurance policy. No, it could not pay for loss of the boat; but at least it would help to ensure our safety. After comparing literature from multiple life raft companies, we ordered a C.J. Elliot 6-man, self-inflating model in a canister. It came fully stocked with solar stills, fish-hooks, and a survival kit. On the day it was delivered, a huge white 18-wheeler semi-trailer pulled onto the residential street where Louis's parents lived. We hauled the raft from the street into the basement. For a short time, we simply stared in awe at the raft's shiny white plastic canister. This was both our biggest single expenditure and an extremely critical piece of equipment. Unfortunately, it had been hermetically sealed at the factory, so that we could not even peek inside the opaque canister to confirm that our raft and survival gear had indeed been packed inside. We simply needed to trust C.J. Elliot.

As we closed in on our departure, we completed a myriad of other prepa-rations. We needed to round out our sail inventory with heavy-weather sails to be used in high winds and perhaps in a storm. We enlisted a sailmaker to add a third reef to the mainsail and to triple stitch our sails for strength. We even ordered a brand-new, heavy Dacron storm jib, including pennants at the head and tack, made exactly to our specifications. I was impressed when the sail arrived in its immaculate bright red sail bag. The growing collection of custom-ized new equipment lent a satisfying air of legitimacy to our budding expedition.

Rhiannon was ready.

CHAPTER 7

To the Gulf Coast

IT WAS LATE July and already two named tropical storms were menacingly churning across the Atlantic. I said goodbye to my parents in the morning and headed to Waukegan. At that time, I was so preoccupied with our imminent departure that I now have no recollection of the farewells or what was said. I knew that my mother was worried but that my father, who enthusiastically supported the voyage, would reassure her along the way. My father even hoped to join us for a week or two if we ever made it to the South Pacific.

Rhiannon loaded on the truck. I am with Clark, Antoine, and Louis.

The "high-lowboy" rig driven by George Snow, a longtime employee of Clark's father Paul, pulled into Larsen Marine in Waukegan. Clark, Paul, and Antoine, a French foreign exchange student who had been living with Clark's family in Iowa, all arrived in Clark's father's sedan. On that morning, the marine travelift loaded our fully stocked sailboat onto the trailer. We removed the bow and stern pulpits and attempted to measure the ground clearance of the highest point of the cabin trunk as accurately as possible. Using a long wooden pole and a tape measure, we variously came up with 13'7", 13'3" and other similar numbers. Along the planned "oversized load route" to Louisiana, the nominal maximum truck height was 13 feet. Though somewhat leery of ramming into an overpass and shearing off the deck house, we decided that there was no choice. We would have to proceed anyway.

Approaching an overpass

Hitting the road just before noon, we made it to a motel in Effingham, Illinois by sunset. Some viaducts on the interstate were labeled 13'3". George slowed the truck to a crawl and moved his rig to the center, straddling two lanes of traffic while shooting for the point of maximum clearance. We had visions of deflating the truck tires in order to get through. Viewed from the trailing car, it appeared that we cleared some overpasses with only an inch to spare, though it may actually have been two inches.

Two days later, we reached southern Louisiana. In a boating magazine, I had seen an advertisement for a boat yard in Slidell, Louisiana, that welcomed transients and offered good prices. I had phoned ahead to Bayou Liberty Marina. I had asked them a few questions and advised them of our anticipated arrival date. They assured me that they could offload the truck, launch the boat, step

the mast, and allow us a week or so in the yard to work on *Rhiannon*, if necessary. When we reached the small back roads leading to the marina, a Sheriff's
deputy pulled the truck over. As northern boys, being stopped by a southern
sheriff just short of our goal caused some palpitations. Fortunately, the officer
was well-intentioned and gave us a welcoming police escort for the final five
miles, leading us to the somewhat obscure boat yard.

Our time at Bayou Liberty Marina was notable for three things. For one, it
was blazing hot. We had lots to do to prepare *Rhiannon* for launching, but it was
exhausting simply standing outside, sweltering beneath the fierce sun, for more
than a few minutes at a time. Accommodating to the heat took us days. The
second remarkable thing was that for the first time we encountered people who
had lived through hurricanes. They all spoke of these dangerous storms with
appropriate reverence and trepidation. Since the hurricane season had already
begun, these encounters did woefully little for our confidence. The third thing
that made an impression was meeting a middle-aged gentleman named Tex.

Tex was working full time on his 45-foot, full-keeled ketch that was also
on the hard, directly across from us in the small boat yard. He told us that he
had been working on his boat for about two years and hoped to launch her in
another year or so to begin a cruise in the Caribbean, and perhaps beyond.
Just watching him for the few days that we were there, it appeared to us that he
would never reach the point where his boat might meet his stringent criteria
for being fully seaworthy.

Although we knew that *Rhiannon* was far less outfitted than his boat, it
was nonetheless satisfying to tell him that we would be leaving imminently
for the South Pacific. This was the point that I first realized a fundamental
truth regarding cruising: one is never completely prepared to leave. At some
point, you must simply find your weather window and head to sea as you are.
Otherwise, you may never untie the lines. (Note that I use the term "weather
window" quite loosely, since we were preparing to depart at the height of the
Atlantic and Caribbean hurricane season.)

We soon celebrated our launching by dropping the "Wide Load" sign from
Rhiannon's transom and sharing a bottle of champagne with the few friends
and family who had accompanied us. For good luck, we stepped the mast over
a copper penny fastened by silicone caulk to the mast step, so that it would not
rattle around. As everyone else departed, Louis, Clark and I moved aboard.
Once the engine was running, we paid our yard bill and left the marina through
the snaking channel leading into eastern Lake Pontchartrain. Our first trip,
mostly under power, took us across the lake to New Orleans, where we tied up
at the Southern Yacht Club's guest dock.

At the yacht club, a charming middle-aged southern woman, Mrs. James,
served as a delightful hostess, taking a motherly interest in the "three northern

boys" beginning their adventure. On the afternoon of our arrival, she was making up a flier in the lobby of the yacht club.

Our launching ceremony at Bayou Liberty Marina

With Clark installing the kerosene running light holders in New Orleans

Sunset at the Southern Yacht Club, New Orleans

She asked, "Any y'all good at ought?"

I initially felt like saying, "I ain't good at naught." However, Louis promptly asked her twice to repeat her question, in order to decipher her drawl. I soon realized that she was actually saying "Any y'all good at art?" Somehow, she thought that I was acknowledging in the affirmative. Unfortunately, I cannot draw worth a damn. Nonetheless, I drew for her my best "Bilge Queen" on a sailboat with an SYC burgee. Fortunately, it worked out okay. In return, she offered us assistance and transportation for any of our business in New Orleans. Some mornings she even fed us breakfast in the yacht club dining room. We remained in New Orleans for about a week. The three of us had to complete boat projects, finish provisioning, acquire charts, and finalize paperwork before we could leave.

We finally obtained our United States Coast Guard registration document. We then arranged a visit from a Coast Guard admeasurer to provide us with a Panama Canal tonnage certificate. Apparently, an obscure, seldom-utilized regulation we had discovered permitted offsite measurement conforming to the unique Panama Canal measurement rules. This represented the first time the New Orleans Coast Guard station had provided this service for a yacht. Even more unusual was another document we obtained called a "Deratting Exemption Certificate." I had read that some countries require all entering vessels to undergo a deratting procedure, to ensure that diseased rodents are not imported by entering ships. Remarkably, in 1976, few if any countries had rules for private vessels or small sailboats that differed in any way from laws pertaining to giant freighters, tankers, or ocean liners. The inspector never even examined our boat. He simply laughed and summarily issued the certificate, which we tucked away in a plastic Ziploc bag along with all our other important papers.

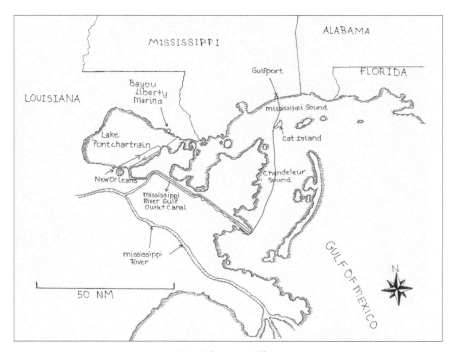

New Orleans to Gulfport

Our next goal was a shakedown cruise east to Gulfport, Mississippi. This seemed a reasonable target for a one-day trip. We wanted to touch land once more in order to complete any tasks we might have overlooked. The charts indicated that the best way to get out of Lake Pontchartrain into the Gulf of Mexico would be to sail 15 miles back east to the far end of the lake, go through the south railroad causeway swing bridge, and then follow the short channels through the bayous out into the Gulf. We had hoped to get out into open water during daylight and perhaps even reach Gulfport by nightfall. Our shakedown sail in Lake Pontchartrain was a glorious one-tack beat across the lake. Clark stood up on the foredeck enjoying his first real sail but complained of queasiness despite the near perfect conditions. Louis and I were worried. Ironically, we later learned that in rougher seas, Clark would be the only one aboard immune to seasickness.

Shakedown sail on Lake Ponchartrain

As we approached the swing bridge before noon, we signaled for the bridge to open, but nothing happened. After a few radio calls to some nearby boats, we learned that the bridge was out of commission on that day. This necessitated retracing our tracks. Late in the afternoon we reached downtown New Orleans, where we waited to pass through the Seabrook bascule bridge to enter the ship canal. Our charts indicated a long path following the main channel of the Mississippi River-Gulf Outlet, which eventually led out to the open Gulf waters. We doused our sails and proceeded under power at about four knots. As we left the city, the canals became straight trenches, barely wide enough for a single tugboat pushing its massive barges. To each side of the canal lay swampy shallow marshland with tall reeds that obscured any visibility beyond the confines of the canal itself.

As darkness fell, we lit our port and starboard kerosene running lamps. We continued slowly forward using moonlight supplemented by a handheld flashlight to help us remain centered within the unlit channel. Based upon our slow progress, we became resigned to motoring through the canal all night. Our engine stopped twice. We unintentionally ran aground into soft mud three times. Once we even needed to throw off a kedge anchor, as we rocked the boat to get free. Though nervous and tired, we all remained hyper-alert while navigating through this eerie tunnel of darkness. We constantly reassured one another to maintain confidence that we would eventually emerge from the bayous.

That all changed quickly when a faint, deep thumping sound approaching from behind became steadily louder, accompanied by a blinding spotlight. Clearly, this was a tugboat pushing barges, which occupied the entire width of the canal. As it relentlessly approached, the thumping morphed into the grinding roar of huge diesel engines. The bright searchlight on the bridge alternately shifted its beam from shore to shore. This scenario was truly reminiscent of Huck Finn on his raft being run down by a riverboat. We had only minutes to devise a way to save ourselves. All three of us envisioned diving for our lives into the canal, as our new home was smashed and overrun by an oblivious tugboat captain. It now seemed inevitable that we would never make it to the sea. Clark revved the engine to full throttle, but outrunning the enormous barge, whose oncoming white bow wave was now both audible and visible proved futile. Our only hope was to head for one side of the channel.

We deliberately drove *Rhiannon* blindly into the wall of reeds to port, quickly running aground in the muck on the margin of the canal. We lassoed a mangrove to pull the stern away from the channel. The wandering searchlight immediately blinded all three of us, as it found us standing on the deck, awaiting our fate. Tug and tow plowed on at full speed with the front barge slightly clipping the reeds on the far side of the channel. We bounced in the mud as the bow wave passed, the entire rig missing us by no more than a few feet. We managed to back out of the mud and clear the vegetation off the deck without resorting to a kedge anchor. Fortunately, the submerged debris in the water did not clog our engine's cooling water intake and the prop never became fouled. Though psychologically traumatized, we continued into the night physically intact. As the sun rose, we reached the open water of Chandeleur Sound where several tugs with their tows passed us with ease. We ate breakfast while we motored down the well-buoyed channel into the harbor at Gulfport, Mississippi.

The waterfront at Gulfport remained a partial wasteland, not yet fully rebuilt after the complete devastation caused by Hurricane Camille, seven years earlier. We tied up to the wall of the large open basin. Later that day, we made a shopping run to the hardware store for a few neglected items and topped off our gasoline tank before all three of us went to sleep early.

Even without alarm clocks, crowing roosters, or loud noises to break the stillness, Louis, Clark, and I were all awake and milling about the cabin nervously with first the rays of dawn. I hopped silently off *Rhiannon's* deck, bar of soap and towel in hand, to wash my face in the icy water from the spigot near the Gulfport harbormaster's office. Following a deliberate pause to listen to some songbirds and the rumble of early morning traffic on the far side of the basin, I glanced at the factory smoke to check for telltale signs of a breeze. It was still calm. ... But that presented no problem. For at that hour calm air signified little.

A tugboat pushing barges passing us in Chandeleur Sound

This was to be our day of departure, August 11, 1976. Our agenda was simple: swing ship both under power and under sail to formulate compass error deviation tables and then head for sea on the first morning zephyrs. The magnetic compass was our primary navigational instrument. Inherent errors caused by metal aboard the boat interfering with the compass' magnetic needle must either be corrected with small magnets or noted on a chart that is easily visible while steering. An error of a few degrees over several days can result in missing a target landfall by many miles. Verifying that our compass' deviation was precisely known was crucial before heading offshore.

I walked back out to *Rhiannon* on the planked wooden dock, just as the sun on my back rose over the treetops into a cloudless morning sky. Tied up just astern of *Rhiannon* was another sailboat, a 20-foot pocket cruiser manned by her solitary crew, Captain Robert Jensen, the jovial, portly master of the Panama Canal Company's steamship, *SS Cristobal.* Captain Jensen was enjoying his vacation, doing what he loves most, both at work and at leisure: sailing in the Gulf of Mexico.

"Beautiful morning, Captain," I called, as I approached his tidy fiberglass boat.

"Would you like some coffee?" He offered, raising the steaming mug in his hand.

"No thanks," I politely declined. "I'm afraid we've got a few things to attend to. We shove off for Panama as soon as we complete our compass deviation tables."

"Well then, I will see you boys in Panama. Look me up at the Panama Canal Yacht Club. ... Bob Jensen, from the *SS Cristobal.*"

As far as he was concerned, we would be snugly moored in Cristobal harbor in a matter of weeks. After all the dire warnings we had received concerning August cyclones in the Caribbean, I still had trouble imagining that we would *ever* safely arrive in Panama, let alone meet Captain Jensen again. Nonetheless, I was tremendously heartened by the confident words of a sea captain who grew up on the Danish coast and was now a ship's master aboard the only regularly scheduled steamship running between New Orleans and the Panama Canal Zone. These were *his* waters we would traverse. We hoped Captain Jensen's confidence in us would prove auspicious.

Captain Robert Jensen (photo courtesy of S. McDurmond)

I continued my path along the dock and stepped onto *Rhiannon*'s deck, sending out concentric ripples over the slick calm harbor surface. Clark walked over to have a few words with the captain himself.

Meanwhile, Louis sat on the cabin top staring intently across the basin. After a deliberate delay, he wheeled in place, looked me squarely in the eyes, and broke the morning's silence:

"What d'ya think?"

"Not much wind." I quipped rhetorically.

Ignoring my useless appraisal, Louis immediately answered his own question. "I think we should swing ship, then set sail. The longer we wait, the worse it's gonna get," he said, referring to the hurricane season, which weighed heavily in our minds.

With sudden impulsive resolution, I replied: "Okay, you start the bilge blower; I'll get the dock lines. ... Let's get the hell out of here!"

Clark jumped aboard. Using a homemade shadow pin pelorus to take bearings on the sun, we carefully swung ship. In this maneuver we used the azimuth (bearing) of the sun, based upon the nautical almanac, as a reference to determine true compass directions from which we could derive our compass error. Just as we finished, a light breeze came up. Clark entered the Greenwich Mean Time and all the relevant navigational information into our official logbook. While sailing at approximately one knot up the channel leaving Gulfport's harbor, Captain Jensen overtook us under power. With a final farewell wave, he turned eastward toward Alabama. We had untied the lines. Our real journey would now begin.

CHAPTER 8

First Passage

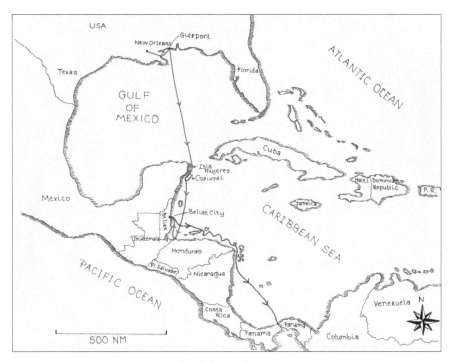

New Orleans to Panama

RHIANNON'S ATOMIC-4 GASOLINE auxiliary engine provided only a 90-mile range in calm weather with our initial full fuel supply. Under power, she could move at six knots using full throttle without adverse current or large waves. But a reasonable motoring speed was four knots. Considering that our background consisted of sailing small boats without engines, we were inclined to motor only in emergencies. We needed to conserve the fuel we carried. We also needed to run the engine regularly for short periods to charge the two 12-volt lead-acid batteries. One battery, the house battery, powered our cabin lights, depth sounder, and VHF-FM radio. We used the second battery primarily to start the engine, though we also had a hand crank.

Under sail, *Rhiannon* could make six knots in favorable conditions and

43

potentially surf down waves in brief bursts up to eight knots. However, we anticipated her average speed to be four knots and often much slower in light winds. Our first intended destination en route to the Panama Canal was Isla Mujeres, Mexico, 565 NM away. This is a small island off the northeast coast of the Yucatán peninsula at the western edge of the Yucatán Channel between Mexico and Cuba.

We devised a cowardly and unseamanlike strategy for crossing the Gulf of Mexico. I will freely admit that we never had any delusions of being either brave or seamen. While in New Orleans, we had bought detailed charts of the entire Gulf Coast, paying special attention to Florida. Although the Yucatán Channel lies almost due south of Gulfport, Mississippi, we intended to sail eastward, skirting the Alabama and Florida coasts, but always remaining approximately 100 nautical miles offshore. This path would later take us westward along the north shore of Cuba, but outside of Cuban territorial waters. Our thought was that if a hurricane threatened, we would duck into a harbor and at least save ourselves, if not the boat as well. We formulated this scheme while Hurricane Belle was already closing in on the eastern seaboard of the United States. Although American yachts were excluded from Cuban waters in 1976, none of us would have hesitated to seek shelter there if extreme weather developed.

We eventually abandoned this entire plan for two reasons. Firstly, the Gulf produced mostly southeast wind, and secondly, our engine quickly proved to be unreliable. In the prevailing southeast wind, we could not sail directly into the wind to skirt the Florida coast. Therefore, we took the offshore port tack, which was a direct course toward Isla Mujeres. After about two days, when we learned that our position was closer to the Cuban coast than to the Florida Keys, we decided to "make a break for it" and cross the Gulf of Mexico directly. In reality, none of us had truly wished to do otherwise, so we accepted the southeast wind with gratitude, as a favorable sign. Yes, we were becoming a bit superstitious, as is customary for sailors. Just as carrying an umbrella prevents rain on a cloudy day, bringing the unnecessary charts of Florida helped to assure us that no hurricane would strike.

Despite exceptionally light air on the first day, we cleared the Mississippi Sound and Cat Island under full sail, losing sight of land at dusk. At under three knots, we slowly wallowed along southward throughout our first starry night in the Gulf. Flashing lightning on the northern horizon signaled the presence of local thunderstorms onshore. The Mobile, Alabama, weather report that we picked up on the radio confirmed the presence of very heavy thunderstorms all along the coast. Fortuitously, none were forecast for our location offshore.

The first light of dawn on the second day revealed an amazing sight. The clear sky was studded with building cumulus clouds, hardly straying from their positions of formation. A few puffy clouds had mushy gray bellies and were dumping their contents as concentrated columns of rain. One cloud was already nearly overhead as it appeared with the daylight. As the cloud overtook us, the wind precipitously increased from zero to a gentle ten knots. Anticipating a more significant squall, we proactively reefed the mainsail. The ragged down-draft visible on the front edge of the cloud seemed to warn us of an impending blow. However, as the rainsquall passed, none of the expected wind materialized. The fleeting moderate wind quickly dissipated to an oily calm in the cloud's wake.

Birds visiting us in the Gulf of Mexico

The calm weather that ensued after the brief squall persisted throughout the following week. Nevertheless, these first days at sea left an indelible impression upon me. The serenity of our vast personal circle of dark blue water fusing with the azure dome of the sky along the horizon was incomparable to any experience on land. This peaceful ring of water, stretching only to the horizon five miles away, constituted our entire world. This circle glided imperceptibly around the globe along with the boat, rendering meaningless all notions of distance or time. Occasionally, a ship would transiently enter our circular world and then quickly disappear over a different quadrant of our horizon. The deep blue hue of the water, the passing schools of fish, the small sharks off the stern with their remoras, and the dolphins surfacing amid floating kelp and jellyfish all lent a mildly animated yet ethereal quality to the calm.

A calm spell in the Gulf of Mexico

Aboard *Rhiannon*, we maintained several logbooks to document our voyage. We kept a traditional ship's navigational logbook, with entries made four times daily and upon significant course changes. That log was shared by all three

A stationary towering cloud with localized rain

of us. Entries included Greenwich Mean Time, magnetic heading, boat speed, sumlog reading, sky cover, wind speed, wind direction, barometer reading, air temperature, sea state, and "remarks." A blank page was also available for longer comments about unusual occurrences. This logbook sporadically included our latitude and longitude. Position information was always carefully recorded on the plotting sheet or nautical chart currently in use. Additionally, we each kept our own personal logbooks, essentially diaries with entries of varying length, written at random intervals. In my personal log on Friday, August 13, 1976, I entered:

The dream lifts only upon the occasional sightings of oil platforms, flotsam, and passing ships. We have not yet settled into any sort of routine. So, the practical aspects of the trip take care of themselves. Laundry, dishes, cooking, and washing ourselves all get done in due time. And surprisingly, the boat is not deteriorating as I had anticipated. Our freshwater is lasting well despite the wicked heat and lack of wind. Sails slat furiously with the rolling swell. When we drop the sails, the halyards and wires inside the hollow aluminum spar clang even louder.

We lost the jib halyard yesterday afternoon and Louis went up the mast in our bosun's chair to retrieve it before dark.

Calm air and persistent swells make us all nervous about getting out of the Gulf before we meet a hurricane. When the wind blows, though, we are all in great spirits... Easy sailing, a beautiful sea, and nobody is seasick! Clark is becoming a good sailor. Having just cooked a delicious cheese, onion, and green pepper omelet, he is also a fine chef.

I would never claim that sailing in the Gulf of Mexico aboard *Rhiannon* was entirely enjoyable or entirely frightening. Before departing I had no experience at sea aboard a small vessel. I had not even considered that sailing might affect my demeanor. I discovered that my mood swings were often abrupt and extreme, in marked contrast to my normally stable disposition. Each morning, I awoke slightly disoriented and afraid, as minor problems and concerns became magnified far beyond their true importance. Tension was heightened after discovering anew the reality of my situation: I had not slept in a secure bed on dry land but was actually adrift in a 30-foot-long plastic shell, out of touch with civilization, medical assistance, repair facilities, fresh food, and a cool shelter.

During these first days at sea, the slightest provocation would start the adrenaline flowing. Immediately, we suspected any "fishing boats" entering our personal realm on the horizon of being either pirate vessels or unfriendly Cuban gunboats. I was not alone in my moods. Both of my crewmates shared my slight morning paranoia. We would all huddle intently around the portable shortwave receiver to hear the latest reports of tropical depressions in the

Caribbean and Gulf of Mexico. We were children tiptoeing in the dark, waiting for some boogeyman to jump out at us. A slight change in the period of the rolling southeast swells would easily heighten our anxiety. One sunny morning, a sonic boom even sent us scrambling on deck, fearing a dismasting.

A page from our navigational logbook

Each day, however, the placid solitude and tranquil sailing reversed the morning's tensions, soothing our troubled minds. The extent of the mood reversal was directly proportional to *Rhiannon*'s progress toward Mexico. By the fifth day, our newest concern became the greasy salt air grime that caked our bodies and converted our clothing to slimy rags. We descriptively named the greasy salt coating we had acquired as "grungoid." Accordingly, this region of the ocean became known to us as "Grungoid City." Adding further to this unpleasant corrosive grunge was the mound of salt crystals spilled onto the galley stove and cabin floor by a ruptured soggy carton of Morton's table salt. With each passing day without a freshwater bath, this proliferating brownish sludge worsened.

In the hot ocean air, our first solution was to dispense with our clothes. We became nudists out of practical necessity, for we dared not deplete our precious freshwater tanks to wash either our bodies or our clothing. We kept the potable water in multiple containers, in case one or two of the reservoirs ever became contaminated. Our water was divided between the 40-gallon built-in tank, the expandable 20-gallon bladder that we had installed, and three additional 5-gallon Reliance collapsible clear plastic containers. Our intent was to replenish the original supply by catching rain whenever possible.

Henceforth, either the rain or the sea provided our bathwater. Though we had seen sharks near the boat, we felt compelled to dive into the Gulf of Mexico at least a couple of times for a refreshing dip. After swimming only 20 yards from our becalmed craft, we looked back toward her. She appeared to be a miniature – a toy boat lost in a pool of infinite proportions. Inspecting her keel with a dive mask from the warm transparent waters below, I was frightened by *Rhiannon*'s tenuous grasp of the sea. While on deck, I had maintained the delusion that the lead keel was firmly rooted in the depths of the water. This impression was quickly destroyed when I saw that her minuscule five-foot-deep fin keel barely nicked the skin of a boundless underwater universe. The boat seemed precariously suspended high above an unfathomable, dark abyss.

As these oppressive days passed, a daily weather pattern emerged. The light morning Gulf breeze would later take a mid-day siesta, leaving us becalmed in a mirror-like sea during the hottest part of the day. Immense, towering cumulonimbus clouds grew steadily from small powder puffs, eventually encircling us. The billowing columns were awesome to watch. However, day after day, neither their wind nor their water would reach us. We watched them dissipate, belching forth all their distilled rainwater precisely where they had formed. We watched this repeating cycle as nearby developing clouds spilled their torrents and broke apart, while a clear blue patch of sky overhead was allowing the glaring sun to parch us mercilessly. Each impressive cycle required no more than an hour to complete.

Despite our most determined efforts to maneuver *Rhiannon* beneath the growing rain clouds, they consistently evaded us. Twice, the cascade of fresh clean water fell noisily only a few hundred yards off, without even affording us shade from the baking sun. Finally, on our sixth day out, when the reflections of the clouds in the glassy water were more distinct than we had yet seen, we noticed a cloud building almost directly above us. In disbelief, we watched as rain spilled forth and once again landed on all sides but not upon us. We had cleared the deck in anticipation, bringing out empty buckets and clean funnels to collect drinking water from the rain running off the sails. All three of us began screaming in a mad rage at the elusive deluge parked only 20 yards off our bow. We could clearly hear the rain hissing and roaring wastefully into the salty Gulf.

After a few minutes of this torture, we finally drifted into the welcome overdue shower, crying out and dancing with delight. A slight wind was blowing in this rainsquall enabling us to sail in circles and remain in the rain for what seemed like an hour. We each lathered up, rinsed off, and enjoyed a cool refreshing drink. A small, harmless waterspout kicked up 100 yards abeam of us, just after we penetrated the limits of the cloudburst. We barely had steerage way when this amazing little demon began dancing mysteriously toward us … a whirling dervish, which was both amusing and ominously menacing. We passed within about 40 feet of its core, then slowly it moved away. I ran to the mast instinctively, ready to free the halyards and drop the sails should we get into the whirlwind's path. But it veered away as unpredictably as it had arrived. Freed from this threat, we played and splashed like puppies until we were almost frozen. Louis ducked below and boiled some of the freshly caught water to make hot cocoa. No sooner had we finished the delicious treat than we found ourselves once again in the sweltering heat, back in Grungoid City.

Small fish were almost always swimming in the boat's shadow. Larger fish frequently joined them. During the first few days we had seen some fishing vessels, though they no longer appeared once we were well offshore. We made a few attempts to catch fish with a heavy line and a variety of lures, but our efforts were fruitless.

Our food was not great. In the light winds and stifling heat, cooking became a chore. To achieve an actual cooking flame, we had to pump the pressurized alcohol stove with a hand pump and then prime each burner for several minutes. The alcohol tended to surge as it flowed, causing frequent large flare-ups of flame in the cabin. Unfortunately, the transparent alcohol flame was often invisible in the sunlight, creating a serious risk of cabin fire. Consequently, part of the cooking routine was to place a large bucket full of seawater near the stove whenever we cooked. We usually consumed two hot meals and one cold meal daily. The cooked meals generally included macaroni or a mixture of canned vegetables, tuna, or meat. We often ate Chef Boy-ar-dee Italian food heated on the stove or directly from the can. We considered a can of sliced pineapple to be a delicacy. Eggs and potatoes lasted well through our first passage.

An interesting trend began in the Gulf of Mexico and continued throughout each of *Rhiannon*'s longer passages. We consistently covered more distance sailing at night when the winds were steadier than we did during daylight hours. This observation, which we confirmed later by auditing our navigational log, contradicted both my intuition and my expectation based upon cruising accounts I had read. Nevertheless, these conditions necessitated efficient sailing throughout the night to maximize our progress. Accordingly, we adopted a three-hours-on, six-hours-off watch system from dusk through mid-morning. With no autopilot or self-steering system, the man on duty steered continuously throughout his watch. The two crewmen off watch were called up on deck only to help shorten sail for a squall or to confirm the course of a sighted vessel.

An encounter with a large ship was alarming if it appeared to be on a collision course. Its crew was unlikely to be aware of our presence and possibly would never even notice a crash that could instantly send *Rhiannon* to the bottom. Once, a colossal supertanker, lit up like a Christmas tree, passed close enough that the churning drone of her engines reverberated through *Rhiannon*'s hull. Nothing matched the gargantuan proportions and power of that vessel passing in the night, not even the monstrous container ships we later encountered in Panama. Another oil tanker that passed us very closely was the *M/V Dauntless Colocotronis*. We later learned that this ship was devastated by a well-publicized grounding and fire on the Mississippi River near New Orleans in 1977, the year after our encounter. When no ships were in sight, the only diversions during night watches were frequent lightning storms, leaping dolphins, and the fairy dust blue-green glitter of bioluminescence trailing in our wake.

Dolphins frequently joined us

I came to dread the wake-up call for my watch, which invariably arrived long before I felt rested. "Mike ... Mike ... Your watch." That irritating, emphatic whisper penetrated the damp, dark cabin air over the rhythmic splash of our bow wave. A mechanical zombie, still half asleep, I would grope my way through the companionway and stagger to the stern pulpit to urinate. Louis or Clark would then update the situation vis-à-vis ships, squalls, compass heading, and wind direction, if we were fortunate enough to have any wind at all. When there was no wind, I would line up three upholstered cushions from the dinette along the cockpit seat, and crawl beneath a blanket leaving one arm outstretched to rest limply upon the tiller. Gazing at the stars directly overhead or at the blinking lightning within a nearby cloud made it simple to remain on course in zero-to-five knot winds. If the wind freshened or if a ship's navigation lights popped up over the horizon, it became easier to stay awake, staring ahead transfixed as *Rhiannon* rushed into the darkness. On overcast nights, I would experience the claustrophobic sensation of riding in a subway car in a narrow tunnel. It would feel as if the boat were confined to a subterranean passage, speeding over a bumpy track, leaving behind a trail of phosphorescent sparks.

Whatever the conditions, the night hours would pass in restless half-sleep until I leaned through the companionway myself to summon the next crewman for his watch. Flashlight in one hand, with one knee propped against a galley drawer, I would check the barometer, then scrawl my entry into the navigational log. Next, before climbing back into my berth, I would habitually fumble for my green plastic mug, which was suspended from its brass cup hook on the starboard side of the cabin. After quenching my thirst by dribbling a half cup full of plasticized water from the collapsible camping jug beneath the dinette into my mug and drinking it, I could resume my slumber.

Sweltering heat, ship traffic at night, and morning angst were far from the worst issues during our first open-seas passage. On August 18, one week after leaving Gulfport, a series of calamities arose. We all knew that a bad day was coming even before it began. The spinnaker had wrapped itself around the forestay into a nasty hourglass at dusk on the 17th, foreshadowing the bad luck. Clark and I had finally managed to lower the tangled red and white chute that evening without having to go aloft. But the next day we were leery of flying the spinnaker despite the downwind sailing conditions. The following account is taken from my log entry on August 18, 1976:

Louis tried to put the jib out with the telescoping whiskerpole early in the morning. Unfortunately, the lightweight aluminum pole jackknifed when the first puff hit us. We had to break off one end of the pole.

A squall came up in mid-afternoon and our problems began in earnest. As the whitecapped waves grew, I went forward to drop the jib, which had been winged out on the spinnaker pole to port. As I quickly dropped the #3 working jib in the 25 knot gusts, Louis screamed to me frantically from the cockpit: "Stop! The forestay's broken! ... Is the forestay broken?!" I looked above me, and holy shit! It was swinging free. I had no winch handle with me at the mast, so I immediately raised the wire luffed working jib back up the farthest I could by hand. The white Dacron sail flogged furiously with deafening staccato reports. - - Clark bore the boat off the wind immediately to relieve any aft-directed pressure on the rig, as I cursorily surveyed the damage. When I saw that the turnbuckle at the tack fitting had actually snapped, I feared that with no forestay our mast would soon be knocked overboard. I shouted to Louis over the cracking sail and strengthening winds: "Should we try to call for help with the emergency beacon?"

I figured that the mast was about to go over the side. Also, not having heard a recent weather forecast, I imagined the approaching cloud system rapidly stretching its wispy sinuous tentacles across the top of the clear sky to be the first leg of a tropical storm. I then yelled back to Louis: "Is there a spare forestay turnbuckle?"

"Yes, in the spares!" Louis reassuringly replied referring to our meager spare parts locker.

In a few moments, Louis appeared on the foredeck bringing forward a spare turn-buckle. As I set to work installing it, Louis informed me that of all eight turnbuckles in the rigging the forestay's was the only one of a larger size...and the only one for which we carried a replacement.

This near dismasting in only moderate winds struck a blow to our confidence in *Rhiannon*'s ability to weather offshore sailing conditions. We worried that there would be a hurricane in the Gulf and now also worried that the rigging was insufficient to withstand even moderate strain. Being exhausted from a nearly sleepless night of lightning and rain squalls, we opted at this point to run under storm jib before the freshening northeast wind. Sailing slightly under-canvassed would enable us to ascertain the cause of the rigging failure. And, if a storm was indeed coming, this was a good opportunity to test this specially made, triple-stitched sail, which we had only seen once out of its bag, in Louis's parents' house.

As Louis pushed the bright red bag containing the pristine new storm jib up through the forehatch, the boat unexpectedly lurched, tossing the sail bag overboard into the waves. With no headsail and only a reefed main up, Clark was unable to sail back to windward where the scarlet bag floated several yards upwind on the surface. I had to physically restrain Louis to prevent him from impulsively diving into the whitecapped waves to retrieve the sail: I certainly did not want to lose Louis as well. Since the sail bag remained afloat, we tried to start the engine. Though the bilge blower worked and the starter motor cranked strongly, the engine itself refused to start. With no engine, no storm jib, an untrustworthy rig, building seas, and a falling barometer, all we could do was watch in desperation as the sail bag slowly slipped down and disappeared under a threatening sky. Despite the waves, we could see its red glow sinking far beneath the surface of the remarkably clear water. *Rhiannon* simply bobbed and rolled, mourning her loss.

Even as the welcome fresh breeze broke our spell of discouraging calm weather, Louis, Clark, and I found ourselves no better-off in spirit. The advent of stronger wind combined with the untimely failure of our engine and the loss of our storm jib seemed to create an ominous warning of impending bad weather. In reality, the dropping barometer and changing weather conditions merely signaled our departure from the huge high-pressure zone that had parked over the Gulf of Mexico throughout the preceding week. Nonetheless, this provided the perfect opportunity for me to review the material that we carried on board describing Caribbean hurricanes and tropical cyclones. Informed by my read-ing, I carefully timed the great swells marching in from the northeast to check for indications of an advancing hurricane. Observing that the swells arrived at regular intervals of under five seconds, I reassuringly told Louis and Clark that there was no cause for concern.

At dusk, we set up the portable 10-band receiver on deck and tuned-in to the shortwave storm forecast for the Caribbean and Gulf of Mexico. We braced ourselves for bad news. We had just passed the halfway mark, putting us closer to our destination, Isla Mujeres, than to any other port of refuge. We had reached the point of no return. Each of us felt certain that some new random disaster would yet arise to thwart our progress. We knew that if a storm was to be our downfall, we would surely hear of it on that evening's broadcast. Louis, Clark, and I huddled around the radio in nervous silence, as Louis raised the aerial and fingered the tiny knobs to adjust the frequency. The faintly audible weather bulletin discussed a third hurricane, whose name sounded to me like "Carol," as well as a new tropical storm, "Dottie," which clearly had been the source of our northeast swells.

Each of us separately noted what we had heard. We concurred on Dottie's announced position. The storm was centered at 24° N, 80° W, within the Gulf of Mexico, while our position was 23° 30' N, 87° W. We were easily within one day's striking distance of her fury. The maximum sustained winds were clocked at 50 knots, with 15-foot-high waves reported. Dottie had not yet reached the 60-knot threshold to attain official hurricane status. We continued listening so intently to the static crackling in the salty night air that we easily heard words that were not even spoken. The expressionless announcer began: "The storm is moving ..." Then his voice abruptly faded into an irritating burst of static, precisely when he began to report the speed and direction of Dottie's progress. Terrified, we each thought we had heard a different variation of "South," "North," "Southeast," or "Southwest." I completely lost any remaining delusion of our immunity to Mother Nature. I sensed that she might find us yet, in the rough currents of the Yucatán Channel. Fortunately, the storm had turned north and never approached our position.

Despite the misfortunes and apprehensions dominating my thoughts, by the end of our first week at sea, in most respects I had become habituated to the new lifestyle. The morning blues persisted, but they became tempered by two newly found coping mechanisms: a strong sense of superstition and a silent search for privacy. Like my "bipolar" mood fluctuations, the superstition and the silence represented a marked contrast to my prior personality ashore.

It is well known that sailors traditionally have held many superstitious beliefs, which are abundantly documented in the literature of the sea. Certain birds and fish bring good luck, while others portend calamity. Some practices are to be avoided, such as renaming a vessel, having a woman aboard, or tying a double half-hitch knot on the date of departure. Many other things bring good fortune, such as stepping the mast on a copper coin, sighting a rainbow, or leaving port in fair weather. Scores of well-known superstitions were adopted and modified by the three of us into invented omens of a similar nature. For example, the small land bird that flew out to our boat and died while onboard was a clear harbinger of ill fate. Ordinarily, the favorable or frightening quality of an omen is self-evident. For example, the presence of a shark or a giant ray forewarns of disaster, whereas the sighting of dolphin or a school of tuna heralds good sailing. The death of a dolphin, on the other hand, would be extremely bad, a sure sign of impending catastrophe.

Conveniently, when I needed a sign to either lift my spirits or confirm my fears, I could conjure one as necessary. For instance, an equivocal symbol, such as a rain shower, calm winds, or a red sky may be interpreted as either bad or good, depending upon what was demanded by the situation. At times, I found myself resorting to this world of fatalistic determinism because the stress of total self-dependence led to a continual need for some foreknowledge of events. Faith and confidence were certainly prerequisites for this voyage, but alone they conferred no predictability concerning the course of daily events. On land, relying upon superstition seems irrational and nonproductive. However, at sea it provided a sense of order, which was both inescapable and satisfying.

Silence as a means of escape was the second coping mechanism shared by all three of us in the Gulf of Mexico. Before our departure I had felt close to both Clark and Louis but had rarely engaged in any deep personal discussions with either of them. During the months of June and July, while I worked intensively with Louis to prepare the boat, the provisions, and the paperwork, our interactions were pleasurable though generally businesslike. We reserved talking about personal sagas, philosophy, and politics for the forthcoming journey. We had anticipated that long periods of monotony would be ideal for heavier conversations.

Although we rapidly grew closer in our mutual trust and understanding of one another, revealing tête-à-têtes were avoided at sea as a means of preserving our only truly private refuge ... our intimate thoughts. Living for extended periods without clothing and without physical partitions in the single cabin of our 30-foot world left our minds as the only remaining sanctuaries of our individuality. We fulfilled our needs to express inner sentiments with a pen and paper, in our haphazardly maintained personal logbooks. Periodically, Louis, Clark, and I recounted funny stories and adventures, but the intimacy of communication never matched the closeness of quarters aboard our vessel. Curiously, boredom never set in, as we each remained busy simply by eating, steering, navigating, sleeping, and absorbing the previously unimagined marvels of the sea.

We played another game to elevate our spirits and improve the morale aboard. Like rats in a Skinner box, we rewarded ourselves for a satisfactory day's progress or nice weather by eating a good meal or some special food. Single-handed sailors are well-known for their personal incentive programs. Sir Francis Chichester would drink to celebrate a birthday, a halfway point in a passage, or a daily speed record. Sir Robin Knox-Johnston would prepare gourmet food to help him get through the rough sailing in the Southern Ocean. Aboard *Rhiannon*, though, we only dared to celebrate in this manner when we felt assured of a safely completed passage.

Crossing the Gulf of Mexico provided me the first true opportunity to apply the celestial navigation techniques I had previously practiced only on dry land. Initially, sextant observations were elementary, because the calm seas provided a good horizon and a stable platform from which to "shoot" the sun. To gain experience, and to teach Louis and Clark the reduction techniques, I deliberately tried to take moon, planet, and star sights, as well. Although some of the plotted lines yielded implausible erroneous positions, each day I made fewer mistakes.

When our progress had moved us onto the chart named "the Yucatán Channel and Approaches," I felt that we had almost arrived in Mexico. To supplement our celestial lines of position, I used our radio direction finder (RDF) to get a bearing on the Cabo San Antonio, Cuba, radio beacon, whose Morse code identifier beeped sharply through its speaker. When this radio bearing corroborated both our dead-reckoning estimated position and our running celestial fix, we knew for the first time with certainty that we were indeed on course. We celebrated reaching the Yucatán Channel. On the balmy evening of August 20, we enjoyed a feast of salami and cheese in the cockpit. We shared jokes and listened to Cuban music well into the night. The next big event was to be our first landfall, a new experience for all three of us.

On August 21, I took several more sights than usual, attempting to verify and update our position. Following our little party, we had a night of poor sailing and probably made only a few miles of progress from our evening position. The adverse current and choppy seas were conspiring to impede our arrival. With dawn, we were once again racked with fear of a storm because of a new southeast swell, mare's tail cirrus clouds, and unexpectedly erratic barometer readings. In contrast, the evening of August 20 had been so peaceful and relaxing that we felt as if we had already arrived in Isla Mujeres. Then, on August 21 we were once again confronted with the reality of the difficult slog ahead.

Fortunately, the wind picked up, and we bombed along through the steepest waves we had yet encountered. Despite the blue sky and hot sun, we had become too lazy to rig our makeshift sun awning. The erratic motion compounded by our anxiety had gotten to all of us. We were queasy. With little appetite, none of us ate breakfast. I remained at the helm all morning as the wind steadily freshened. After making two tentative sail changes, we arrived at our 175% Genoa jib and a full main as the optimal combination for the conditions. With that canvas, we made six to eight knots all day. A midmorning sun sight followed by a running fix at noon revealed excellent progress against the current. The Cabo San Antonio beacon and depth soundings over the coastal shelf both reassuringly confirmed the accuracy of our celestial fix.

Finally, by midafternoon, I took an additional sun shot. After a hurried reduction and plot, I found that we were only five nautical miles northeast of Isla Contoy, a small Mexican island which serves as a bird sanctuary, located just off the tip of the Yucatán Peninsula. I called to Clark, who was already up on deck. He immediately spotted trees and a tower poking out above the hazy horizon to the southwest. Land was right where it should have been! We were elated about the perfect landfall, our first sighting of land since Mississippi, 10 days earlier. Naturally, I was tremendously relieved by the precision of my previously untested navigational skills. In this current era of GPS, the satisfaction derived from accurate celestial navigation in 1976 is probably difficult to understand. We were exactly where we wanted to be, 28 nautical miles north of the entrance to Isla Mujeres, still charging southward at over six knots.

Though it proved futile, Clark cleaned the carburetor, checked the spark plugs, and cleared the fuel lines in a final attempt to start our recalcitrant engine. As the engine stubbornly refused to do its work, we began preparation to enter the unfamiliar port under sail. This planning posed no problem, for we had a detailed chart of the island and were most confident in *Rhiannon*'s superb maneuverability under sail.

As we raced the fading daylight toward our destination, our thoughts turned toward cold drinks and freshwater to wash the caked salt grime off the boat and our grungy bodies. A sudden change in the late afternoon weather caught us off-guard as we had no access to any local weather forecasts. Ferocious looking, gray squalls suddenly materialized both abeam to port and ahead of us. Black columns of rain streaked down into the churned-up seas. As we continued sprinting to the south, a great man-o-war frigate bird circled high above us, its sharp swept-back wings distinctly silhouetted against the graying sky. All three of us eyed a building rainsquall moving in off the port bow. Just then, a giant manta ray heaved itself high into the air then quickly dropped its shadowy 12-foot mass onto the surface of the water with a shuddering belly flop. The powerful crash raised a tower of spume beneath the approaching cloud. Our excitement rapidly diminished as the prospect of attaining safe anchorage by evening faded.

Unfortunately, darkness was almost upon us when we finally sighted the steep cliffs of Isla Mujeres carving their outline against the fading red glow of twilight. Utilizing our two detailed charts and the latest issue of the American *Sailing Directions*, we devised a plan for sailing into the anchorage at night.

However, as darkness fell, the crucial navigation beacons on shore did not illuminate as indicated on the charts. Two important lights were missing altogether, while a third, critical "group flashing every five seconds" light appeared to be located at the wrong end of the four-mile-long island. There was a "flashing eight-second" light where we determined the five-second light should have been. In short, there was no agreement between the charts and what we observed.

A late afternoon squall in the Yucatan Channel

With no visibility in the dark, we dared not approach the dangerous shore too closely. Crashing surf pounded the rocks at the base of the unlit cliffs. Twice, we attempted cautious approaches but conservatively turned back. Should our conclusion that the navigational lights were mis-charted prove incorrect, we might be dashed uncontrollably onto the rocks by foaming breakers, with no reasonable hope of sailing off.

A violent electrical storm ensued, bringing fluky winds and steep confused seas, running against the stiff two to-three-knot northbound current. All three of us were utterly exhausted by the excitement and tension of this long eventful day. Fitful sleep and the anxiety during the preceding two nights, combined with the disappointment of seeing the land yet not being able to go near, were too much to handle. We decided to stand offshore until morning. As the thunderstorm continued, the seas became increasingly dreadful. The spidery mats of lightning in the clouds and the purplish daggers extending to the water thundered around us with alarming frequency. Since Clark had slept all morning, he was able to stand the first watch, while Louis and I slept below. We carried only our working jib, a sail just sufficient in size to maintain our position off the island. Without a steadying mainsail, *Rhiannon* rolled and pitched erratically.

When I returned to the cockpit for my watch, it was 2:15 a.m., time to head back toward the coast in the agitated water. Before long, a steep breaking wave lifted us up and violently hurled *Rhiannon* onto her beam-ends with a smashing blow. Though tethered by a harness, I grabbed a stanchion, so as not to be flung into the roiling water. Dishes, books, and gear flew wildly from the starboard to the port side of the cabin below me. Eventually, my nightmarish watch ended. Louis then manned the helm until daybreak.

At dawn, Louis woke me as we sailed past the dusty brown cliffs. At the southern promontory of Isla Mujeres, the crumbling ruins of a Mayan lookout tower caught the first orange beams of light from the east. Sure enough, the daylight proved that the beacons were incorrectly charted, just as we had suspected during the night. As the sun rose, the last of the rain clouds dissolved into another clear hot day.

Under full sail once again, *Rhiannon* reached into the sheltered turquoise passage, skirting the shoaling ledge in the shadow of the Mayan ruins. The patchy yellow rocks and olive-green brush on the jagged cliff top slid past as we sailed over the coral-strewn white sand. Soon the cheerfully painted forms of wooden Mexican work boats surrounded us. In 12 feet of crystalline water over a sandy bottom, we luffed the sails and planted the hook in our first foreign port.

Entering Isla Mujeres at dawn

CHAPTER 9

Mexico

THE MOMENT LOUIS released the halyards at the mast, dropping the sails, all three of us breathed a collective sigh of relief. We high-fived one another and then sat quietly, taking in the scene, and reflecting upon our accomplishment with pride. It had taken us over 10 days to cross the Gulf of Mexico, for a trip that we had anticipated would require at most four or five days. However, we were not embarrassed about the duration of our voyage, considering that the wind had propelled us the entire way, without use of the engine. In one 24-hour period we had traveled less than 20 miles, with much of that day spent drifting backwards. Our arrival boosted our collective self-confidence. We had completed this passage in total isolation, with no possibility of contacting the outside world, relying solely upon the wind and our wonderful little boat.

The anchorage at Isla Mujeres

Louis, Clark, and I sat in the cockpit gazing at the striking waterfront scene at Isla Mujeres. A large Coca Cola billboard, visible on the side of a building on shore, seemed to promise us some long-awaited cold drinks. We had anchored a couple hundred yards offshore, among a fleet of brightly painted wooden Mexican fishing boats. There were no other yachts, either power or sail, in sight. In the early morning, the sun was already hot, and we saw few signs of life other than some pelicans swimming near the shore. We soaked in the unfamiliar smells, sights, and sounds. Our sailboat had successfully delivered us to a foreign port. We erected our sun awning and raised the yellow code "Q" flag to signal that we were awaiting pratique. Since it was a Sunday, we were uncertain if we would be able to obtain official clearance to go ashore that day. It made little difference, as we were quite content to remain in the cockpit, at anchor, watching the comings and goings on shore. We tidied up the boat a bit and then cooked pancakes for breakfast.

The Coca Cola sign on shore

A Mexican fishing boat at Isla Mujeres

At 10:45 a.m. while still eating, we were astonished to see the local officials heading out to *Rhiannon* from shore. Their small unmarked launch pulled alongside, and we helped four men climb clumsily aboard. One wore a blue uniform, while the other three were shirtless and potbellied, looking quite unofficial. One man represented immigration, another was from customs, and a third represented health. We surmised that the fourth fellow was simply driving their boat. When they had almost completed their business, they began asking for money. We knew from our reading that there should be no official fees for clearance. However, bribery, known to be ubiquitous in Mexico at that time, was virtually compulsory.

On this occasion, the excuses for payment included Sunday overtime, launch service, and anything else that they could verbalize in their broken English. They wanted $50. Following some negotiation, we finally gave them $40, which for us was a lot of money. We barely carried that much cash between us, though we each had some traveler's cheques that we planned to exchange into local currencies along the way to cover expenses. They continued to ask for more, but we did not relent. Eventually, they left, taking our passports, which they informed us could be picked up from the Capitán de Puerto "mañana, mañana."

We hoisted the Mexican courtesy flag, which we had stowed aboard, used a foot pump to inflate one of our two Sevylor dinghies, and rowed ashore. My first steps on land were unsteady due to an annoying illusion that the land was moving. Surprisingly, quite a few places were open for business on Sunday. Our priority was to find that cold Coke, promised by the large conspicuous sign. We craved that luxury, having drunk nothing but lukewarm water from a plastic container for the preceding ten days. Only one problem … we had no Mexican money!

We walked out onto the unpaved dusty streets of Isla Mujeres, the Isle of Women, originally named by Spanish explorers who, in the 1600s, had found Mayan fertility statues there. We did not see any fertility statues, but what we did see was even better. It was the first time we had seen "real" women in over ten days. After walking in the scorching heat for over an hour, we finally managed to pay for drinks with U.S. dollars. What bliss!

Although we were primarily concerned about our boat, we did know that our parents were anxiously awaiting word from us. We had each promised our respective families that we would contact them as soon as we arrived in any port. In 1976, phoning home was not trivial. On Isla Mujeres, there was only one small Telephone and Telegraph Office, marked by a small sign hanging askew from a rusty chain. Unfortunately, this office was closed on Sundays. Therefore, word of our safe arrival would need to wait. In the meantime, we each wrote postcards that we planned to mail to friends and family the next day from the tiny island post office.

The telephone and telegraph office at Isla Mujeres

Shortly before noon, a large blue and white ferry arrived from the mainland, disgorging a boat load of Mexican tourists coming from Mérida for the day. The island became much more animated. There was a festive, carnival-like atmosphere. Everyone was out in the streets. We noticed many European tourists and a few Americans as well. By afternoon, a welcome sea breeze had moderated the heat. A modern church and tidy plaza with electric lights strung all around contrasted with the crumbling plaster buildings and dusty unpaved roads elsewhere on the island. That evening, we treated ourselves to a delicious dinner in a restaurant. Louis had filet of turtle. I ate chicken. And Clark tried some meat that may have been beef. Today, I feel ashamed that we all ate sea turtle in Mexico in 1976, at the time being completely oblivious to their endangered and protected status.

The next day, we somehow managed to retrieve our passports, obtain Mexican pesos, and contact Clark's family after waiting in line for the only long-distance telephone on the island. Clark instructed them to reach out to our respective families and notify them of our safe arrival. We found a spigot to wash ourselves a little and then rowed back to *Rhiannon* as she danced in the wind from side to side about her anchor. While in the dinghy, we reviewed the projects we hoped to attack.

The ferry arriving at Isla Mujeres

Our primary imperative was to troubleshoot and repair the fickle engine. We anticipated spending about a week in Isla Mujeres to sort things out, even though we were anxious to get south of the hurricane zone as expeditiously as possible. In a pinch, we could live without an engine for a while. However, auxiliary power would be absolutely necessary for transit through the Panama Canal. Not only was sailing into the canal locks impractical, it was strictly forbidden. Without the engine to charge our two 12-volt lead-acid batteries, we conceivably could continue without the benefit of electricity. We would only need to forego our crude first-generation depth sounder, our five-channel VHF-FM radio, and our electric lights. The VHF-FM radio was only capable of broadcasting at most 25 nautical miles anyway. We could still listen to our portable 10-band short wave receiver that had its own batteries. Although neither radio could provide us with any offshore weather forecasting to inform us of expected sailing conditions, we could receive intermittent reports of major storm tracks on the short-wave receiver.

Knowing that we could someday be in a situation without our engine to charge our batteries, we had brought traditional low-tech backups. Aboard *Rhiannon,* we carried a lead line to check depths, a full complement of signal flags for communication, and kerosene lanterns for lighting. The lead line even had one advantage over the depth sounder. We could pack soft wax into a recess in its lead weight. This wax would pick up bits of sand, mud, or gravel, alerting us to the seafloor's composition. Our barometer and an eye to the sky were always our best clues for approaching weather. In any case, the engine would eventually become necessary for us and thus demanded our serious attention.

An unpleasant surprise awaited us as we climbed back aboard *Rhiannon.* The distinctive odor of gasoline fumes permeated the cabin. Before we could work on the engine, we needed to address this more urgent, dangerous risk. A quick survey revealed that fuel was leaking from beneath the built-in 28-gallon steel gasoline tank. Clark and I rowed back to shore. We bought some large plastic Jerry cans. We siphoned the 18 remaining gallons of rusty gasoline into the cans. Using a hacksaw, we cut away large sections of the starboard quarter berth structure to access the built-in tank. Upon removal, we saw a small hole through the floor of the tank apparently caused by rust. Leaving the tank up on deck to air out, I rowed the dinghy ashore alone to find a replacement. Unfortunately, the only tanks in town were outrageously priced six-gallon portable tanks for outboard motors.

The next morning, I once again went into the village to inquire further about replacing or, alternatively, repairing the tank. I first found the Capitán de Puerto smoking a cigarette in his office. He outright refused to speak to me without an interpreter. (Due to his unwillingness to deal with us, we never received either port check-in or departure clearance papers from him. It probably would have required one more bribe anyway.)

I next wandered over to the Mexican Navy base at the edge of town. There, I was approached by armed guards as I passed through the gate. I smiled broadly and strode confidently to the first building, where I climbed the stairs. A sailor in a white uniform with big brown eyes and a well-trimmed mustache greeted me cheerfully. He introduced himself as José. I explained our problem, and he replied, "No hay nuevo tanque aqui." Attempting English, he helpfully continued, "Maybe es possible repararlo, come back in two and half."

So, Louis, Clark, and I put the tank into the dinghy and rowed it directly to the Navy base's dock before 3 o'clock. In the shop on the base, the Mexican sailors thoroughly washed the tank and applied an excellent metal patch using solder. They were afraid to weld it, fearing a gasoline vapor explosion. Interestingly, after the tank was cleaned, we saw that the hole had been caused by a puncture rather than corrosion. We thanked them for their generous, much appreciated help, bought them all beers, and returned the fuel tank to *Rhiannon*.

Although we did not really want to impose further upon the Mexican Navy, it appeared that the base was our only recourse for assistance. On the following day, we returned to the Navy base, with our two dead batteries to be charged. The officers graciously charged them. From there we went back into town and bought 10 gallons of gasoline at the local station. Once back aboard *Rhiannon* we began a final valiant attempt to troubleshoot our engine. We cleaned the carburetor and spark plugs once again but to no avail. The three of us were resigned to finding a mechanic in some other port, as there were none on Isla Mujeres.

Bringing jerry cans to remove gasoline from our leaking tank

Louis paddling out to *Rhiannon*

During our stay on Isla Mujeres, we rented Honda 50 motorcycles and toured the island, visiting the Mayan watchtower, the south lighthouse, and the fringing coral reef. Given my long-standing interest in herpetology, I enjoyed observing the antics of a few local lizards and snakes. A striking poster featuring a female *toreadora* was posted conspicuously throughout the island, publicizing a bullfight to be held the following day in Cancun. Cancun at that time was a sleepy little-known town only four miles to the south, consisting of a bullring and a pristine beach with a few palapas. The first hotels were being constructed, though only a few new buildings were visible from the water.

Poster for a bullfight in Cancun

We considered stopping in Cancun to check out the bullfight, but instead we opted to sail to Cozumel. We hoped to find a mechanic there. While still on Isla Mujeres, I grabbed one of the engaging bullfight posters off a fence and kept it as a souvenir. Clark and I bought some postcards with pictures of the Isla Mujeres fishermen working alongside their colorful traditional boats. As we made our way back toward our dinghy on the beach, we recognized one of the weathered old fishermen depicted on the postcards. Upon our request, this newfound celebrity graciously autographed our cards.

Fresh water was still an issue for us. Since our arrival, there had been absolutely no rain. Massive rain clouds were visible over the Yucatán each day, but the easterly winds kept the convergence zone well inland of Isla Mujeres. This was a problem as we only dared fill our drinking water tanks with rainwater. There was no reasonable source of potable water ashore. Additionally, we craved a freshwater shower before heading back to sea. One evening, I met an American couple, Carol and Rick, who kindly permitted all three of us to use the shower in their hotel room. In return, we shuttled them out to *Rhiannon* for lemonade, chocolate, and conversation. We later solved our laundry problem, as well. We found a local woman to do all the washing at an incredibly reasonable price, considering the large quantity and the disgusting grime involved.

Having known Louis quite well for many years, I was aware that he was capable of very deliberate, cautious, and meticulous planning. However, he had always tended to be at least a little careless or absent-minded in other respects. Soon after our arrival in Isla Mujeres, Louis placed his only footwear, a pair of well-worn canvas deck shoes, on top of our cockpit awning to dry. In short order, a gust of wind flipped up the canopy, flinging both shoes into the drink. *Rhiannon* quickly pivoted about her anchor, moving away from the spot where Louis's shoes had fallen. Given no other option, and perhaps to punish himself for his own temporary lapse of judgement, Louis spent the first couple of days in Isla Mujeres walking on the hot unpaved streets in his bare feet.

Fortunately, the water adjacent to our boat was so clear that the bottom was plainly visible even 30 feet down. Though we had anchored *Rhiannon* in about 12 feet of water, the depth beneath the boat varied as she swung with the changing wind direction and currents. A few days later, I spotted his shoes on the coral sand about 25 feet down. Louis, still barefoot, became determined to retrieve them. Although a good swimmer, he had little experience with free diving. Nonetheless, after several attempts and without using fins, he recovered both shoes. In this case, Louis's stubborn streak paid off.

As new live-aboard cruisers, without mentors or other sailors to observe as models, Louis, Clark, and I gradually discovered for ourselves the answers to some fundamental questions. For example, when voyaging under sail, how does one decide when to depart from a secure harbor and return to the open sea? Most sailors will tell you, "When the time comes, you simply know it." Perhaps you have exhausted the activities or sites of interest ashore. Perhaps a window of good weather provides a perfect opportunity for the next passage. Perhaps you have just completed some critical repairs. Or perhaps you have become persona non grata and are forced to flee. Whatever the case, you "simply know it" and begin to stir. Just as birds become agitated and begin to flock before a long autumn migration, there is an instinctive sense that tells you when it is time to leave. We did not understand this before our journey began. But after our brief time in Isla Mujeres, we knew when the time had come.

In the late afternoon of August 28, we went ashore to recover our fully charged batteries, for a small fee, at the Navy base and to enjoy one last meal on Isla Mujeres. This time we ate at a small local restaurant named Peko's. The family running the restaurant seemed thrilled to host us as their guests. Though it proved far less than palatable, I forced myself to down a bowl of spicy red soup that I had unknowingly ordered. I posed for a picture with the family of smiling girls, the oldest of whom was probably about my own age.

Peko's restaurant in Isla Mujeres

Back aboard *Rhiannon*, we deflated and stowed the dinghy in preparation for departure. Later that evening, still engineless, we dragged out the large genoa, hanked it onto the forestay and tied on the sheets. After hoisting both sails, we weighed anchor and set sail for the island of Cozumel. We cleared the shoals at the south end of Isla Mujeres by sunset, hoping to arrive at Cozumel by morning. With a good breeze and minimal waves, we charged south through the water at six knots. Unfortunately, we were once again bucking the three-to-four-knot northbound Yucatán current, which feeds the Gulf Stream. So, we progressed toward our destination at only two to three knots. During the night, I came down with severe gastroenteritis, including sweats, chills, vomiting, and diarrhea. I am certain that I had a high fever that night, perhaps suffering from a case of *Salmonella*. Louis and Clark were charged with finding a safe harbor, while I was hopelessly debilitated and miserable in the cabin.

By late morning, Louis and Clark began steering *Rhiannon* toward the large pier and buildings in the town of San Miguel on Cozumel. Still fighting a stiff current, they spotted a tiny gap or cove in the shoreline just north of town. A couple of sailboat masts were visible inside. Prior to that, we had not even known that a marina existed at Cozumel. Louis and Clark performed a series of short tacks to reach the tight harbor mouth, while traveling over a coral-strewn sandy bottom, distinctly visible through the clear turquoise water. Though unsure of the depths, Louis and Clark reasoned that the water must be deep enough because a few sailboats appeared to be docked inside the basin.

Skillfully maneuvering *Rhiannon* through the inlet and out of the current, they spotted a concrete pier to which other boats were tied in a Mediterranean (Med) mooring fashion, stern to, with anchors securing their bows. Still under sail, the two of them managed to drop the anchor and glide backwards perfectly, shoehorning between neighboring boats just as our transom neared the concrete dock. Fortuitously, a helpful couple from a 45-foot motorsailer caught our stern lines. Louis then lowered the luffing sails after a perfect engineless docking maneuver in the exceptionally challenging marina. Meanwhile, I remained ill down below, exhausted and totally spent following a miserable night. I could hear the conversations and scrambling footsteps on deck above me. All I knew was that we had safely arrived in Cozumel.

The marina at Cozumel

The couple living aboard their motorsailer in this small marina warned us that el Capitán de Puerto de Cozumel was a difficult man. After a short rest, I mustered the strength to go ashore with Louis and Clark. We soon found this Port Captain in his office. He promptly demanded the clearance dispatch from the Port Captain in Isla Mujeres. Of course, we did not have one because the Port Captain in Isla Mujeres had refused to speak with us.

The motorsailer docked at Cozumel

We explained that we were only planning to stay long enough to deal with our broken engine. For a moment, he glared angrily at the three rag-tag gringos who had unexpectedly descended upon his quiet office. Dismissively, he told us to return to him on our day of departure to check out. Fortunately, he did not collect our passports, our official documents, or any of our money. We did not mean to be disrespectful. We simply did not know the rules. As far as we were concerned, this gave us the freedom to remain in Cozumel for as long as necessary and to do whatever we pleased.

The marina itself was an unexpected windfall. It provided complete shelter from the weather. The water beneath the boat was pristine and perpetually teemed with brightly colored fish. Running water, though not drinkable, was available right on the dock. And, best of all, the marina was completely free of charge. It was probably due to the hurricane season that we never encountered a single other transient cruising sailboat during our entire sojourn in Mexico. Compared to Isla Mujeres, Cozumel at that time was more luxurious, more populated, and more expensive. A jet airport located just behind the marina serviced daily flights to Miami, bi-weekly flights to Houston, as well as regular flights to Mérida in Yucatán.

After making a few inquiries, we located a marine mechanic, named Miguel Barrera. However, before resorting to outside help, we made one more stab at the Atomic-4 ourselves. We replaced the condenser coil, the points, and yet again cleaned out the carburetor and fuel lines. No go! We tracked down the mechanic. Miguel was a pleasant diminutive gentleman with a broad smile who moved at a slow but deliberate pace with a pronounced limp.

We learned that Miguel spoke English, French, and German, as well as his native Mexican Spanish. He had been a successful self-made entrepreneur in several businesses, including a boat charter company. At one time, he had owned a marine dealership that was the exclusive supplier of OMC & Johnson outboard motors for Cozumel, Cancun, and Isla Mujeres. He reportedly acquired that franchise by winning an argument with J.C. Clark, the president of the firm that supplied OMC with gaskets and valves.

His charter business in Cozumel had made him many friends around the world, especially in the United States and Canada. He had become a personal friend of Pierre Elliott Trudeau, the Canadian Prime Minister. Unfortunately, in 1973, Miguel had been involved in a horrible road accident in which he nearly lost his right arm and leg. He had been hospitalized for a year and consequently lost his business empire along with much of his money. Back on his feet again, he had started a new business in Cozumel selling marine engines, repairing engines, and running boat charters.

Miguel boarded *Rhiannon*, confidently walking across the splintered wooden board that served as our precarious gangway. Once inside the cabin, he attempted to start the engine while spraying ether into the air intake. Next, he fiddled with a few connections and then looked at the exhaust elbow. After contemplating the engine silently for several more minutes, he told us that the entire engine would need to be removed from the boat. He needed to work on it in his shop several kilometers away. Already, the three of us had become concerned that this repair might be well beyond our budget. We quickly reviewed our three alternatives. We could either have the engine fixed, replace it with an entirely new *diesel* motor, or simply continue with no engine at all.

We voiced our apprehensions to Miguel concerning the cost. But, without providing even a ballpark estimate, he reassuringly told us not to worry because it "should not cost mucho." We asked him about the cost of a new diesel motor because he was the regional Westerbeke marine diesel dealer as well. He would not quote a price but instead expressed confidence that he would be able to fix our engine. He mentioned that he might need to send away for some parts but would not know the extent of the repair until he began the work. Louis, Clark, and I looked at one another and decided to trust him. After all, the engine was no good to us in its current state … and we had little choice.

Minutes later, Clark and Miguel set about removing the 330-pound engine. The propeller shaft coupling was disengaged from the transmission, the throttle and choke cables were disconnected, the fuel line was removed, and the exhaust pipe was detached from the exhaust manifold. Next, the starter power cable, the electrical connections and the cooling water hose were all removed. The alternator and the engine mounts were unbolted as well, freeing the engine for extraction. While this was happening, Louis and I secured both the main halyard and our spare masthead halyard to the boom to serve as a crane. We suspended our 4:1 boom vang block and tackle directly above the heavy engine.

Three young mechanic's assistants, all smaller than Miguel himself, spontaneously appeared barefoot on the dock. Within moments, our troublesome engine was hoisted up through the companionway and hand-carried across the narrow gangplank to the concrete dock. The engine was quickly dispatched to who-knows-where by the barefoot men. Miguel took off with his crew, promising to let us know what he had found within a few days. For the three of us, it was strangely shocking to see the cavernous void where *Rhiannon*'s engine had once been.

Our engine and the gangplank

Miguel's helpers carrying the engine

In the days that followed, I regained my strength on a diet of rainwater, canned food, and local bread. Before long, I was able to walk with Louis and Clark into San Miguel, two kilometers down the road. The weather pattern began to change, and many people in Cozumel remarked that the beginning of the rainy season had arrived earlier than usual. We did not comprehend the significance of this. But we knew that we were now far into the hurricane season and would not find reliable refuge until we reached Panama. Though the days remained sunny and hot, every night heavy rains would suddenly appear, forcing Clark to pull his bedding quickly into the cabin from the cockpit, where he preferred to sleep. The clatter of the downpour and Clark's movements on the deck would awaken Louis and me just long enough to secure the overhead hatches.

The empty engine compartment

In Cozumel, we easily topped off our drinking water supply with filtered rainwater, and always added the prescribed amount of chlorine bleach to counter bacteria. We had read that while cruising, the minimum necessary drinking water ration was one half gallon per person per day. During the first days of passages, we stuck to that guideline. Once assured that we could catch rain off the sails to replenish our supply, we eased the restriction. While in Cozumel, with the advent of the rainy season, no water rationing was required.

While our engine was out for repair, the three of us had plenty of time to relax, explore and enjoy Cozumel. One day, we rode together on rented Honda 50s across the island to its eastern shore. The straight road was monotonously devoid of buildings or any signs of civilization. The terrain was flat, covered by dry scrubby vegetation. An occasional grey lizard scurried across the road. At the eastern side of the island there really was not much more to see, except the open Caribbean Sea. The surf crashed heavily onto the beach, in sharp contrast to the placid waters of Cozumel's western shore. As we straddled our bikes and squinted into the bright morning sunlight to gaze at the sea, the stiff east wind blew sand and dust into our faces.

The vast rolling Caribbean waters instilled both awe and fear, which none of us dared to express aloud. We were still strangers to the sea, Midwestern boys far from home. I was filled with ambivalence at the prospect of setting out once again in our diminutive vessel onto a vast ocean, so powerful, and unpredictable. Nonetheless, I felt excited to face the inevitable challenges ahead and to experience the unknown wonders of the water-world that covers two-thirds of our planet.

As the days passed, we received word that Miguel and his crew were hard at work on our engine. He had reground the valves and was inspecting the pistons. We also knew that he was fabricating a new head gasket. We learned the problems had been caused by corrosion secondary to seawater intrusion. Somehow, saltwater had gotten into the engine through either the fuel or the exhaust system. The mechanics would need a few more days.

Meanwhile, I got to know the other people aboard boats in the marina. A middle-aged couple, Cal Surtees and his wife Barbara, lived aboard a red-dish-brown motorsailer with a ketch rig. In contrast to *Rhiannon*, their boat was well equipped with hot and cold running water, an air conditioner, two dogs, a cat, and many of the amenities of a comfortable home. Initially, I was a bit envious of their lifestyle, watching them sitting around and relaxing most of the day as I varnished our teak cockpit coaming.

Cal was quite a character. He had a large tattoo on his chest, which he apparently had acquired while in the U.S. Navy during the 1940s. He possessed a wry sense of humor, was quite talkative, and frequently offered unsolicited advice. Cal made a living drawing caricatures and portraits. Owing to health issues, including high blood pressure and risk of a stroke, he had not yet begun to work since they had arrived from Miami months earlier. I felt grateful to have good health. Although their boat appeared comfortable and well-appointed, I concluded that I was fortunate to be voyaging rather than sitting on a luxurious boat in ill health.

At the time of our arrival in Cozumel, a large Mexican yawl named *Attila* was berthed in the basin. The authoritarian Port Captain mandated their departure. They had a dangerous eight-month-old Doberman and a rowdy young skipper, who apparently was in some trouble with the police. We only saw them for a couple of days but were not disappointed to see them moving on.

The only other inhabited vessel in the marina was a 45-foot Chris-Craft cabin cruiser en route to Fort Lauderdale, Florida, from Cartagena, Colombia. The crew of young South Americans aboard, usually shirtless with dark sun-tanned skin, were fun-loving and always entertaining to watch. They spoke some English with heavy accents and never divulged their motive for crossing from Colombia to the U.S. during hurricane season. They appeared to be on some type of mission, which we were fairly certain was related to smuggling. I was learning that the seafaring characters one meets on a sailing trip are often eccentric, unique, and fascinating in a way that I had never experienced back home. As Dorothy said in the *Wizard of Oz*, "Toto, I've a feeling we're not in Kansas anymore."

The clear marina water, chock-full of tropical fish, beckoned us to dive beneath *Rhiannon*. This was our first opportunity to attempt some underwater photography. The only camera that we had brought along was a 35mm single-lens reflex camera. We had purchased a large acrylic underwater housing that sprouted an array of external levers to control the shutter and all the settings. Putting the camera into this bulky contraption and latching it closed always took at least 10 minutes. Consequently, we left the camera in the water-proof housing most of the time, which had the benefit of keeping the camera dry in the damp cabin. We shot a few underwater pictures in Cozumel, but had no idea if they came out okay, as the 35 mm film roll remained in the camera, to be developed months later.

On the morning of September 4, after five days of work, Miguel arrived at our boat unannounced, with his men holding our refurbished Atomic-4 engine. The barefoot men reversed the removal process, carrying the bronze-colored engine block back across the teetering gangplank. Miguel, assisted by Clark, reinstalled the engine. The propeller shaft flange was meticulously aligned and double-checked. Everything was reassembled. We added four quarts of fresh oil to the crankcase and installed a new impeller in the raw water pump. The engine started easily on the first try. Miguel adjusted the timing by rotating the distributor housing until the engine ran smoothly. We tested the transmission at the dock and then hauled in the anchor for a quick trial circuit around the marina. The three of us were ecstatic that we did not have to throw the engine overboard. The engine ran better than ever!

With the boat returned to her Med mooring, the time had come to discuss the price of the repair with Miguel. Louis, Clark, and I all thought that negotiations would go better after Miguel had downed a few drinks. We proposed this to Miguel, offering to take him out for lunch in town. He readily agreed. Louis and I hopped onto the bed of Miguel's small pickup truck, and Clark rode up in front with Miguel. Once in San Miguel, we sat at a table in an open-air restaurant at the south side of the main plaza. After plying Miguel with several beers and some small talk, we asked him what we owed. Miguel began by calculating aloud what was involved: "four quarts of oil, four spark plugs, a new head gasket, a new impeller, two piston rings, and five days of labor including re-grinding valves, cleaning cylinder walls, and reinstalling, aligning, and tuning the engine."

There was a pause. Our hearts dropped to our stomachs, as we each anticipated a bill that might seriously impede our entire voyage. I feared that the price I was about to hear would cause me to regret not buying a brand-new diesel engine.

Miguel then continued, "For all of the parts and the labor, how does $70 U.S. sound?"

Quickly calculating that my share was a mere $23.33, I suppressed my astonishment at the amazing bargain, as did both Louis and Clark. Immediately, we agreed that the price was fair and handed the cash to Miguel. In disbelief, we bought one more round of cerveza. Then, with grins of appreciation, we walked back to the marina to prepare for our departure toward Panama.

CHAPTER 10

A Change of Plans

ON THE MORNING of our departure, Sunday, September 5, 1976, we walked over to the Port Captain's office, exactly as he had suggested upon our arrival. Not surprisingly, his office was closed. The weather appeared favorable, with a steady barometer and fair wind. We decided to leave anyway, once again without any departure papers. This time we knew that we were breaking some rules. But, having no intention to return to Mexico, we did not care. The Port Captain likely figured that we would not be good for much of a "fee" anyway. Perhaps, he had let us slip away, turning a blind eye to formality, leaving us to face the eventual consequences of our neglect.

As usual, we planned to proceed entirely under sail, without using our engine. Although the engine was now operating flawlessly, we intended to reserve motoring strictly for entering ports, emergencies, or brief periods of time to top off the batteries. We did carry an extra five-gallon container of gasoline on deck. We knew that gasoline jugs openly exposed to lightning could be dangerous. However, we hoped to use the extra five gallons as fuel, rather than jettison it, unused during a thunderstorm. We left the marina heading south in a gentle breeze, fighting a persistent adverse northbound current. Initially, under full sail there was sufficient wind to propel us south past the Port Captain's office and the long ferryboat pier in San Miguel. Magnificent hues of tropical blue and green water fringed the western shore of Cozumel. Thankfully, the hazardous areas of reefs and shoals were well marked on our charts. Through the impossibly clear water, the white sandy bottom, occasionally strewn with rocks, weeds, and outcroppings of coral, slipped beneath *Rhiannon* as we fought the oncoming current.

We certainly wanted to make tracks and sail clear of the island before the Port Captain might spot us. However, our plan did not work. By midafternoon, as we were nearing the south end of Cozumel, the wind had died to the extent that our forward motion through the water was no match for the opposing current. Watching the stones and shadowy weeds on the bottom below us, we could plainly see that we were sailing backwards! We were unwilling to waste our precious fuel so soon to buck the current under power. Immediately, we dropped our anchor, temporarily furled the sails, and patiently awaited stronger wind.

Two hours later, the wind picked up. Our siesta was over. We were off in a flash, as 12 knots of steady wind from the east-northeast finally facilitated our flight from Mexico. The Port Captain never saw us. Two brilliant rainbows in the late afternoon provided an auspicious beginning to our continued dash toward Panama, at the height of the hurricane season. Although we saw rain in the distance, we stayed dry aboard *Rhiannon*. By 10:30 p.m. the last glow of light from Cozumel had faded imperceptibly beyond the horizon astern. We found ourselves once again at sea. Under full sail, we experienced exceptional, blissful sailing. We were making seven and a half knots, occasionally surging to eight, in a new, favorable current. In my journal, I noted:

> *With this kind of weather, we'll be in Panama in no time. I spotted one freighter going past us toward the north but no other action besides some jumping schools of fish.*

On September 6, with continued optimal conditions, Louis and I experimented with a variety of sheet-to-tiller self-steering arrangements, attempting to liberate ourselves from our perpetual bondage to the helm. We had brought with us a book describing multiple self-steering rigs that relied solely upon dynamic feedback between the tension of the jib sheet and the turning forces of the tiller. Using turning blocks, accessory lines, and elastic rubber surgical tubing, we spent hours testing different mechanisms. Despite our careful attention to sail balance, nothing would stabilize the course of our lively fin-keeled boat for longer than 20-minute runs. Defeated, we resolved to install a self-steering wind vane in Panama, before eventually crossing the Pacific Ocean.

Later that day, I wrote:

> *Sailing tonight should be enjoyable in the absence of squalls. However, we may have some nighttime rain judging from the clouds on the horizon. Louis has been a great cook today. He made pancakes (with eggs), and a macaroni and cheese casserole with tuna. Clark has a toothache, which is really the most unpleasant thing left ... Rainbows every day, clear sky, warmer, clearer, bluer water than ever... Perhaps we will catch a fish. I imagine we will be able to collect rainwater on this leg, so the caked salt should not be as bad as in the Gulf. 'A fast passage is a safe passage' and we really need to move! I am sure that this will not be possible the entire time, but I imagine we can now make Trujillo [Honduras] by the time any storm materializes.*

Being preoccupied by sailing, navigation, boat maintenance, and simply habituating to our new life, we had never made a concerted effort to fish. We had seen large schools of jumping fish and even commercial fishing vessels. Clearly, there were fish in the sea. We occasionally threw out a fishing line with a lure to troll in our wake, but we caught nothing. As evening approached, we reeled in our line, and performed our navigational duties.

While offshore in the Caribbean, we did our best to plot a position fix on the chart at least twice each day. Navigation in 1976 was an art, not a science. The cardinal rules were: 1. Exercise constant vigilance and 2. Never rely upon a single source of navigational data.

We relied on many data sources, incorporating all available information every time we calculated our position. The following is a list of our routine navigational resources:

1. Visual bearings of known landmarks or navigational aids, such as mountain peaks, distinctive clouds over land, or lighthouses, to triangulate a position.
2. Dead reckoning by calculating speed through the water, true course, and time from a previously known position. Dead reckoning requires corrections for current, leeway, compass error, and inaccuracies of speed averaging.
3. Depth readings (obtained either by depth sounder or lead line) compared to the soundings noted on a chart.
4. Bearings to charted radio beacons obtained with our radio direction finder (RDF).
5. Celestial observations of the sun, moon, stars, and planets by sextant, necessitating both a visible horizon and an adequately clear sky. A pitching and rolling deck also hindered accuracy.
6. Information procured from a passing ship.
7. Changes observed in the temperature or color of the water.

This is a much-abbreviated list that does not convey the complexities or uncertainties involved with each method. Inaccuracies in all these techniques mandated integration of as many sources as feasible, especially when approaching land. On this passage, southward from Mexico, the radio direction finder, dead reckoning, and sun sights constituted our principle means of navigation.

By the morning of September 7, we had been out of sight of land for one and a half days. We awoke to a cloudy sky and freshening breeze. Although we were uncertain of our exact position, a favorable northeasterly wind drove us southward on a broad reach toward Honduras, our provisional destination. Though the Panama Canal was our actual goal, we had not firmly decided upon our next port-of-call. Sailing our own vessel imparted an incomparable sense of freedom. We did not need to pick a definitive destination. With a simple flick of the tiller, we could instantly alter course to set sail to any country in Central America, or perhaps to a Caribbean island, Europe, or beyond. Deserted islands, hidden coves, and exotic ports unreachable by other means were all attainable, simply at the whim of the helmsman. In contrast to flying on an airliner, cruising on a ship, or riding aboard a train, we were not bound by itineraries or schedules.

On that morning, a queasy stomach thwarted my fanciful daydreaming of obscure romantic destinations. The waves were building, and I found the motion increasingly uncomfortable. It always took a few days for my equilibrium to adapt to the rhythms of the sea. Ever since an ominous red dawn that morning, the sky had remained overcast, augmenting my mounting gloom. Intermittent squalls gave way to more steady rainfall. All three of us felt lethargic, and we soon became fatigued from lack of nourishment. Though Clark did not experience mal de mer, he was still recovering from his toothache. We had difficulty acquiring a reliable radio beacon. The cloudy skies precluded celestial navigation all day. As we slogged southward through a lumpy seaway in the rain, we became more uncertain of our position. We did not know how much the current had set us. We also had no access to any weather forecast. The deteriorating weather was an additional cause for concern.

At dusk, we sighted the silhouette of a northbound ship traveling on a parallel and opposite course, approximately a quarter mile to port. Louis was able to hail the vessel on our VHF. This was the *Muser*, a British freighter bound for the Florida Keys. In a reassuring English accent, the radio operator advised us of "continued good weather" for the next two days but warned us of a depression over the Lesser Antilles that was moving westward. He related our latitude and longitude, which informed us that we had made less progress than we had assumed, despite our bursts of speed and consistent headway. We also came to understand that this overcast rainy day with choppy seas represented "good weather," at least to men aboard a large ship.

Nonetheless this chance encounter at sea cheered us immensely. It was amazing that simple things, such as knowing our position with certainty and getting a general weather forecast, thoroughly buoyed our spirits. Re-energized, I lit the kerosene running lanterns in the cabin and carefully carried them forward to secure them in their brackets at the shrouds. Clark heated a meal for dinner as we prepared for the night of "good weather" to come.

While eating, we tuned-in our Sony radio to the station with the strongest signal. An announcer speaking English rapidly, with a most delightful Caribbean accent, vividly described a fabulous celebration to come. Upbeat music with infectious dance rhythms emanated from the radio. This 10-band receiver was our sole connection to the outside world. It spoke directly to us. The broadcast originated in Belize. I knew embarrassingly little about Belize. I had first learned of British Honduras in elementary school. I had read more recently that the name had been changed to Belize about three years earlier, though it remained under British rule.

There was not yet any tourism in Belize; and it certainly was not a cruising destination whatsoever in 1976. The announcer spoke of St. George's Caye Day, an approaching festive holiday. I fell into the enchanting calypso and reggae rhythms, so different from the music I had enjoyed in Mexico. All three of us thought that it might be a worthwhile stop. But, for now, pressing southward toward Panama, beyond the reach of hurricanes, took priority.

Lacking a single captain, we developed a unique system for making command decisions aboard *Rhiannon*. Louis, Clark, and I knew that maritime and naval traditions have long recognized the necessity of a supreme captain as a commanding officer. There are numerous reasons for this tradition. Life on a vessel is most easily organized when a single authority carries final responsibility for decisions related to navigation, safety, equipment management, provisioning, crew duties, discipline, etc. Given that none of us possessed an extensive knowledge of cruising, we decided to devise a creative solution.

Louis, Clark, and I were equal owners. But Louis and I both had more previous sailing experience than Clark. We therefore agreed that Louis and I would share the traditional duties of captain related to managing the boat. In advance, we determined how we would implement this in practice. For official matters, such as paperwork when entering ports, the three of us would alternate serving as the nominal captain. For matters of immediate decision, including emergencies, the one who was on watch at the time, or alternately the first on deck, would act as skipper to coordinate activities and assign tasks to the others.

Concerning issues suitable for more prolonged deliberation, such as determining the next port of call, or purchasing new equipment, we would discuss it together as a group to reach a consensus. The overriding rule in the case of an impasse was to follow the safest, most conservative course in every situation. For example, in the event of a conflict concerning whether to enter a harbor at night or stand off until morning, the more prudent standing off would prevail. Other duties on board were to be divided equally or as most practical according to an individual's skills.

Many autocratic captains had cautioned me that this system could not work. I have subsequently utilized this system aboard other boats for the past 45 years, always with good success. The 21st century concept of "crew resource management" (CRM) is based upon similar principles. CRM has been widely adopted in both aircraft cockpits and operating rooms. In those situations, one person remains in charge, while team input is strongly encouraged. In government, democracy has proven to be as successful as autocracy, and in the cyber world, crowdsourcing can solve problems beyond the capacity of an individual mind. As a result of our procedures aboard *Rhiannon*, an occasional risky adventure may have been bypassed in the interest of safety. However, overall, our system worked exceptionally well.

While we slogged southward after dark, still on a broad reach, the sky remained overcast, creating a pitch-black night. As the wind picked up, we shortened sail to a triple-reefed mainsail and working jib. The waves steadily grew in height. The wind increased to the point that we ended up dropping the main altogether. Sailing under jib only, with the wind consistently over 25 knots, *Rhiannon* began to surf. On this night of tricky steering, Louis and I did not allow Clark to take the helm. Our path ahead was lit only by the glow of the red and green kerosene lanterns, reflected by the sparkling spume of the bow wave. We were riding a rocket ship through the night, furiously careening down the faces of waves, with a phosphorescent trail in our wake.

Louis and I steered entirely by feel, a skill well-ingrained through our experience surfing Albacores in Lake Michigan. As the stern rose with each approaching wave on our quarter, I would tug firmly on the tiller, to overcome the sudden weather helm and maintain our course without rounding up. A loud roar would ensue as the Cal 2-30 exceeded her hull speed, surfing to over 11 knots. I would then relax my strong pull on the tiller, using quick, finer adjustments to extend the exhilarating ride for as long as possible. *Rhiannon* would inevitably settle back onto her haunches with a distinct hiss, ready to catch the next wave in line.

In the morning, following our first rough night at sea, we discovered that there had been some minor damage. The molded rubber rubrail that capped the hull-to-deck junction had fallen loose and was slapping against the topsides with loud reports. Two mainsail slides had broken, and our gear in the cabin had been strewn all about. We effected temporary fixes and continued sailing through yet another cloudy day. The wind had veered to the east, which was the direction we needed to travel around Nicaragua on our way to Panama. We elected to continue southward toward Puerto Cortes, Honduras, which appeared to have a large sheltered bay as a harbor. Our RDF received strong signals from the beacons at both Swan Island and Belize, providing us a reasonable working estimate of our current position. The wave heights remained at six to eight feet all day.

At dusk, we expected to pick up the Puerto Cortes radio beacon. It never happened. Once again it was an overcast night. Through a small break in the clouds at dusk, I attempted a moon sight with the sextant. It was too rough for me to reduce the sight. Shortly after dark, steady rain began. We were proceeding toward a lee shore in extremely limited visibility, navigating by dead reckoning alone. Based upon our calculations, we should have found ourselves within five to ten miles of shore by 11 p.m. A bright lighthouse with a 20-mile range should have come into view during my watch.

By 11:30 p.m. the following seas were becoming steeper and closer together, relentlessly driving us toward the coast. I wiped off my eyeglasses frequently and scanned the horizon with binoculars through the rain, searching for the anticipated light. I thought that I saw the silhouette of distant mountains. I am not certain whether I only imagined or truly heard breakers ahead. But, without a fix and no lighthouse in sight, there was just one reasonable course of action to be taken. I called Louis and Clark up on deck. We reversed course to a heading of 360°T and sailed close hauled under jib only. We gave up on Honduras and opted to backtrack north for two days toward Belize to join the holiday celebrations. We simply pushed the tiller to reverse our course and set sail for an unplanned destination that had beckoned us with its siren song of festive music.

However, the night was not over yet. As my watch continued in the rain, I held our course carefully to remain east of Glover Reef, a 15-NM-long atoll composed of hazardous coral. Lightning flashed intermittently in the clouds, momentarily illuminating the night. Looking upward, I saw an eerie bluish light emanating from the VHF antenna at the masthead. It was St. Elmo's fire. I was concerned that the static discharge might predispose us to a lightning strike. But the mysterious phenomenon only lasted for a few minutes before complete darkness returned. At one point, a small pocket freighter came up from astern, passing close aboard on the port side. As she passed, she slowed for a while as if to inspect us. Through my binoculars, I saw men upon the well-lit bridge deck gazing back at me through the rain, using their own binoculars as well. Their lights rapidly disappeared into the night.

I wrote in my journal:

We did this all night, taking turns on watch. We were bombarded horribly, beating jib only into some huge waves. -- I saw one freak breaking wave, which came to a point just in front of the bow, towering at about spreader height. Being drenched, despite foul weather gear, I began to get cold. I sang at the top of my voice, all of the songs that came to mind. Most incongruously, I sang Oh, What a Beautiful Morning, as well as some oldies and Gilbert and Sullivan songs from HMS Pinafore.

Eventually, I became mesmerized, in a state of half sleep, hunched over the tiller, intermittently monitoring the bulkhead-mounted compass. Suddenly: Wham! I was punched hard in the chest and awakened with a start. Totally stunned, I cried out in pain, with no idea of what had happened. Louis and Clark immediately appeared at the companionway to see what was wrong. An eight-inch-long flying fish lay flopping on the cockpit floor with buzzing wings. Apparently, this fish had launched itself somewhere ahead of *Rhiannon*'s bow and flown with great speed over the deck and into the cockpit, striking me. Only the fish was more surprised than I was. I scooped it up in my hand and hurled it back into the waves. My watch was over. I retired below for some uninterrupted sleep.

By daybreak, we encountered much better weather. Listening to Belize Radio, we learned that the information from the British freighter *Muser* had been correct. A depression, more specifically a tropical wave, was approaching from the east. Finding shelter became more urgent. We carried no harbor charts for Belize. However, sailing directions written for large ships provided detailed instructions. We knew that we could depend on the Belize radio beacon. Therefore, we were not concerned about determining our position. The sky had been clear all morning, which allowed me to obtain a reliable line of position from the sun. I derived an excellent fix by crossing that line with the radio beacon bearings from Swan Island and Belize. We meticulously updated our dead reckoning position throughout the day. By evening, under full sail, we reached Cay Bokel, a tiny uninhabited island at Turneffe Atoll, where we anchored for the night in the lee of the reef.

On the morning of September 10, we raised our anchor for an early start. We were 20 nautical miles from Belize City, our goal for the day. A barrier reef lies 12 nautical miles to the east of Belize City and much of the coast of Belize. Shoal water of approximately five-foot depths occupies most of the area between this barrier reef and the coast. A narrow channel, like a meandering river, cuts through the reef to the deeper waters adjacent to shore. We sailed northward from our anchorage toward English Cay. This tiny islet with a few small buildings on it housed local pilots who could guide ships through the channel into the open roadstead south of Belize City. As we approached the opening to the unbuoyed channel, we attempted to start our engine. Although we had run the engine briefly the previous day to charge our batteries, our recalcitrant Atomic-4 would not start. Once again, we would need to sail *Rhiannon* into port.

Based upon our only local chart, it appeared that the channel would be a straight shot directly toward the deeper water along shore to the west. We proceeded under sail, traveling at four-knots past English Cay. Monitoring our depth sounder and observing the shades of the water, we knew that we were within the deep channel. The next thing we knew, we were sailing along at four-knots directly over the massive shoal. We had no idea where we had lost the channel or which direction to turn to get back into deep water. *Rhiannon* continued to fly forward, perilously close to running aground. This great plain of coral remained clearly visible beneath us. We needed to cover several more miles to reach the deeper water along the coast. The depths appeared consistent with less than a foot of clearance under our keel. We had discovered through pure luck that our boat could sail safely outside of the channel, across the shoal, directly to Belize City.

English Cay marking the channel to Belize City

The sailing directions, written primarily for large commercial vessels, advised anchoring in the expansive open roadstead south of town. As we approached this designated area, we saw no anchored ships or vessels of any kind. Clark made a blind radio call on the VHF hailing frequency. Fortuitously, someone replied almost immediately. The return call was from a British gentleman living in Belize City who enjoyed using the radio as a hobby. Though not a sailor or port official, he knew the layout of the city and offered some helpful advice. He recommended that we proceed around the point of land at the far eastern end of the city, toward the broad mouth of the Belize River, called Haulover Creek. He had seen boats tied up there at the customs dock but noted that he rarely saw yachts or visiting sailboats there. He warned us of a mud bar crossing the mouth of the river. He reported speaking recently to a vessel of four-foot draft that had successfully cleared the bar to enter the river. He was not sure if we would clear it with our five-foot draft. Louis, Clark, and I were determined to try.

With 10 knots of wind and flat water, we rounded the southeastern point, gradually turning westward toward the mile-wide mouth of Haulover Creek. A fleet of several dozen wooden workboats with tightly furled canvas sails lay at their moorings along the southern bank. At the northern shore, we spotted a barge and some other vessels tied up to a concrete wharf. Peering through binoculars, we chose that as our goal. We dropped the jib onto the foredeck and pressed forward toward the dock under main only. *Rhiannon* decelerated rapidly, almost stopping, as her keel plowed into the soft mud. With the mainsail still drawing and our weight to assist, she heeled gently to starboard. Suddenly, we broke free into the river. We dropped the mainsail at just the proper time to glide alongside a vintage wooden cabin cruiser secured to the wharf. Fenders in position, we safely rafted *Rhiannon* outside of the aging power boat and raised our code "Q" flag.

Tied up in Belize City at the mouth of Haulover Creek

CHAPTER 11

St. George's Caye Day

SHORTLY AFTER WE tied up in the early afternoon, the customs, immigration, and health officers climbed aboard wearing tidy white shirts and street shoes. We all crowded together in *Rhiannon*'s cockpit. The check-in process involved some pleasant sociable conversation along with the routine formalities. Although most of our documents appeared complete, the immigration officer had expected some official clearance papers from Mexico. We simply needed to answer a few additional questions. We explained that Belize City had not been on our planned itinerary and that our engine was inoperative. This easily satisfied their bureaucratic requirements. In addition to being very hospitable to us as foreign visitors, the customs officer was quite solicitous, readily volunteering his assistance in troubleshooting our recalcitrant engine.

Checking-in with port officials in Belize

As soon as the others had left, Clark and Charles, the customs officer, set to work on the engine. Fortunately, the trouble turned out to be a few fouled spark plugs—an easy fix. With the engine back in operation, we thanked Charles, sent him on his way, and for the first time shifted our attention to the strange new world surrounding us. Our eyes were immediately drawn to the only other vessel that appeared incongruous to Belize City.

A derelict wooden sailboat, slightly shorter than *Rhiannon,* sat tied to the wharf just off our stern. None of us had seen a boat like her before. Her rotting wood deckhouse was cloaked in faded white paint. Most striking was the mysterious carving or tiki nailed to the front of her wooden mast. Her furled mainsail was lashed to her boom, suggesting that this questionably seaworthy vessel inexplicably had recently sailed. We walked closer to examine the rigging, the deck gear, and the tiki. As we stood gawking, the cabin hatch suddenly sprang open, and out came ... Bob.

Bob was one of those legendary characters transported directly from a Robert Louis Stevenson pirate novel. A cross between a skid row bum and an unkempt hippie, Bob's appearance made us look like choir boys. And none of us had bathed in over a week. Bob sported sandy, shoulder-length hair, a straggly beard, a stained t-shirt, and wild tattoos. He hopped up onto the wharf and introduced himself in plain American English. A cigarette dangled from his crusty lips, and a gold earring hung from one ear. He reeked of body odor and marijuana.

As he was the only other transient sailor we had encountered since leaving Gulfport, we were anxious to gain wisdom from his experience. He told us that he had been sailing in his little boat, singlehanded or with an occasional female crew, throughout the Caribbean for many years. Louis, Clark, and I were still wondering whether we had been foolhardy, or perhaps even crazy, to set out during the Atlantic hurricane season. We had been questioning our own judgement all along. The total absence of other cruisers had underscored our doubt ... until that day. This was our chance for vindication. We had finally met someone who had survived Caribbean cruising for years, even during the tropical storm season.

After we had learned that Bob sailed from country to country, or island to island, picking destinations on a whim, we wanted to learn his secrets.

"Bob," I asked. "How do you navigate?"

Brusquely, he reached into his pocket, pulling something out. Instinctively, I jumped back. I feared he was drawing a knife. Instead, it was a small, 1960s-style, plastic transistor AM radio.

He replied, "I use this!"

Curiously, I asked, "Okay? What do you mean?"

"I tune it in to the strongest AM station, like from Havana, or Kingston. Then I turn the radio around until the music is loudest, so I know where it points ... Then I know where I am."

Bob's derelict boat (The man standing is not Bob.)

"Aren't you worried about running aground?"

He continued, "At night, I can see the light from cities on the horizon, so I know when I'm close. I don't carry any charts."

Louis then chimed in, "What about hurricanes? Aren't you concerned about storms?"

Bob, apparently quite stoned, frowned in disbelief at the question before retorting, "Hell, no. I've never been in a hurricane. When a hurricane gets near ya, it'll just blow you away, man! It'll blow you away!"

After that less than reassuring interchange, we asked Bob where to eat in town. He directed us toward a place called Mom's Diner, and off we went. Clark remembered that someone had famously advised never to eat in a place called Mom's. It made no difference. Mom's diner, an apparent relic of the 1920s, turned out to serve the best food in town. We ate there every day.

Holiday decorations in Belize City

Belize City

In short order, we discovered that the alluring celebration which had drawn us to Belize was the national holiday on September 10 called St. George's Caye Day. This major event is the local equivalent of Bastille Day in France or Fourth of July in the United States. The holiday commemorates the expulsion of the Spanish by local British settlers, called Baymen, during a battle on the tiny island of St. George's Caye in 1798.

The Post Office

The weather map

One hundred seventy-eight years later, in 1976, banks, public offices, and many businesses were closed. The residents of Belize, though mostly impoverished, were all outfitted in their finest clothes, milling about the streets. Belize was predominantly populated by tall handsome men and strikingly beautiful women, all descendants of African slaves. Young women wearing bright print dresses of all colors walked seductively through the crowded streets and across the swing bridge at the center of town. Red and blue banners draped the storefronts and utility poles. Rhythmic music emanated from phonographs in clapboard houses and small shops. This was no ordinary day in the city. We had arrived on the perfect day.

The heart of Belize City was the swing bridge crossing the Belize River at the city's commercial center. The white colonial-style wooden post office building dominated the north bank, just opposite the bridge. On the porch of the post office, inside a glass case mounted on the wall, hung a prominent hand-drawn map. This was the weather map, the only source of forecasts accessible to the public. It was also our sole indication of an impending storm or potential weather window that could guide our departure. At the time of our arrival, a sweeping white arc on the map stretched across the Caribbean, just offshore to the east. This arc represented a tropical wave of low pressure, expected to arrive imminently.

The swing bridge in the center of town

Directly across the river from the post office stood the immense animated marketplace, covered by a corrugated tin roof. Walking across the bridge, I looked eastward toward the mouth of Haulover Creek, where *Rhiannon* lay secured in the distance. A band of black, low-lying rain clouds edged toward the city beneath an already overcast sky. A single sailing workboat glided gently up to her mooring near the market. The first cold drops of rain began to fall. I hurried down to the market to seek shelter from the approaching deluge. The market stalls pulsed with life, as everyone prepared for the holiday. The smell of fish, the sounds of animated bartering, and the wild colors of fresh produce assaulted my senses as I walked among the crowded aisles. I could only decipher occasional words of the rapidly spoken Creole. Young men flirted with women in Spanish. I was intrigued to learn that people preferred to speak Spanish for social intercourse in Belize, while they spoke English for business. As the rain clattered down on the metal above, I realized that the marketplace roof had been designed to keep out the sun but was no match for a downpour. Torrents flowing from gaps in the metal roofing created rivers in the aisles of the market. Nobody seemed concerned. Shopping continued routinely.

The covered market and sailing workboats

Sailing workboat in Haulover Creek

Knowing that the weather would keep us in Belize City for at least a few days, Louis, Clark, and I decided to take advantage of the layover for some boat maintenance and repairs. A commonly quoted definition of *cruising* is: "Fixing your boat in exotic places." This is less funny than true. I was still puzzled as to why our forestay turnbuckle had broken in the Gulf of Mexico. I studied the forestay and its attachment, shaking the forestay fore and aft, then side to side. I finally realized that the direct attachment of the turnbuckle to the stem chainplate only permitted motion in one plane. I concluded that all along we had been missing a toggle to create a proper universal joint. I had no idea how this had been overlooked, but finally the problem was plain to see.

The approaching rain

I needed to do more about this oversight than just smack myself on the forehead. But we were in Belize. There were no other sailboats in this country with contemporary stainless-steel rigging. There were no boat chandleries, either. So, I walked over to the only hardware store in town. It was a surprisingly well-stocked establishment, located on the animated main street, not far from the swing bridge. Brooms, shovels, axes, and hand tools were abundant. At best, I was hoping to find a suitable fastener or a piece of metal that could be fashioned into a makeshift substitute for the missing part. As a longshot, I asked the proprietor if he had any sailboat fittings. He thought for a moment, then climbed a tall wooden ladder to drag down an old shoebox from a dusty shelf.

He offered, "I have a few things in here. But there isn't much."

I began rummaging through the half-dozen small items in the box. Generally, I do not believe in miracles. But I was completely astonished to find that the only piece of stainless hardware in the box, and perhaps in the entire country, was a toggle of precisely the correct size for *Rhiannon*! And it even had a matching clevis pin. He sold the priceless part to me for mere pennies.

Belize City canals

A typical house on stilts

With that problem neatly solved, it was time to address another issue. We had lost our new, unused storm jib overboard at sea. The storm jib represented a critical component of our arsenal to battle the inevitable gale in our future. Louis, Clark, and I reasoned that Panama would likely have a sailmaker or at least other sailors from whom we might buy a used sail. However, we had become increasingly superstitious. If we obtained a storm sail while in Belize, it could potentially ward off bad weather on our way south. Conversely, fate might curse us with a tempest if we remained nakedly exposed, without a storm jib on board. We also reasoned that the traditional sailing workboats in Belize must require a local sailmaker. Thus, there had to be a sailmaker somewhere nearby. An hour of queries around the waterfront eventually led us to a name … Kenny. I found a young girl who knew where Kenny lived. I set out with her toward Kenny's house.

Belize City was laid out around a convoluted network of sewage drainage canals because no municipal sewer pipe system existed. Getting away from the center of town into the quiet back streets and paths, I observed endless rows of tightly packed, one-and-two room wood-frame houses, many of them resting on tall stilts. Flooding had ravaged Belize City in the past, and the poor residents could ill afford to lose their homes again. The houses were painted in a variety of primary colors or simply left unpainted with grey weathering walls. People had nailed planks, somewhat haphazardly across damaged parts of most buildings. Stray mongrel dogs patrolled the streets, foraging for scraps. Scrawny chickens scurried beneath tin-roofed shacks. Old men walked with canes, while barefoot children played happily in the mud. Everyone we passed greeted me warmly, always eager to converse with a stranger. My guide eventually led me down a narrow alley to a grey house on stilts with a screen door at the top of the stairway. I could hear a treadle-driven sewing machine whirring loudly inside. The young girl called up to Kenny. A short aging craftsman soon emerged, grinning broadly.

I asked Kenny if he could make us a sail. In a thick local dialect that I could barely comprehend, he explained that he owned a sewing machine, but we would need to procure all the required materials. Although a sailmaker, he stocked no raw materials, obtaining them only as needed for each individual job. He requested rope for a boltrope, grommets for hanks, durable thread, and sailcloth. We would also need some wire rope for the head and tack pennants. Heavy-duty canvas was the chosen material because Dacron and Nylon were nonexistent in Belize. Kenny ushered me into his unlit single-room home. The walls were painted green. The floor was bare, with furniture sparsely scattered around the periphery. An antique sewing machine sat conspicuously on a simple wooden table. We agreed upon a price equivalent to $85 U.S. and shook hands.

Back at the boat, Louis and I designed the new sail on paper and calculated the quantities of material needed. We cannibalized some of our three-strand nylon anchor rode for a boltrope. We grabbed a few of our spare galvanized steel shackles to substitute as jib hanks. A fabric store in town carried the heavy-duty canvas and thread that we needed. At the big hardware store, we found grommets. Within hours, we had delivered all the requested components to Kenny.

Kenny making our canvas storm jib

Louis, Clark, and I had a few days to hang out while Kenny completed our sail. In contrast to the defensive unsociable attitudes of strangers in cities back home, the people in Belize City were totally unreserved and constantly reaching out to make contact with us on the streets. Dealers pushed drugs more openly than in Harvard Square, though I was never tempted to buy. Despite the endemic poverty, the mood of the people on the streets consistently appeared joyful and optimistic. We did not encounter panhandling. However, at the quay, near *Rhiannon,* several people warned us of thieves boarding vessels. For this reason, one of us usually stayed behind to guard, while the others went into town.

In addition to Bob, we did eventually encounter a few other Americans hanging out in Belize City. There were dopers, radicals hoping to get to Cuba, and a few adventure travelers who had come to experience the jungles, the creole food, the Mayan ruins, and the rhythms of the people. The spectacular beaches and reefs of Belize had not yet been discovered as a premier tourist destination.

Belize remained a part of the British Empire in 1976. Consequently, British diplomats, government officials, and businessmen frequented the city, but they generally remained within their own social sphere. The Fort George Hotel was the place to find the Brits. On Saturday night I went there to have a drink and to dance. There was a great band playing at the time, though I was not really feeling it that day, due to some fatigue and an annoying skin rash.

In the back streets of Belize City

During our stay, Louis, Clark, and I gradually cleaned up the boat. The heavy rains helped by washing the caked salt from the deck and the rigging. But the cabin required considerable direct intervention by all three of us. Examining our store of potatoes and onions that had been kept in a sack beneath the galley sink since New Orleans, we discovered an advanced infestation of writhing maggots and furry mold. Clearly, none of us had been diligent or even satisfactory housekeepers within the cabin. Therefore, we were not the least bit amazed to make this long overdue discovery. As enjoyable, vibrant, and uplifting as

Belize City had been, its drawbacks were rapidly intensifying. Nights were often sleepless and hot. Voracious mosquitoes and invisible sand fleas swarmed in the muggy air. When our new canvas sail was at last finished and the post office tracking board promised clear weather, it was time to move on.

CHAPTER 12

Gracias a Dios

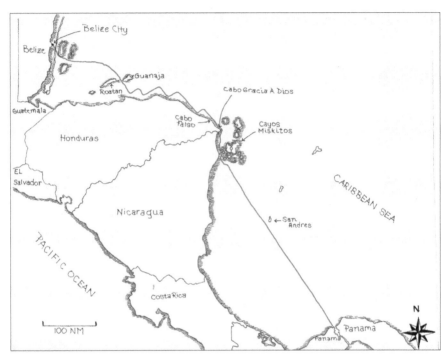

The route from Belize to Panama

ON SEPTEMBER 15, 1976, we cast off *Rhiannon*'s dock lines and cleared the mud bar at the mouth of Haulover Creek. We were officially destined for the Panama Canal Zone, conservatively estimating arrival within two weeks. We had already learned from experience that potential calms, equipment failures, and headwinds precluded overly optimistic predictions for any passage. In letters mailed from Belize to our families back home, we even added a few extra days to our estimates. We never wanted relatives to believe that we might be overdue in port. If we did not contact them when they expected, we feared that perhaps they might initiate some sort of search for us. Furthermore, we were already dealing with enough angst of our own without having any added concerns about someone launching an unwarranted search for us. We never filed any sort of float plan or formal itinerary. In most places we were travelling, no organized search agency or rescue authority even existed. Louis, Clark, and I knew that we were always alone, completely dependent upon our own ingenuity and the limited resources aboard our fragile little boat.

A quick glance at any map or nautical chart of the Western Caribbean immediately reveals the most prominent coastal feature. The eastern point of land in Central America, where the Coco River forms the border between Honduras and Nicaragua, is a cape known as Cabo Gracias a Dios. When voyaging southward along the Central American coast, one must travel eastward against the prevailing contrary wind and current to pass this formidable promontory. The name, meaning "Thanks to God," is attributed to Christopher Columbus. On his fourth voyage in 1502, coincidentally also during the month of September, Columbus required 29 days of rough sailing to reach this cape from Trujillo on the northern Honduras coast. He endured horrible storms and endless headwinds before finally turning south into fair weather. The passage was so miserable, even for the great "Admiral of the Ocean Seas," that he gave thanks to God for rounding this point of land. Louis, Clark, and I definitely were not bold explorers. But we fully understood the reputation of Cabo Gracias a Dios and, accordingly, girded our loins for the impending battle.

Our course took us toward the southeast after passing the south end of Turneffe Island. Cabo Gracias a Dios lay some 325 NM away. We remained well offshore of Glover Reef, attempting to make as much easting as possible. We then continued south on a port tack in moderate southeast winds. On the second evening, I noted that "we saw a magnificent rainbow, a meteor that lit up the area as day ... and several flying fish landed on the deck." Later that night, we tacked back and forth, rail down, as we were struck by intermittent gusty squalls packing 35-knot winds. *Rhiannon* punched into the steep waves. Despite the slog, we only made 10 NM of easting all night. During that night, we spoke to a nearby freighter by radio. They provided a favorable weather forecast for the next day. This was welcome news, especially considering our disheartening progress.

On the following day, we reached the Bay Islands of Honduras: Roatan and Guanaja. In the distance, a rain squall including a waterspout was drifting away, leaving us in fair weather. We were sailing on port tack in an ideal 12-knot southeast breeze with our track leading directly toward the gap between the two verdant Bay Islands. We held our course, cautiously avoiding the shoals east of Roatan. That morning, the sailing was perfect! The sea was absolutely calm, the air was warm, the skies were clear, and the islands looked magnificent. We saw no other people or vessels, even as we later tacked toward the east, following the south shore of Guanaja.

This was our first taste of enjoying an idyllic paradise all to ourselves. Our thoughts turned in awe to the feats of the early European explorers who, amazingly, had sailed through these same waters, without even a chart. We had no clue of the tourist playground that this virgin region would become in the following

decades. I noted in my journal that if severe weather were to crop up over the following days, we now knew of a place where we could easily return to seek shelter.

After passing the Bay Islands, we continued to tack eastward, experiencing
rainsqualls alternating with calms. On the short-wave receiver, we were able to
pick up the Caribbean weather forecast from Miami relayed through a repeater
on Swan Island over 2.8 MHz. Thankfully, there were no storms predicted for
the following three days.

On September 18, during one of several rain squalls, Clark suddenly called
out, "What was that?! ... I just saw a huge dorsal fin." Louis and I wore eyeglasses, so we could see little through our rain-covered lenses and even less with
our glasses removed. Nonetheless, I also soon spotted our visitors. It was a pod
of small black whales. Their smooth sleek backs repeatedly broke the surface, as
close as 10 feet from our starboard beam. Although we could not identify them
at the time, these most likely were pilot whales. They disappeared as quickly as
they had arrived. We sighted no other whales during our time in the Caribbean.
In 1976, populations of the great whales had become alarmingly small, as most
species had been decimated by the active whaling factory ships prowling all the
oceans at that time.

Unlike whales, dolphins were more abundant in the 1970s than they are
today. Over-fishing had not yet critically depleted their food sources. Dolphins
have always been man's greatest companions at sea. They consistently thrilled
all three of us whenever they arrived. Sometimes solitary but usually in groups,
dolphins loved to play around the bow wave, dive beneath the keel, and perform acrobatics while keeping pace alongside the boat. I was always delighted
by the random appearance of dolphins during my night watches. Frequently, I
would be alerted unexpectedly to their presence by the characteristic breathy
"puh-heee" sound of a dolphin exhaling and inhaling as it broke the surface.
Soon others would join the first one, cheering me through my night watch.
Often, the lively underwater chatter of a pod would reverberate loudly through
Rhiannon's resonant hull, waking the off watch as well. We frequently observed
dolphins who probably were also observing us. This was great entertainment.

Sailing a small boat offshore is a form of stark isolation. An appearance
within our circle of view by any animate creature was always a significant
event. During this passage, I became acutely aware of the pelagic birds, the
flying fish, and the leaping tunas, as well as the playful cetaceans that entered
our world. In truth, we were the strangers invading their world, aliens to the
sea. But, occasionally, other members of the land-based world also paid us a
visit. Fishing boats frequently appeared and disappeared over the horizon as we
neared coasts. Aircraft contrails occasionally crossed the sky.

However, to me, the most notable visitors were the ones who, like us, were most
removed from their own element. I easily empathized with the shore birds that

had been lost or blown off course, ending up at sea. I imagine that those birds, not accustomed to long overwater migration, would often meet death in the waves as soon as they became exhausted. A few were lucky and found *Rhiannon,* the witch, transporting her own "three birds." Off the coast of Honduras, just beyond sight of land, on September 18, two small land birds came aboard. One was a finch, and the other a smaller yellow-throated bird. They walked over Clark as he lounged in the cockpit and took turns exploring the cabin. As we tacked back toward the coast, they swiftly departed the moment land was in sight. These visits aboard our floating home were always magically uplifting.

With Clark in the cockpit

A small visitor

Fortunately, we never met the fierce storms and daunting conditions described by Christopher Columbus. However, consistent east winds forced us to tack back and forth repeatedly in our quest of Cabo Gracias a Dios. Other than the wind direction, the weather became fair as we eventually beat into smaller diminishing waves. All afternoon on September 19, we could see a headland that we had hoped was the fabled cape. But as we drew near, the contours of the coast and alignment of the shore informed us instead that this was Cabo Falso, the "false cape" that had given Columbus false hope of having reached the true eastern promontory.

Beyond Cabo Falso, with 21 NM left to Gracias a Dios, we tacked to within 100 yards of the beach just before sunset. A lone man was walking at water's edge along the calm seashore. Even though we had been sailing for four days and were so close to the Honduran coast, we did not land. As darkness fell, we cautiously came about onto starboard tack to head back offshore. As long as the wind blew, we needed to continue toward Panama without stopping.

Louis, Clark, and I then faced our greatest navigational dilemma thus far on our voyage. The sky had become overcast, and the wind had backed slightly to the northeast at about 15 knots. This wind was perfect for a night rounding of the Cape. However, there were no lighthouses, buoys, or other aids to navigation. The charts indicated multiple areas of shoal water inshore, as well as many small reefs and islets, called Miskito Cays, extending well offshore from the Cape. A cloudy sky prohibited celestial navigation. Coastal piloting without any visible landmarks on shore would have been impossible in the dark. We knew that dead reckoning using the compass would surely be helpful. But strong uncharted currents of uncertain direction precluded safe rounding of the Cape using only the compass and sumlog. Unfortunately, the nearest radio beacons were scores of miles away.

Therefore, we carefully studied the charts to consider our alternatives. One plan would involve sailing far offshore, bypassing all the hazards near the coast. But that would add a full day to our trip. Just then, I saw another possible way forward. I ran my idea past Louis and Clark. A contour line on the chart denoting a depth of four fathoms (24 feet) described a broad meandering arc that rounded the entire Cape while threading between all the obstacles. The northeast wind would enable us to navigate the entire passage, sailing on a comfortable reach. We all agreed that this would be our plan. Next, we confirmed that our depth sounder was functioning properly. Just in case the depth sounder might fail, we readied our lead line as a backup. All three of us were game for the challenge.

The flashing red dot on the face of the circular depth sounder indicated we were in 50 feet of water. We eased the sails, falling off toward shore. Slowly, the bottom rose toward *Rhiannon*'s keel as we met the shallow water. At just under

25 feet, we intercepted the imaginary four-fathom contour line and adjusted our course. For the next four hours, all three of us remained vigilant on deck. We passed several unlit fishing stakes but otherwise kept well clear of hazards, as we walked a virtual tightrope between the prominent point and the treacherous reefs. Once we had successfully passed Cabo Gracias a Dios, feeling immense relief, we set our course offshore, toward Panama. Louis, Clark, and I had accomplished in days what had taken Columbus weeks.

The Night Was Not Over Yet!

It was midnight. None of us had yet slept. Our routine watch schedule had been disrupted by the navigational test that we had just passed so cleverly, with high marks. I took the first watch. We continued sailing briskly on a reach toward the south southeast. By 1:30 a.m., tired and bleary-eyed, I spotted the lights of a ship. I immediately took its bearing, using our small hand bearing compass. The vessel was nearly dead ahead. Although I saw white lights, even through binoculars I could not make out her green or red navigational lights. It appeared to me that this ship was steaming directly toward us. I altered course to port, expecting the ship's bearing to progressively change, passing us to starboard. When I next looked up, the ship's lights again appeared to be coming directly toward us, although I still could not make out the structure of the vessel herself.

I called Louis up on deck to help. By now, it was time for his designated watch. To both of us, it appeared that the ship was now moving across to our port side. In response, Louis veered to starboard as we continued charging forward at four and a half knots. Still unsure of the ship's course, we altered our course once again. Multiple lights on the deck of the huge freighter rapidly loomed up before us, blinding our night vision and obscuring our view of the immense vessel.

We had approached to within less than 100 yards of an imminent collision when suddenly, to our astonishment, we both realized that the ship was anchored! We had been inadvertently homing in on her towering steel hull all along. This was an optical illusion in the night. We had still been sailing over the coastal shelf, in only 100 feet of water. It had never occurred to us that something might be anchored there, beyond sight of land. We had learned an important lesson from this bizarre, nearly disastrous, self-wrought error. As we sailed around the anchored ship, Louis and I looked at one another and burst into laughter at our own foolishness. Our laughter awoke Clark, who staggered on deck, just in time to see us gliding alongside the brightly lit stationary ship.

As we headed back into open water, the waves grew, and the wind picked up once again. We sailed all morning under a triple-reefed main and working jib.

We were making a steady six knots with occasional bursts of seven and a half to eight knots. By noon we were abeam of San Andrés Island. We had travelled approximately 150 NM in 24 hours, our best day's run since New Orleans. This fascinating Colombian island of white sand beaches and pristine reefs loomed on the hazy horizon to our east. Lively Caribbean and Colombian music, broadcast from San Andrés, played loudly on our radio. It was enticing. We debated finding an anchorage and checking in. But we were well on our way to the Canal Zone. Our true goal was to get to the Pacific Ocean. Panama was finally within reach, and for once we had great wind. With bittersweet feelings about bypassing this intriguing island, we continued south.

While at sea, *Rhiannon*'s port quarter berth became my own personal space. It is essential for every crew member aboard a vessel of any size to have a refuge, a designated space to which he or she may retreat. Although there might be little true privacy without separate cabins, a defined zone in which one may sleep or find solitude on board is essential. Living in close quarters with others for an extended period requires interludes of separation. Small-boat sailors must learn to respect the needs of the others for "alone time" throughout their time off watch. During these down times in our private spaces, we were free to read, write letters, complete journal entries, explore the radio dial, or sleep.

Falling asleep aboard a constantly moving sailboat heeled to one side required skill. The entire experience of sleep on *Rhiannon* was far different from that of slumber ashore. First one must find a secure position. Wedging flexed knees against the sides of the quarter berth was a start. Propping cushions or pillows all around may help a bit more. But this was only the beginning. Finding a position of security in a pounding seaway required more finesse, gained only through experience over time. Adequate ventilation generally demanded some fiddling, as well. As soon as the proper arrangement was found, transitioning into a relaxed meditative trance was essential. Sleep would remain elusive if one's muscles were allowed to contract reflexively in response to the lurching of the hull. Once asleep, my dreams were generally based on land. Awakening from such a dream and finding myself far out to sea, being thrown about in my tight quarter berth was almost always disorienting and frightening.

On September 23, 1976, following one more day of heavy, wet sailing past San Andrés, we planned our final approach to the Canal Zone. Once again, with cloudy skies and intermittent thunderstorms, we depended upon our radio direction finder for navigation. We did not know the RDF frequency of France Field, which was located near the Cristobal Harbor breakwater entrance. Instead we used the radio beacons from Taboga Island in the Pacific and Puerto Limon, Costa Rica. Additionally, we found medium-wave broadcast stations in Panama City suitable for homing. The clouds parted just long enough to obtain a noon sun sight with the sextant. In a dying wind, we found ourselves 26 NM out.

For the first time in our journey, we cranked up the Atomic-4 and used the engine instead of the sails for propulsion. We powered along for five hours, reaching the Cristobal Harbor breakwater after dark. We narrowly avoided a few large freighters as they picked up steam heading out into the Atlantic following their eight-hour canal transits. In my journal, I wrote:

We almost smashed into a can to which a barge was moored in the breakwater entrance. It should not have been there. Apparently, it was involved in salvaging a wrecked vessel.

We had spent the entire afternoon cleaning out the boat while under power that day. All three of us had noticed that the cabin had taken on what we thought was a "maritime smell." It was a kind of pungent fishy odor that would surely have been offensive to anyone unaccustomed to the stench. We were embarrassed that we had acquired a fishy smell despite having never caught a single fish to eat since we left.

Due to the tight stowage aboard *Rhiannon*, we always left our frying pan on the gimbaled stovetop at the base of the companionway steps. Since we left Belize, I had remained barefoot, leaving my deck shoes right at the foot of the stove. I picked up my shoes, knowing that I would need to wear them soon to go ashore. I immediately found the source of our malodorous boat: A large flying fish had died in one of my shoes. Apparently, this unlucky fish had flown from the sea on its own wings, missing our frying pan by mere inches. The irony of the situation did not escape us. A fish that died trying to get into our frying pan was the closest we had come to catching a meal.

We were well rested and in fine shape as we finally dropped our CQR anchor in "the Flats" of Cristobal Harbor. Sharing the anchorage with a variety of small freighters, we raised the code "Q" flag. We opened a bottle of wine to celebrate and tuned-in to the Armed Forces Radio station to listen to the Ford vs. Carter Presidential debate.

CHAPTER 13

In the Zone

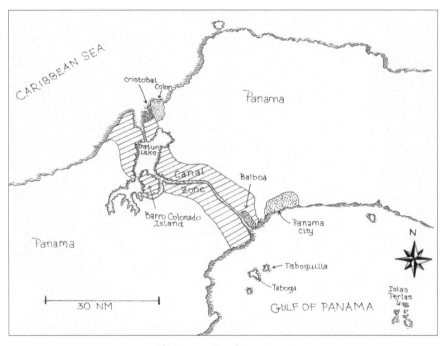

The Panama Canal Zone in 1976

The Panama Canal Zone

The Flats, where we anchored the evening of our arrival, were a dreary wide-open wasteland at one side of the dirty commercial harbor of Cristobal. This roadstead served as a compulsory purgatory, where arriving boats without a fixed destination were relegated to anchor. Tramp steamers, rusty 100- to 300-ton cargo ships, and a variety of workboats lay at their anchors, randomly spaced across its gloomy waters. Louis, Clark, and I had barely begun to toast our safe arrival when a Coast Guard launch carrying some officials motored up in the dark.

This was our first occasion to witness the skillful maneuvering of the pilot boats and launches in the American-controlled Panama Canal Zone (CZ). They always approached us from abeam at an alarming speed, as if planning to ram us broadside. Next, the driver would dexterously shift into reverse gear, bringing the bow of the launch to an impressive halt inches from our topsides. In a well-orchestrated maneuver, the official would then step effortlessly from the bow of the launch onto our deck, just as the launch would begin to back away with a roar to wait nearby.

That night when the officials checked us in, we discussed the Panama Canal Tonnage Certificate that we had obtained in New Orleans. The officer informed us that the tonnage as measured in New Orleans would not be recognized by the authorities in the Canal Zone. Panama Canal tonnage, in 1976, was based on a unique archaic formula devised in 1914 specifically for cargo ships. Neither container ships nor yachts had been considered when the rule was written. Permanent treaties had always precluded updating the original formula. An example of gross bureaucratic bungling, this measurement calculation included cargo tonnage below deck, engine room tonnage, and a variety of other parameters that were totally irrelevant to our pint-sized sailboat. Following some discussion, we produced the obscure regulation verifying the validity of our measurement certificate from New Orleans. The officer still insisted that we would need to be re-measured. But happily, for us, the $50 re-measurement fee would be waived. All we would need to pay was the canal transit toll. We would have to wait several days to learn what that would cost.

The CZ that I experienced in 1976 represented a living crossroads of cultures, commerce, and ideologies embroiled in conflict. The Canal Zone had been leased by the United States from Panama since the canal's construction early in the 20th century. The CZ included the canal, which traverses the isthmus via manmade Gatun Lake, as well as a narrow buffer of land on either side of the waterway itself. An engineering marvel of the world, excavated at the expense of thousands of lives, the Panama Canal has been a strategic and economic asset since its construction.

Effectively a territory of the United States, the CZ divided the impoverished country of Panama into two halves. The geography of the CZ is confusing. Due to a winding S-curve in the Central American isthmus, the Pacific outlet of the canal paradoxically lies east of its Atlantic opening. Situated at the Atlantic end of the canal in 1976 was the town of Cristobal, contained within the confines of the CZ. The neighboring city of Colon lay immediately adjacent to Cristobal, but within the country of Panama. Similarly, on the Pacific side, Balboa was the American enclave within the Zone, located directly alongside the sprawling Latin American metropolis of Panama City, which is in Panama.

When we arrived, during the fall of 1976, Panama was rife with political tensions and social unrest. The official American buildings within the CZ sported immense red, white, and blue banners celebrating the American Bicentennial that year. American flags were ubiquitous. Simultaneously, the Panamanian radio waves were dominated by constant anti-American propaganda broadcasts emitted by the military dictatorship of General Omar Torrijos, whose official title was "Maximum Leader of the Panamanian Revolution." Torrijos commanded the Guardia Nacional, the rifle-toting military police force that patrolled the country with an iron hand. The Panamanian quest to gain sovereignty of the lucrative canal linking the Atlantic and the Pacific was reaching a crescendo. The presidential election in the U.S. further escalated Torrijos' anti-American rhetoric.

The CZ was home to the service members and families stationed at the various American military installations found within the enclave. The American-owned Panama Canal Company managed all activities associated with operation of the canal itself. The historic Gorgas Hospital and the Barro Colorado Island outpost of the Smithsonian Tropical Research Institute were also located within the American CZ. Neatly landscaped early 20th century colonial-style government buildings lined the tidy CZ streets in the areas away from the canal itself.

In contrast to those streets, the parts of the Canal Zone immediately flanking the canal resembled any other busy industrial seaport. In both Cristobal and Balboa, monotonous commercial wharves were lined with cargo ships, dry docks, and rows of tuna boats. Tugboats, pilot boats, and dredge barges charged back and forth between the big ships. Day and night, a steady procession of ships transited the canal in both directions.

Within the CZ, an old-fashioned passenger railroad line traversed the isthmus. In 1976, one-way train fare between the Atlantic and the Pacific was exactly one dollar. Merchant seamen, shipping agents, American service members, and government officials, all conducted their business entirely within confines of the well-secured CZ, often oblivious to the squalor in neighboring Panama City.

Unfortunately, for cruising sailors, the Panama Canal was never the quick shortcut linking the seas that they had anticipated. Instead, it was a bottleneck. Panama had a way of sucking you in, then chewing you up slowly before spitting you out on the other side. In 1976, sailboats arrived at a rate of two or three per week. It was the rare boat that stayed less than a week. Most yachts remained for more than a month. No one left Panama unchanged. The unrest, the variety of fascinating people, the impressive canal … all had a profound impact on me.

With Panamanian Independence Day approaching, the Torrijos government launched a heightened anti-American campaign. The xenophobic attacks incited by Torrijos added to the violent crimes that were already rampant in the poverty-stricken streets of Panama City. Americans were prime targets. Shortly following our arrival, we learned that transient yachtsmen were banned from shopping in the commissaries and co-ops within the CZ. Only Canal Zone residents were permitted. As a result, Louis, Clark, and I had to venture into the dangerous streets of Colon or Panama City to purchase all provisions and equipment for *Rhiannon.*

After anchoring and clearing-in, we inflated one of our flimsy Sevylor dinghies and rowed three-quarters of a nautical mile into the night to the nearest commercial wharf. We fought a strong current, with four oars pulling at once, to get through the choppy harbor. The shrill whistles of tugboats and the deep sounds of loud engines punctuated the darkness. We tied up next to a giant container ship, the *Falcon,* registered in Monrovia, Liberia, a common port of convenience.

Anchored among small freighters in the Flats

The streets of Cristobal were desolate. The shuttered offices of shipping agents were marked by simple placards on the quiet warehouses. Louis, Clark, and I made our way together past the widely spaced streetlamps in the dockyards. Eventually, we reached the Panama Canal Yacht Club, tucked into the deepest recess of the harbor. The three small piers at the yacht club were fully occupied, primarily by cruising sailboats of all descriptions. Despite our wobbly legs, we arrived at the yacht club bar and each had a drink. Somehow, well after midnight, we located our dinghy and, more amazingly, found our way back to *Rhiannon,* swinging happily around her anchor in the Flats.

By dawn it was raining steadily. At 8:00 a.m. a strong squall came through. Our anchor began dragging in the gusty wind, pushing us toward a 200-ton freighter anchored nearby. Fortunately, our engine started, and we were able to motor forward in the blinding downpour. We re-anchored with greater scope in a better position.

Later that morning, Louis rowed ashore in the drizzle to see if we could secure a spot at the Panama Canal Yacht Club. Unfortunately, the club was completely full, and we were not able to obtain clearance to move out of the Flats for four more days. Early-morning squalls in the Flats became routine. Eventually, we were able to move to the club. Following a short period tied to a huge steel mooring ball there, we managed to obtain a comfortable spot on a pier.

On a large mooring ball at the Panama Canal Yacht Club

On a dock at the yacht club. *Sagarmatha,* belonging to our friends Paname and Paul Paris is tied aft

Meanwhile, Clark had contacted his mother, Betty Lou Pellett, and older sister, Marlene (Mutsy), who arranged to fly to Panama to join us for our eventual transit through the canal. Both loved to travel and were looking forward to seeing Clark. Clark's mom relished the idea of transiting the canal on her son's boat. We had three weeks in Panama before they arrived. We spent our days working on *Rhiannon* and getting to know the other cruisers.

While we were waiting, we strongly considered sailing to the San Blas Islands (Guna Yala), to see the native Kuna (Guna) villages and picturesque diving spots. We had seen the Kuna people with their distinctive piercings and jewelry walking through town, selling the beautiful reverse-appliqué molas for which they are known. However, during our first few days at the Panama Canal Yacht Club, we had encountered four sailboats that recently had been struck by lightning. Three of those had been hit while in the San Blas Islands. When we saw the insidious internal damage to the structures of those boats, we decided that we should stay put.

Besides, this was our best opportunity to pursue critical boat projects. We had to repair the detached rub rail, build ratlines for climbing aloft, construct a wooden whisker pole, and procure a self-steering wind vane. Each week, I looked forward to listening to the latest music on Casey Kasem's *American Top 40*, broadcast every Saturday on the Armed Forces Radio. Popular songs at that time included *Magic Man* by Heart, *The Wreck of the Edmund Fitzgerald* by Gordon Lightfoot, and *Fernando* by Abba.

Completing our projects required daily forays from the CZ into the dangerous neighborhoods of Colon to shop for needed supplies. One afternoon, Louis, Clark, and I went to a lumber yard in town where we bought boards made of some tropical mystery wood to build a long, hollow whisker pole for *Rhiannon*. Panama was the only country in which I had ever travelled where old women and strangers on the city streets repeatedly warned me to turn back due to the danger. We learned to travel in groups of two or more when walking through the streets of Colon. We always moved swiftly, maintaining a watchful eye toward the rear, never lingering longer than necessary to complete the business at hand.

When the day's work was complete, or we were simply too tired and hot to continue, we hung out at the yacht club, where an odd mix of fascinating individuals always gathered. Cuba libres at the bar cost 30 cents during happy hour. Late afternoon drinks quickly became routine. One evening, walking into the yacht club, all three of us recognized a familiar face. Captain Bob Jensen was drinking at the bar. The master of the *SS Cristobal* was sitting exactly where he had told us to find him, when we had originally met him in Gulfport, Mississippi, over two months earlier. He was less surprised to see that we had made it to Panama than we were ourselves.

The *Cristobal* was in port, tied up along a pier for another two days. He offered us a tour of the ship, which we enthusiastically accepted. We thoroughly enjoyed our extensive tour of that stately old steamship, soon to be retired from service. The archaic control bridge, the engine room with its massive boilers, the cargo hold, and the captain's quarters were all impressive marvels of a bygone era. Louis, Clark, and I appreciated the confidence that Captain Jensen had instilled in us back in Gulfport, more than he ever realized.

While in the CZ, I contacted John Pickering, a former biology teaching fellow of mine at Harvard, who was doing post-graduate research at the Smithsonian Tropical Research Institute on Barro Colorado Island. When canal building engineers dammed the Chagres River to create Gatun Lake in 1914, this island had been left as a natural tropical rainforest. It had been used continuously over the years as a field station for biological research. While in Panama, I was able to arrange an overnight visit to this fascinating island, spending two days on its trails observing the amazing variety of flora and fauna along with some of the researchers.

Transiting the Canal

We soon learned that sailboats frequently were damaged during their hazardous transits through the Panama Canal. Tales of crushed hulls and toppled rigging caused by careless boat handling in the locks had spread through the yacht club grapevine. With time on our hands and a desire to familiarize ourselves with the canal transit procedures, Louis, Clark, and I each arranged to crew as line-handlers on other boats making their transits before *Rhiannon's*.

I crewed for a fellow named George Miller, a brash '65 Harvard graduate, former Peace Corps volunteer, and advertising filmmaker. He was single handing his modified Grampian 30 from New York to Los Angeles, supposedly to meet his fiancée. Despite his professed plan, George had deservedly gained a reputation as a womanizer at the yacht club. I picked up a few tricks during our transit, but only related to line-handling. My practice transit with George Miller went without incident. It was an essential learning experience for me.

Louis made his practice run aboard *Caravela of Exe*, a beautiful Alden Caravelle being circumnavigated by a lovely British couple named Ted and Mary Lyne. Clark also found a boat for his own practice run. Following these exercises, we felt thoroughly prepared for our own trip through the canal.

In 1976, all yacht transits were accomplished in a single day, under power. Small engineless sailboats needed to temporarily fit an outboard motor to make the passage. The Panama Canal has three locks at the Atlantic side and three at the Pacific side, with the manmade Gatun Lake situated at a higher level at mid-isthmus. There were three methods of lockage available for sailboats.

"Center chamber" lockage involved using four heavy dock lines, two at the bow and two at the stern, all secured on bollards at the sides of the lock, while the boat rode in the center. These lines were tended by line-handlers aboard the boat. The four line-handlers, to be supplied by the yacht owner, would take in or let out their respective lines progressively as the boat rose or descended in mid chamber. Center locking was safe if the lines were well handled because the mast and rigging were unlikely to strike a wall when the turbulent water rushed in. Woe is the boat whose line-handlers lose control when the massive culverts belch forth their swirling eddies of churning water or a giant ship's propeller creates a powerful backwash.

The second method was "side chamber" locking. Side locking involved tying up to one wall of the chamber using old tires as fenders. As the boat scraped up or down against the rough pitted concrete wall, the spreaders, mast, or rigging could easily be damaged.

The third type of lockage involved rafting alongside a bigger boat, such as a tugboat, while that bigger boat was side locking. This required no active line-handling while the water level changed. It was therefore the safest and easiest of all.

If a yacht carried the requisite four dock lines, the captain could request center lockage. Otherwise, the boat would be relegated to the treacherous wall. Rafting to a tug or workboat was a matter of random chance.

Sailboats were permitted to transit, by reservation, on any day of the week. Yachts were usually accompanied in each lock chamber by a large ship. The Panama Canal Company always placed a professional canal pilot aboard each transiting vessel, to remain in command throughout the transit. Interestingly, the Panama Canal was the only place in the world where U.S. Navy ships temporarily gave up their military command to a civilian pilot. The entire 25-mile transit for a sailboat would take a whole day, from dawn to dusk.

Our long-awaited transit began early in the morning on October 12, 1976. We motored to Manzanillo Bay just outside of the Gatun Locks to await our turn. We were the only transiting sailboat on that day. Clark's mother and sister had joined us in Panama as planned and were part of our crew for the transit. Additionally, John Pickering, my biologist friend from Barro Colorado Island, was aboard for the adventure. Scotty, our Panama Canal Pilot, was in charge at the helm. We had paid our canal toll, which amounted to $9.46 U.S. In contrast, today a typical 30-foot sailboat transit costs over $2000 U.S.

Scotty was a 50-year-old man with a neatly trimmed grey beard. He wore a dark blue baseball cap and chain-smoked cigars. He lounged in the cockpit with one hand on the tiller, keeping a hand-held radio at his side. We kept Scotty well supplied with Kentucky Fried Chicken and beer throughout our transit. Later in the day, when rain showers arrived, he put on a yellow slicker and pith helmet. He looked to me like a cross between a Grand Banks fisherman and a 19th century African explorer. For him, working on a small sailboat was a walk in the park compared to conning a container ship. The Panama Canal Company paid Scotty $200 U.S. per transit regardless of the size of the vessel. Our toll did not even begin to cover the Canal's expenses for our transit.

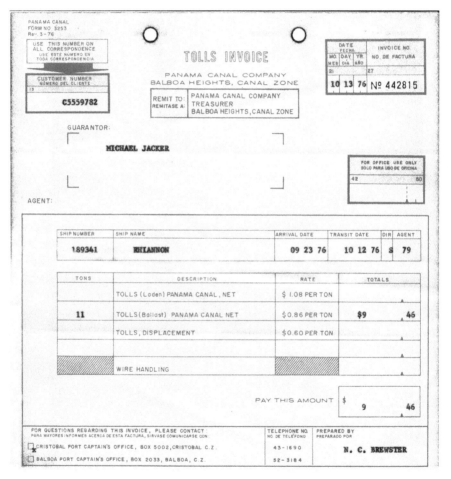

Our Panama Canal toll receipt—A great bargain

After we motored into the first lock chamber, the shore workers threw four heaving lines out to the boat, two from each wall, using monkey's fists. Some transiting cruisers I had watched wore helmets to protect their heads from the hardball-like monkey's fists. Others caught them with baseball mitts. On *Rhiannon,* we let the attached messenger lines fall across the deck then scrambled to pick them up before they dropped into the water. We tied our four heavy dock lines to the lightweight messenger lines leading ashore. The canal workers then pulled the dock lines up to bollards atop the chamber walls. This was repeated for four of the six locks that day. We were fortunate to raft up to a canal tug that happened to be passing through, in the final two descending locks at Miraflores, near the Pacific terminus of the canal.

Scotty our Panama Canal pilot

In the first lock, an immense container ship pulled up close behind us, guided by electric locomotives known as "mules." The ship's bow loomed above us in the chamber, underscoring *Rhiannon*'s diminutive size. Thanks to our practice runs on other sailboats, the locking was uneventful. Throughout the day, Clark's mother and sister relaxed on deck, enjoying the varied scenery of the canal. They alternately sunned themselves or sheltered beneath the cockpit awning during rain showers. Unfortunately, an injury on board eventually marred the day. John Pickering was standing on the foredeck when a ship passing us in Gatun Lake generated a steep bow wave. As *Rhiannon* abruptly pitched, John was flung into the forestay, gashing open his forehead. Scotty radioed for help. A Canal Company launch soon evacuated John to Gorgas Hospital where he was sutured, while the rest of us completed the transit. At sunset, we arrived at the Balboa Yacht Club where we picked up our assigned mooring. After a few days of local sightseeing, Clark's mother and sister flew home.

A container ship shares a lock chamber with us

Clark and his sister on the foredeck, Louis, and Clark's mother in the cockpit

Louis tending lines on the foredeck while center chamber locking

Rhiannon advancing into the next chamber. Note the U.S. Bicentennial decorations on the building

Balboa

At Balboa, the tides were extreme. Every six hours, the water level changed an average of 15 feet, with an 18-foot difference between high and low water during spring tides. This meant that there was almost always a strong current in the mooring field at the yacht club. Additionally, the yacht club moorings were located immediately alongside the main ship channel for the canal. Every 20 minutes the wake from a passing ship would cause all the boats to roll vigorously from side to side. As a result, in 1976, both anchoring and the use of private dinghies were prohibited. Launch service ran until 12:30 a.m. To get the attention of the launch driver to take us ashore, we had to wave vigorously or flash lights.

About the time we arrived in Balboa, Clark decided to apply to law schools. The application process was lengthy; mail correspondence was slow. We had to spend several extra weeks in Panama while Clark slogged through the applications. In the hope of speeding up this process, Clark temporarily moved into the home of Professor Jenkins, a CZ resident whom he had met, while Louis and I remained on board *Rhiannon*.

While Clark applied to law schools, Louis and I tackled our self-steering issue. We had encountered several boats with self-steering windvane systems. *Prospero, Zingara V, Sea Oak,* and some others all used RVG vanes. *Sagarmatha* had an Aries vane. Dave Shields of *Sea Oak* and his wife were finishing their cruise and returning to Florida. We offered to buy their RVG. They would not consider selling it at any price.

Then we met Louis Cibulka, a Czech engineer aboard his Morgan 41, *Dragon*. He had designed and built his own windvane. When he got word that we were looking for a self-steering system, he immediately offered to sell us parts of his. He loved his design and assured us that it had worked well for four years. The only problem was that it was sometimes a bit too small to handle the steering loads on his 41-footer. He said it would be perfect for *Rhiannon*. He was planning to build a similar but bigger system for *Dragon*. As the seller was a bit of a wheeler dealer, Louis and I were not 100% confident that he was offering us worthwhile parts. Nonetheless, we paid him $235 U.S. for two items: a vertical-axis vane made of welded stainless steel covered by cloth fabric impregnated with airplane dope and a wooden auxiliary rudder with a trim tab. It would be left for us to design, fabricate, and install all the mounting brackets and linkages necessary to make it work. He provided us with a general idea of how the system was supposed to function, but the rest was up to us.

Rhiannon had a steeply raked reverse transom. We knew that the mounting brackets would be complex. Since we had purchased the major components we were committed to the project. There were four major challenges: 1) designing the mechanism, 2) determining the complex angles and dimensions for the parts, 3) traveling through the dangerous streets of Panama City to find stainless steel pipe and welders, and 4) installing the device on *Rhiannon*'s transom while hanging over the side of our bobbing dinghy at the Balboa yacht club mooring, amid strong currents and ships' wakes.

Panama was in turmoil. In response to ongoing bomb threats by Panamanian terrorists, the CZ authorities had imposed martial law. For several days we could not leave the yacht club grounds. During a lull in the violence, we were able to find the parts we needed. For the two of us, building the self-steering system from our dinghy in the turbulent water was an engineering feat rivaling the construction of the Panama Canal itself. We managed to get the job done.

Installing George from a dinghy

While in Panama, I once again attempted to obtain official permission to cruise in the Galapagos Islands. Now that we had arrived in Panama, we needed a definitive plan. I made a trip to the Ecuadorian embassy in Panama City, which once again proved futile. I spoke with administrators at the Smithsonian Tropical Research Institute. They had no inside track with the Ecuadorians either. We had met a few other cruisers heading west, who had their own ideas of how to get into the Galapagos.

Don Sandstrom, a Californian circumnavigating with his family aboard their home-built Cross 40 trimaran *Anduril*, also had tried in vain to obtain a permit. He was simply going to go anyway. Circumnavigators Don and Sue Moesly, aboard their beautiful double ender *Svea*, planned to stop in the Galapagos on their way across the Pacific, but had no inside connections either. "Paname" and Paul Paris on *Sagarmatha*, along with some French friends of theirs from the

Club Nautico in Colon, were planning to stop at the Darwin Station on their way to the Marquesas. None of them had Ecuadorian documents. Louis on *Dragon*, from Czechoslovakia, also planned to head to the Galapagos without a permit.

Ecuador was severely restricting access to their Islas Encantadas. We had exhausted all our avenues to acquire official permission to cruise there. We decided simply to improvise a plan — and go.

I Almost Lose Louis

In the evenings, after working on *Rhiannon*, we had no place to hang out besides the Balboa Yacht Club restaurant and bar. Louis was stir-crazy, though he seemed to enjoy partying along with a heavy-drinking crowd at the bar. I was seriously concerned that Louis was depressed. Long days spent bobbing on our mooring working in the sun, with no departure date in sight was frustrating. One evening, I had had my fill of drinking by 11 p.m. I hopped aboard a launch to ride out to our boat. I immediately went to bed. Louis remained at the yacht club, drinking with his friends.

An hour or so later, I was awakened in my quarter berth when I heard the launch from the club banging into *Rhiannon*'s side. This was followed by a loud thud in the cockpit above me as Louis stumbled aboard. Although I was half asleep, I distinctly heard Louis coming into the cabin. Noisily, he dumped out tin cans of stored food from an old canvas sail bag. I then heard Louis climb back into the cockpit, followed immediately by an ominous splash. It was approximately 1 a.m. I knew that the launch service had stopped running for the night.

I called up to Louis, but he did not reply. I went up into the cockpit, tripping over cans of food on the floor. There was no sign of Louis. I shined a flashlight into the dark night as I shouted in all directions. There was still no sign of Louis. I was terrified that Louis, depressed, discouraged, and drunk, had thrown himself into the fierce tidal currents at the edge of the canal's busy ship channel.

I immediately attempted to raise other nearby boats and the yacht club on the VHF radio with no success. I dreaded telling Louis's parents and Clark what had happened. With the strong currents and abundant sharks, I doubted that his body would ever be found. It looked like the end of our journey. Several minutes later, as I was still trying to raise help on the radio, I heard splashing in the water several yards off the stern. I trained my flashlight beam on the sound. There was Louis, swimming steadily back toward our boat! Louis was wearing only underpants. I helped him aboard in his exhausted, wet, inebriated state.

As I later understood, based upon his drunken logic, Louis had decided to continue partying aboard a neighboring boat. Since the launch service had stopped for the night, Louis had decided to swim to the other boat. To keep his clothes dry he had put them into the only empty bag he could find. He said that by the time he reached the other boat they had all gone to sleep. He lost the sail bag and all his clothing in the water. Incredibly, he had been able to swim against the moderate current near slack tide and miraculously find our boat in the dark.

The Cruising Community

In 1976, Panama attracted an intriguing cross-section of cruisers sailing a variety of boats and heading in multiple directions. Not all of them were transiting the canal. Some were coastal travelers from South America or North America. Some were on deliveries from the west coast to the east coast of North America or vice versa. Some had sailed down the west coast of Central America from the U.S. or Canada on their way to the Galapagos or the South Pacific. Many people were voyaging from an assortment of European countries. There are far more cruising sailors today than in the 1970s. But today's sailors fit the same stereotypes and have similar stories.

Although cruising sailors continue to depend upon one another for technical assistance, spare parts, tools, advice, camaraderie, and entertainment, these dependencies were greatly magnified in 1976. Without the Internet or cruising guidebooks, they depended on word of mouth and exchange of paper charts to acquire critical information. Neither the Panamanians nor the American residents of the CZ regularly socialized with the transients. Consequently, the people living aboard yachts quickly developed strong bonds and intense relationships with one another. The following are a few of the transients I remember most vividly.

Xochitl (pronounced Soh-chee)

I met Janet Howard Ross, a woman in her early 20s, while transiting the canal with George Miller. She was a holdover flower child, a somewhat loose, barefoot, blue-eyed blonde vegetarian, who resembled a *Mad Magazine* cartoon character. She had previously travelled overland to Costa Rica from Mexico, where she had adopted the Aztec name for flower, Xochitl. She was a maritime hitchhiker, without a boat of her own. She had arrived in Panama on some long-departed boat. When I met her, she was looking for a ride out. Perpetually smiling and flirting, she seemed to have boyfriends on several yachts. Xochitl was friendly with everyone at both yacht clubs in the CZ. At the Panama Canal Yacht Club, she fixed a rip in my shorts with a beautiful reverse applique patch in the style of the Kunas. I remember her telling me that she previously had been a big believer in astrology but that "it doesn't work on travelling people."

At one-point, Xochitl wanted to join the three of us on *Rhiannon*. Fortunately, she hooked up with a British single hander named Sean instead. She hoped to continue voyaging with him on his catamaran. In my journal, I declared that she was "bad luck." I wrote:

> *We may have taken her were it not for this fact. On the boat that brought her to Panama, one guy was thrown overboard, and another guy was thrown down and hurt. She had known John Pickering, who unluckily sustained a severe laceration as a line handler while going through the canal on* Rhiannon. *When she went out on a date with Sean in Colon, he was knifed in the back and has been in the hospital for over a week.*

I have one more "bad luck" story regarding Xochitl. One evening, she assembled a group of a half dozen cruisers to walk together into the dangerous streets of Colon to visit Sean in the hospital. While we were quickly moving together on a busy sidewalk, a Jeep carrying two of the Panamanian Guardia Nacional pulled up and summoned me to their car. At the time, I had curly brown hair and a red beard, but I did not appear particularly different from the other Europeans and Americans walking with me toward the hospital. In Spanish, the Guardias demanded to see my papers and to know where I was going. When they learned that I was an American and was not carrying my passport at the time, they threatened to arrest me. They did not believe that I was walking to visit a friend in the hospital.

The others waited on the sidewalk and watched to see what would become of me. The Guardias said some insulting things, which I barely understood, and ordered me to leave Panama. Luckily, following this brief harassment, they let me go. As a suburban boy from Illinois, I realized with fear that if I were assaulted on the street, the police would be against me. I had a momentary glimpse into the subjugation that threatens half the world. I understood that there was no security for me in Panama.

Paname

Jean-Paul Paris, known as "Paname," was a French nuclear physicist and world-class mountaineer. In 1971, he had played a pivotal role as a member of the successful French expedition to the west ridge of Makalu, the fifth highest peak in the Himalayas. In 2020, he remains a well-known internationally respected alpinist.

By 1974, Paname and his wife "Paul," both in their mid-40s, had been inspired by Bernard Moitessier, the famous French solo circumnavigator and author. Moitessier is best known for "dropping out" of the original Golden Globe Single-handed Round-the-World Race in 1969. He left the race to continue sailing around the world one and a half times, eventually reaching Tahiti. Moitessier had continued to sail in his double-ended steel-hulled sloop *Joshua* for many years, finally settling on the island of Ahe in the Tuamotus.

Paname and Paul, extreme adventurers themselves, had decided to follow in the path of Moitessier. In the same boat yard in France where *Joshua* had been built for Moitessier, they commissioned the construction of a nearly identical sister ship. They christened her *Sagarmatha*, the Nepali name for Mount Everest.

Always thorough planners, Paname and Paul outfitted their bright red 38-foot double-ender with the most robust and reliable equipment available. They planned to sail to Ahe to visit Bernard Moitessier at his home. Ultimately, they hoped to move to Tahiti where Paname might find a job with the French government as a physicist. In the mid-1970s nuclear weapons testing on Mururoa, in the southern Tuamotus was in full swing.

The two of them kept *Sagarmatha* spotless. At the Panama Canal Yacht Club dock, Paul would appear in her bikini, mopping the deck every morning. Several times while in Panama, I was lucky enough to be invited to dinner aboard their boat and totally enjoyed their good wine, Paul's French cooking, and our stimulating conversations over dinner. We often discussed technical aspects of cruising and navigation strategies for the Pacific Ocean.

Paname was eager to share his amazing photos and the harrowing true stories of the Makalu expedition. In contrast, our trivial "adventure" in *Rhiannon* seemed insignificant. This was not to be the last time our paths would cross.

D'Arcy Whiting

The pre-eminent stalwart of the New Zealand yachting community, and a legendary gregarious character, D'Arcy Whiting was in Panama en route to New Zealand, on the final leg of an extended family cruise. D'Arcy, his wife Mollie, their daughter Debbie, and future daughter-in-law Annie, were aboard their sloop *Tequila*. *Tequila* was an immaculate 47-foot, custom racer/cruiser designed by D'Arcy's naval architect son, Paul Whiting. The boat's sleek kauri wood hull was painted sky blue. Her interior was exceptionally well appointed for cruising, especially considering that she had been successfully campaigned by the Whitings for several years in the competitive New Zealand racing circuit. They had just completed a cruise in North America.

I was inspired by their gracious hospitality and wealth of sailing experience. After being treated as an equal aboard *Tequila,* I for the first time truly felt welcomed into the fraternity of world sailors. I knew that we would meet them again somewhere down the road.

Yvonne Larsson

Two interesting sailboats arrived at the Balboa Yacht Club within days of each other: *Cimarron,* an Islander 44, and *Santa Maria,* a 50-foot traditional double-ended wooden ketch from Chile. A large Swedish flag flew conspicuously from *Santa Maria's* mizzen mast. Rumors initially spread that four Swedish women were traveling aboard *Santa Maria.* As the truth unfolded, I learned that her crew was comprised of two Swedish men and two women. The *Santa Maria* crew quickly befriended Greg and Carol, the delightful California couple who were preparing for a canal transit to cruise the Caribbean aboard their boat *Cimarron.* One evening, I was invited to dinner with the entire group from both boats at the American Legion restaurant located above the Balboa Yacht Club.

The two fair-skinned, full-bearded Swedish men, Jurgen and Gustav, had previously been seamen aboard a Swedish bulk carrier. These two outgoing, personable mariners had left their ship in Chile and set sail on a voyage of their own. I began to spend time around the yacht club with these two delightful twentieth-century Vikings. They spoke passable English with lilting Swedish accents. It was a pleasure to be around these Swedes. Their engaging sea stories and fascinating backgrounds were an entertaining diversion from the local unrest. Gustav, *Santa Maria's* captain, was planning to rejoin his merchant ship as a first mate. Jurgen was also planning to leave *Santa Maria* in Panama to join a huge sloop, *Lonesome I,* before eventually finding work on an oil rig.

The two women accompanying them, Yvonne and Eivor, both missionary nurses in their early 20s, had been working in indigenous villages in Peru. Disenchanted with their work, they had left Peru aboard *Santa Maria,* reaching Panama with the two men. During their voyage, Eivor had linked up with *Santa Maria's* captain, Gustav. Nonetheless, both women intended to leave *Santa Maria* aboard *Cimarron* for her canal transit and a short trip to the San Blas and Colombia. Their plan was to return to Balboa for their belongings on *Santa Maria* before eventually returning to their mission in Peru.

Although neither of the women had previously sailed, they both had taken well to the ocean. I began to hang out increasingly with these beautiful, engaging Swedish women. Making a slow waving gesture with her downturned palm, Yvonne described with delight the gentle motion of the Pacific Ocean swells.

Often, voyagers whom I met appeared dejected or tired. Not these Swedes. This entire group consistently was enthusiastic and full of energy and good humor. Their spirit was infectious. For once, I had met a crew that enjoyed living, appreciated fun moments, and accepted their disappointments with grace and charm. In Peru, the women had lived among poor people with little hope in life. With their worldly perspectives, they were unfazed by the spartan conditions aboard *Santa Maria*. Yvonne and Eivor were grateful for the lives they were privileged to lead. Both women laughed heartily at my comical attempts to speak Swedish.

Yvonne and I developed a great rapport and started spending more and more time together. I hitchhiked with Yvonne to eat at Napoli Pizza in Panama City. We explored the CZ for hours. One night, we strolled through the streets of Ancon and Balboa. On another night, we hiked to the middle of the arch suspension bridge of the Pan-American Highway that spans the canal. We wanted to spend all our time together. Yvonne transited to Cristobal with her friends on *Cimarron* and returned to Balboa the next day on the train to stay with me and Louis aboard *Rhiannon*.

Yvonne Larsson

Troubles in Taboga

As soon as we had completed the self-steering windvane installation, I spent a day in Colon walking from office to office paying fees and collecting official stamps in order to obtain a proper cruising clearance (zarpe) to sail *Rhiannon* to Taboga Island. Taboga is a small, hilly Panamanian Island, located nine NM from Balboa.

Taboga, Panama

Rhiannon at Taboga

Louis and I were anxious to test our new wind vane. We named it George, after the truck driver who had taken our boat to Louisiana. We also wanted to scrape the forest of gooseneck barnacles off *Rhiannon*'s fouled bottom prior to crossing the Pacific. At Taboga there was a "grid" of steel girders upon which a boat could rest as the tide went out, permitting dry access to the keel for several hours. We hoped to careen *Rhiannon* on that grid to clean her bottom. Louis, Yvonne, and I sailed to Taboga at dusk, successfully testing George en route. We set our anchor near some other sailboats and went to bed.

The next morning, Yvonne and I were enjoying an intimate moment in the v-berth when a vicious squall suddenly erupted. Being thus occupied, I definitely did not want to spring out of the forward cabin the moment we sensed the telltale lurch of a dragging anchor. We heard Louis in the cockpit cranking up *Rhiannon*'s engine and, moments later, urgently calling for our help. I jumped out of bed, grabbing only my glasses on the way.

The engine had already stopped because a jib sheet dangling in the water had fouled our prop. We were continuing to drag in the gusty cloudburst, rapidly approaching the bowsprit of a neighboring vessel. Louis jumped overboard with a knife to free the prop, with the overhanging bowsprit of the other boat looming above him. Simultaneously, the neighbor's crew was frantically paying out their anchor chain, to retreat from *Rhiannon*.

Louis was quickly able to free the wrapped line without cutting it. As he climbed back aboard, I started the engine, and we safely motored away. Yvonne helped us re-anchor. She had become a valuable crewmember during her short time on board.

It was Saturday morning. Louis and I rowed ashore hoping to secure permission for us to careen *Rhiannon* at Taboga, as planned. We found a uniformed officer, Señor Cunningham, who directed us to the local Guardia office. Dutifully, we walked up the hill through the sleepy village to a tiny white-washed building with an opened door.

The inside of the shabby one-room office was dark and cold. I saw a single wooden desk flanked by three jail cells, reminiscent of an old western movie. A framed black and white picture of General Torrijos hung on the peeling plaster wall above the desk, beside a limp Panamanian flag that dangled from a wooden pole. Behind the desk sat Señor Corbes, the sergeant.

Louis and I presented our paperwork and our request to careen *Rhiannon*. Immediately, he unequivocally denied us permission, citing a missing stamp that we should have obtained in Panama City. When I asked specifically what was needed, Señor Corbes made a sham search through his desk for an example of the proper document, which of course did not exist. Then he changed his story to tell us that our documents would be good in Colon but not here on Taboga.

He changed his story twice more. First, he claimed that our papers permitted cruising but not boat work. Then he said that we should not careen because the grid was located near a tourist beach. He really could not make up his mind. However, we clearly comprehended his message. Neither Louis nor I relished the thought of being locked up in the small dank jail cells we had just seen.

Disappointed, Louis and I returned to the boat with no choice but to clean her hull at anchor. Louis, Yvonne, and I set to work scraping barnacles. We had finished half the job by early afternoon. All three of us were in the water when, unannounced, a launch approached from the island. As we climbed back on deck, dripping wet in our bathing suits, the launch slammed carelessly against *Rhiannon*'s topsides. A uniformed Guardia, wearing heavy military boots stomped aboard carrying a submachine gun. Both Señor Cunningham and Señor Corbes, the only full time Guardia stationed at Taboga, remained on the launch, watching reverently.

The soldier aboard our boat apparently was a more senior officer, who was visiting Taboga for an inspection. Clearly, the two local Guardia had intentionally directed their commander to harass *Rhiannon*. This was the weekend before Panamanian Independence Day; anti-American activities had reached a crescendo.

The menacing officer demanded to see our vessel's documents. I promptly complied, producing all our papers. Our crew list included Clark, but not Yvonne. He next demanded to see Clark's passport, which, fortuitously, we had kept with us, even though Clark remained in the CZ to work on his applications. In Spanish, the Guardia brusquely informed me of several perceived violations: 1) Clark was not aboard, 2) Yvonne had no papers, 3) the Guardia stamp was missing from our zarpe, and 4) a Chicago Yacht Club burgee was being flown at the same height as our Panamanian courtesy flag.

The flag issue in particular seemed to enrage him. He became increasingly agitated as he scolded me: "In my country, the Panamanian flag is above all others!" Immediately, I dropped the burgee, even though we had been following proper flag etiquette.

He then commanded us to leave Panama by "three hours." I was unsure if he meant "by three o'clock" or "in three hours." But it was noon, so it made no difference. He climbed back into the launch with the others, and they motored off.

We did not want *Rhiannon* confiscated by the Panamanians, so we complied. Weighing anchor, we set sail into the Gulf of Panama. Once again, we put George through his paces, making final adjustments to fine tune our installation. We still needed to clean half of the bottom. So, we sailed to another smaller Panamanian island, Taboguilla, to finish the work. We knew that no Guardia patrolled that island.

In 1976, Taboguilla was the home of a fish meal factory. We anchored *Rhiannon* near the factory. White rotting fish parts littered the water of the cove. Louis and I took turns in the water scraping, while Yvonne kept watch for the foraging sharks feasting on the floating fish meal. Fortunately, we finished without incident.

Scraping the hull near the fishmeal factory at Taboguilla

The following day was Sunday. Yvonne had planned to return to *Santa Maria,* which was then anchored at Taboga. We were persona non grata in Taboga, having just been deported from Panama the previous day. Louis and I devised a scheme to get Yvonne back to her boat. We suspected that the visiting Guardia official would have returned to the mainland by Sunday and that the local Guardias would most likely be sleeping in, after a late night of holiday drinking. We decided to smuggle Yvonne clandestinely to Taboga.

We set out before sunrise, maneuvering *Rhiannon* through the calm quiet anchorage under cover of darkness just as dawn was breaking on the horizon. Stealthily, we drew alongside *Santa Maria.* We silently transferred Yvonne to the Swedish ketch before heading back once more to the CZ to find Clark.

Rather than returning directly to Balboa, Louis and I decided to anchor for one more night at Taboguilla. Checking into the CZ on a Sunday would have been challenging. That day, as we sailed, the Gulf of Panama was spectacular. Flocks of pelicans and solitary boobies were winging back and forth across a backdrop of blue sky while towering cumulus clouds were hanging over the isthmus.

Final Days in the Isthmus

Louis and I sailed back to the CZ, arriving at the Flamenco Island check-in point during a torrential rainstorm to await boarding by a U.S. immigration officer. We were itching to leave Panama for the Pacific, but Clark was not yet ready. We ended up waiting for Clark at the Balboa Yacht Club for one additional week, our sixth week since arriving in Panama.

But for me, there was a silver lining inside this dark cloud. I had one more week to spend with Yvonne. She had moved off *Santa Maria* to meet her friends on *Cimarron* in Cristobal. She would be joining them for their upcoming cruise to the San Blas.

I rode the train across the isthmus to visit Yvonne and all my friends on the Atlantic side one last time. Captain Jensen was back at the yacht club bar. In the time since we had first arrived, the *SS Cristobal* had already made four round trips between New Orleans and the CZ. Yvonne and I ate a delicious dinner aboard *Sagarmatha* with Paname and Paul. Later, we drank at the bar and played pool before joining a raucous party aboard *Cimarron*. Even Xochitl the free spirit was there, on the eve of her departure with her newest boyfriend, the helmsman of a freighter bound for New Orleans.

I spent the night aboard *Cimarron* and said my goodbyes as they cast off for the San Blas the following morning. I was sad to see so many good friends leave. Our own departure seemed long overdue.

Back in Balboa, more arriving vessels joined the Panama cruising fraternity. There were new cruisers to meet. A few days later, Yvonne and Eivor returned by air from the San Blas. I rode the morning ferry with Yvonne out to Taboga, where *Santa Maria* had remained anchored for weeks. Yvonne and I picnicked together on an island hillside and roamed the seashore. I spent the night aboard *Santa Maria* with Yvonne and the three other Swedes.

The next day we went back to Balboa together to join Louis on *Rhiannon*. Clark, having completed his law school applications, moved back aboard. After final provisioning, Louis, Clark, Yvonne, and I departed the CZ for the last time. We would spend one final night at Taboga before heading to sea. It had been several weeks since our run-in with the Guardia on Taboga. We felt confident that *Rhiannon* would not be recognized by the Guardia on shore this time.

At Taboga, we rafted *Rhiannon* alongside *Santa Maria*. The Whitings from New Zealand were also in the anchorage aboard *Tequila*. That night they were hosting a 22nd birthday party for their soon to be daughter-in-law Annie. The party doubled as a bon voyage party for us. We finally would be leaving Panama the next morning.

Yvonne contemplated joining Louis, Clark, and me on *Rhiannon* for our passage to the Galapagos. Deep down I knew that bringing Yvonne with us on *Rhiannon* would be a bad idea. As much as we wanted to stay together, we both knew that a fourth person would aggravate the already tight quarters and upset the social dynamics. Leaving Yvonne was especially hard.

On the morning of November 9, we hoisted *Rhiannon*'s sails. As we slid past *Tequila* to leave the anchorage, Debbie Whiting and Annie laughed and hollered as they lobbed water balloons at us from their foredeck. Tragically, four years later, Annie and her husband Paul Whiting were both lost at sea while returning home from Tasmania on their sailboat, *Smackwater Jack*, following the 1980 Sydney to Hobart race.

Bon voyage from *Tequila* at Taboga

Our six-week sojourn in Panama had felt like a lifetime. But for me it had been transformational. I had learned of fear and helpless vulnerability. I had experienced subjugation through abuse of power. I had witnessed unprovoked violence. I had befriended inspiring people. And — I had fallen in love.

CHAPTER 14

Depression

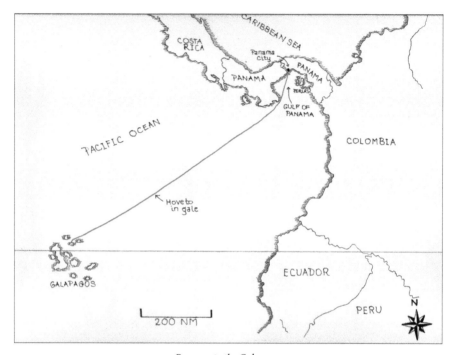

Panama to the Galapagos

LEAVING PANAMA, I was ambivalent. We had been delayed in the Canal Zone far too long. It was well past the time to move on. The vast Pacific Ocean loomed ahead. As a Midwestern boy, I found the scale of this ocean to be beyond my comprehension. We were finally setting out on our first open-sea passage, the heart of our journey. It had been a major accomplishment just to reach the Pacific Ocean. However, what lay ahead was daunting and unknown. We had long ago buckled ourselves into this roller coaster car. The clacking ratchet chain had steadily brought us to the top of the first summit. *Rhiannon's* wild freefall was about to begin. As we sailed away beneath a gloomy overcast sky, our friends anchored at Taboga slowly receded into the distance. The water's surface was slate gray. I was lost in my private thoughts. During the first hours of our sail, I felt hollowed out, empty. I missed Yvonne. My feelings were a mixture of excitement, anticipation, gratitude, fear, and profound sadness.

Before leaving Panama, we had provisioned *Rhiannon* for a 60-day stretch. We did not know whether we would be able to stop in the Galapagos. And if we did stop, we did not know if we could provision there. Upon our departure, we began a strict regimen to conserve our fuel and drinking water. We followed our rule of one-half gallon of water per person per day.

We no longer had any means of communicating with the outside world. We had written our final letters to our families, warning them not to expect to hear from us for 60 days. We did tell them that we would try to contact them sooner from the Galapagos, if possible.

We had not been able to find any useful advice, from either books or other cruisers, concerning the best route from Panama to the Galapagos. The weather in this stretch was reputed to be unpredictable. Other than our eyes to the sky and our barometer, we had no means of forecasting the weather. It had taken some famous small-boat sailors over 20 days to complete this passage. The Gulf of Panama was notorious for prolonged calms and strong, shifting ocean currents. Several authors had experienced miserable heat for days, becalmed in these doldrums, waiting for wind.

We had anticipated calm seas and light winds throughout the 850 NM voyage to the Galapagos. We were therefore greatly encouraged by the 10 knots of wind from aft of our beam on the morning of our departure. We made good progress at approximately five knots through the Gulf of Panama. Anxious to get to the Galapagos, we bypassed the Perlas Islands. We had been warned that recent flooding in the Darien had washed countless logs into the Gulf. Striking one of these giant logs at five knots would have been disastrous. As forewarned, we passed numerous floating trees in the inky water throughout the day. George steered flawlessly, while all three of us sat on deck scanning for flotsam. Freighters and tankers heading to and from the canal passed us continuously. As we approached Punta Mala that night, we finally began to head offshore into the great Pacific Ocean.

The next day produced a mixture of calms and squalls that brought with them, at most, moderate winds. We were out of sight of land. The floating logs and shipping traffic had disappeared overnight. Our initial progress greatly encouraged us. As we settled into the passage, we attempted fishing, trolling a lure behind us. Unfortunately, the lure, hook, and half of the line were all stolen by a large fish.

By the third day, conditions began to deteriorate. The sky became completely overcast, with no possibility of celestial navigation. Our moods became gloomier along with the progressively darkening sky and ashen gray sea. We directed our best efforts toward keeping an accurate dead reckoning position, frequently updating our estimated position on a plotting sheet. With George steering perfectly, our workload thankfully had diminished. Long night watches became easier. If we dozed off in the cockpit for a brief period, *Rhiannon* would remain precisely on course. George was better than a fourth crew member. He required no food or sleep. He never became seasick. He was reliable. And he had no annoying habits.

By the fourth day, the anticipated doldrums still had not materialized. In fact, the wind and waves were steadily building under the dark cloudy sky. As the hours passed, the wind veered until we were eventually beating into a headwind and rougher seas. On that day, all three of us became depressed. This was no fun. Conditions were deteriorating further, rather than improving. We had expected calms, blue skies, warm air, and long, rolling Pacific Ocean swells. Instead, it began to rain. It was a steady rain, not just a passing rainsquall. Our port lights and hatches leaked horribly. The cabin was damp and cold. The barometer was falling. Each pressure reading was lower than it had been at the same hour on the preceding day. As the waves grew taller and steeper, the wind-driven rain obscured our vision. I was blinded by the water droplets and salt crystals on my eyeglasses.

To top it off, our engine would not start when we needed to charge the batteries. Fortunately, during a brief lull Clark managed to clean the carburetor while Louis changed the spark plugs. This time the finicky engine did start. But by the time they had finished, a storm had begun to materialize in earnest. The barometer plummeted rapidly, paralleling our spirits in the drenching rain.

Late in the afternoon, in visibility of less than a quarter NM, a vessel drew alongside about 75 yards away. She was a white-hulled 150-foot Japanese fishing boat. She slowed and paralleled our course for about five minutes. Several of her crew lined the deck to take our picture with their cameras. Other than a cursory hand wave, we did not communicate with them. They clearly were as curious about us as we were about them. When they left, we heated up a can of Chef Boy-ar-dee ravioli for dinner. At nightfall, I lit the kerosene running lights and walked them forward in the rain, as we prepared to resume our night watch routine.

The fifth day was a bad day marked by a series of ominous signs. First, my wristwatch stopped running. Next, I found a dead bird on the deck. Later, Louis lost a bucket overboard. The wooden tiller delaminated and broke. On top of that, our radar reflector came crashing onto the coachroof and the mahogany cockpit coaming broke. On that same fateful day, the rubrail that we had so carefully repaired in Panama fell off again. This time it fouled itself on *Rhiannon*'s keel. We had expected to face adversity. But we were not expecting it all to happen at once on our first rough day at sea. Continuously wagging our auxiliary rudder, George held a flawless course. This freed the three of us to mitigate all the new damage with temporary repairs. We used c-clamps to mend the broken tiller, and we lashed the detached rubrail to the stanchions.

Encountering a storm in this region came as a complete surprise. Louis, Clark, and I proactively began to prepare in earnest for what appeared to be an impending gale. We pulled out our storm preparation checklist. We secured our homemade oak barricades across the companionway hatch. We screwed deck plates over the vent openings. We closed seacocks and battened down the hatches. As the wind strength grew, we progressively shortened sail, adding reefs to the mainsail and exchanging jibs from the 175% genoa to the 100% working jib and eventually to the canvas storm jib made in Belize.

The three of us looked in awe at the oncoming waves with their heavily breaking crests. We had no idea how to estimate the wave heights. As waves began to crash over the bow, we gave George a break and steered by hand. Although none of us had any more experience steering in these conditions than our mechanical wind vane, we were nonetheless concerned that George might unexpectedly err, leading to disaster.

Throughout the next day we fought the worst of it. *Rhiannon* continued to press forward, close reaching into the teeth of the gale. Thirty-five knot winds with periods of higher gusts blew all day. Interestingly, there was never any lightning. Louis and I were seasick. Nevertheless, we stood our watches. Clark fared much better. Our foul weather gear, sweaters, and bedding all became soaked. Our sparkling white cabin transformed into a grayish black den as black mold invaded. Dripping with water, the cabin resembled an underground catacomb. Dead flying fish lay stranded on the deck. We pumped out the bilge with the little energy we had left.

In this state of seasickness, fatigue, and uncertainty, I was miserable. This certainly was not my Pacific voyage "dream come true." We were experiencing a meteorological phenomenon aptly termed a "depression." The well-known eighteenth-century author, Dr. Samuel Johnson, famously wrote: "Being in a ship is like being in jail, with the chance of being drowned." I had read that quotation many times before, but on that day, I fully appreciated its truth. Even Clark began to feel queasy. That night, we dropped the storm jib, lashed the tiller, and hove to under only a triple-reefed main. We all slept until dawn.

In the morning we were able to tune our 10-band shortwave receiver to WWVH, the station that broadcasts accurate time signals for navigation. Transmitted from Hawaii, WWVH also announced, at hourly intervals, the latitudes and longitudes of Pacific Ocean storms. These alerts were primarily based upon reports radioed from commercial vessels at sea. Storms located in areas of sparse shipping traffic often remained unreported. The lack of satellite weather forecasts rendered this system quite crude by today's standards. By the time our gale was first mentioned on the air, the news was far too late for us to take any evasive action. We were already well into the depression.

Fortunately, we were far out at sea and had no concerns about potentially running aground on a lee shore. However, we had been dead reckoning for a few days already, and our assumed position could have been off by over 100 NM. For a brief period at 10:00 a.m. and again at noon on the sixth day, the disk of the sun fleetingly revealed itself through the totally overcast sky. I grabbed my sextant. At each of those times, I quickly sighted the cloud-cloaked sun without requiring a single shade glass to shield the barely visible disk. Amazingly, our dead reckoning position was only 25 miles off, after over three days of sailing in unknown currents.

After the gale abated. The storm jib is still flying.

On the seventh day, the storm finally passed. Abating seas and an encouraging rising barometer signaled better weather to come. The sun emerged, and the clouds gradually disappeared altogether. For the first time since leaving Panama, the Pacific Ocean appeared in its glorious splendor. *Rhiannon* was like Dorothy's house, suddenly flung from the tempest into the colorful Land of Oz. The ocean was a deep emerald blue, set against the white foam of the breaking crests. The sky was clear. Schools of flying fish shimmered above the waves. A black frigate bird circled overhead, as a lone white albatross gracefully soared between wave tops. The wave pattern became more regular as the wave heights diminished. We hanked on the working jib and comfortably drove forward at six knots carrying a double-reefed main. A pod of dolphins joined us, welcoming us to the "true" Pacific Ocean.

As the sailing improved, so did our spirits. We ate. We rested. We were once again enjoying the voyage. On the ninth day, I took a morning sun sight and estimated our position to be about 100 NM away from the Galapagos. For the first time, we spread out our large chart of the Galapagos Islands. Of the hundreds of nautical charts that we had procured, this one always intrigued me the most. It depicted a distinctive grouping of round and lobe-shaped islands. Shaded elevation contours graphically highlighted numerous prominent volcanic craters. This chart's mysterious, exotic appearance embodied my image of an antique pirate's map. While charging forward in the general direction of this archipelago, we carefully studied the awesome chart. Without an official Ecuadorian cruising permit, we needed to quickly devise a final strategy for visiting the islands. Accordingly, we discussed our options.

One option was to sail into one of the two official ports of entry, Wreck Bay (Puerto Baquerizo Moreno) or Academy Bay (Bahia de la Academia). Based upon the International Laws of the Sea, as we understood them, we should be permitted four days in port. However, this did not imply permission to cruise or even to disembark from our boat. We had also heard that if we arrived in port in disrepair, we should be granted temporary entry in order to restore our vessel to a seaworthy condition. Of course, none of this might actually have been true or accurate. But it was our understanding at the time.

A second option was to enter the island group far from the ports of entry, then cruise through the archipelago, gradually working our way toward one of the two ports. If we were not stopped, we could respectfully visit uninhabited areas en route. As we had incurred visible damage during the gale, we could potentially exploit the damage as justification for our entry.

By consensus, we agreed on the second option. For several reasons, we selected Wreck Bay as our eventual port of entry. First, the harbor at Wreck Bay is well sheltered. Additionally, it is located in the eastern part of the archipelago. This would give us the opportunity to sail past other islands upon our ultimate departure toward the west. Moreover, we had heard that the authorities at the Darwin Station in Academy Bay were more restrictive toward visitors.

Therefore, we decided that if our course and the sea state were favorable, we would attempt to make our landfall at Isla Genovesa (Tower Island) and possibly go ashore there. We knew that in heavier winds, landing at Genovesa would be dangerous due to its steep rocky coast. We selected Isla Marchena as a backup landfall.

Once we had found our position, at noon on the tenth day, Isla Genovesa lay dead upwind. However, a single port tack beat upwind would easily bring us near the uninhabited islands of Marchena and Pinta. Marchena thus became our goal. Squinting into the hazy sun, we soon made out the silhouettes of two separate conical volcanic peaks just breaking the horizon. We had *found* the Galapagos! And we were still sailing in great wind! We were thrilled!

Glorious sailing in sight of the Galapagos

Today, in the 21st century, it sounds almost comical to be using the word "found." Navigation by GPS, coupled with readily available marine weather forecasts, trivializes the entire undertaking. In 1976, with the overcast sky, the gale winds, and the strong uncharted currents, we felt it was conceivable that we could have missed the Galapagos altogether. I had read accounts of sailors before us who had been unable to find these islands. It is difficult now to convey the extent of our uncertainty during the long days when we knew neither our position nor when the sky would ultimately clear sufficiently to permit celestial observations.

Aboard *Rhiannon,* the British Admiralty publication of *Sailing Directions* was our only guide to navigation in the Galapagos. I do not know if another guide even existed at that time. There were no lights, no buoys, and no natural or manmade harbors on uninhabited Marchena Island. The coastline was noted to be rocky throughout and generally unapproachable. However, the *Sailing Directions* described a small black lava sand beach. It noted that local fishermen sometimes anchored off this beach in calm conditions. That note was our only clue to where we might land after having spent over 10 days at sea. Absurdly, we had run this miserable gauntlet simply to reach a questionable anchorage off a God-forsaken beach, on a rocky shore.

It was November 18, 1976. Although we sailed at over six knots all day, we were unable to arrive with sufficient daylight to locate the beach described in the *Sailing Directions.* The beach was not even marked on the chart, so we would need to explore the coastline of Marchena during the day to find it. The wind was blowing steadily from the south at about 10 knots. We were approaching from the northeast. Despite the tall, gently rolling swell coming down from the north, the waves in the lee of the island were small. Arriving just after dark, we needed to stand off. We dropped the main in order to reach comfortably back and forth under working jib only. The waning crescent moon shed no useful light upon the island. Starlight alone enabled us to keep track of the black volcanic island's position during the night.

In contrast to the unpleasant night of standing off Isla Mujeres months earlier, this was a night of pure magic and awe. The clear sky was resplendent with stars. It was so dark and so clear that the gaps between the brighter stars all seemed filled by a solid dome of fainter stars. As I lay stretched out on the cockpit bench, shooting meteors flashed too brightly to be ignored.

Then, the dolphins arrived. This time they were different. During my watch I sat up, grasping the lifelines with my hands to watch the show. As they whizzed past, their underwater wakes left bioluminescent trails, perfectly describing their paths. Then, in an alarming repeating sequence, a solitary dolphin would speed headlong toward *Rhiannon* from directly abeam. The approaching fiery phosphorescent wake resembled the trail of an oncoming torpedo. Just when it appeared that our boat would be struck, the dolphin would dive or veer away at the last possible moment. As a dolphin leaped, the trail of luminescent droplets streaming off its body would transform into a shower of blue-green fairy dust. This unusual display lasted all night. The dolphins mesmerized Louis and Clark as well. Eventually a spectacular sunrise broke the fantasy night, and we altered course to advance cautiously toward Isla Marchena.

CHAPTER 15

Las Islas Encantadas

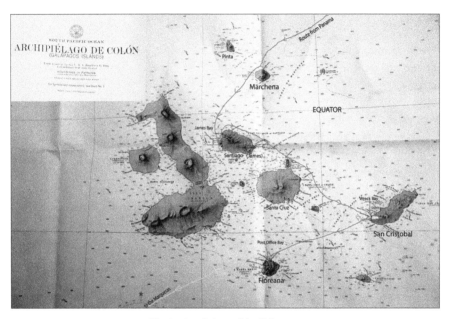

Navigational chart of the Galapagos

Isla Marchena

Rhiannon eased forward toward the north shore of Marchena. In the distance, to starboard, the perfect volcanic cone of Isla Pinta rose majestically, illuminated by the rising sun. Louis, Clark, and I scanned the forbidding coast ahead, searching for the "beach" referenced in the *Sailing Directions*. A breathtaking expansive moonscape unfolded before us. The north side of the island appeared totally barren. We saw nothing but jagged black and rust-colored boulders of lava, marked by occasional small craters. The closer we approached, the more inhospitable the shoreline appeared. Crashing breakers launched wind-whipped spray high into the air along the entire hellish coast.

A small black patch on the shore, perhaps 50 meters in width, seemed to be devoid of the wave driven spume. Using binoculars, we concluded that this must be our beach. Even this cleaner stretch of land was dotted by sharp lava boulders. The wind funneled down the 1100-foot volcanic slope straight out to *Rhiannon*. We turned on our depth sounder. We were about a half NM offshore when we dared not get any closer. We wanted to remain well outside the surf break. At six and a half fathoms, we set the Danforth anchor. Although the boat sailed around on her anchor in the gusty wind, we finally felt secure, once again attached to terra firma.

The wind was blowing at about 15-20 knots. We debated whether to go ashore. Leary of the crashing waves, we decided it would be best to wait until conditions died down a bit. We were also wondering if Ecuadorian patrol boats were in the area. We wanted to monitor the situation longer, before leaving the boat. Furthermore, it was cold! We were now only miles from the equator, and yet we were chilled. For the first time since leaving Illinois, we put on our long pants and heavy sweaters, even while sitting in the bright morning sun. The Humboldt Current, bringing frigid water from Antarctica up the South American coast, courses directly through the Galapagos. We surveyed the beach through binoculars. At first glance, the entire island appeared dead to us, a barren wasteland totally devoid of life. This surprised us. After all, this was the Galapagos, a renowned haven for fascinating fauna.

I am feeding a lava gull while at anchor at Isla Marchena. Though near the equator, the air is cold.

Resigned to stay aboard, at least until the afternoon, we decided to clean up the cabin and repair whatever we could. But first, it was time for a good breakfast. Clark prepared a large stack of pancakes, which we ate on deck with margarine and syrup. Although we had elected not to go ashore to explore that morning, the local wildlife had decided to visit us at anchor. First, the small finches and grey lava gulls arrived. As I held leftover pancakes up in the air, lava gulls hovered on the breeze overhead to snatch them from my grasp. Others waited on our horseshoe life ring, laughing and calling out as they awaited their turn to be fed. Next, the sea lions came. Big, plump sea lions with doglike faces circled our boat. One of them reminded me of a fat old lady taking a leisurely Sunday dip in the ocean. It smiled at us, refused an offer of pancakes, and then slowly moved on. A large green sea turtle bobbed up and down near our anchor rode as it, too, curiously eyed our boat.

With the wind increasing, and chores for the day completed, all three of us took a nap. By the time we awoke, it was already late afternoon, too late to mount a shore expedition. After dinner, we gazed at the stars before sleeping for the night. We reasoned that the next day ought to be calmer. We were psyched to set our feet on dry land in the morning.

The next day was again cloudless and cold. Katabatic winds rushing down the slopes were even stronger than on the previous day. It was blowing at 25 knots, with even higher gusts. Swell from the north was creating well-developed surf inshore of *Rhiannon*. We could easily see the tops of the curling breakers being sheared off into spray by the contrary wind. Nonetheless, we were determined to get to shore. Clearly, one person needed to remain on board *Rhiannon* while the other two went ashore. The wind was blowing offshore. If *Rhiannon* were to drag anchor, she would rapidly drift northward out to sea. We would never be able to catch her by paddling the dinghy. The nearest land to the north was somewhere in Mexico, well over 1000 NM away. If we were to be stranded on this barren, uninhabited island without shelter, we would not survive.

We decided the best way to get our cheaply made dinghy ashore was for each of us to row with two paddles. We hoped that by pulling the four paddles through the oarlocks in unison we would make slow progress upwind toward shore. Before setting off in the dinghy from *Rhiannon*, we tethered ourselves with a long line to the boat. We needed to test our ability to row against the fierce wind prior to setting ourselves free. Before landing, we would try to inspect the beach from beyond the surf line, to see if there was any safe beach area that was free of the sharp basalt boulders. If the dinghy ruptured, we knew that we could be stranded. We would have no radio or means of communication between the beach and the boat. This was our best and only plan. We had come this far and gone through so much. We were compelled to explore this desolate moonscape.

Clark and I would be on the landing mission, while Louis remained alone on *Rhiannon*. In the dinghy we securely tied a bailing bucket and a canteen of water. The four-oar idea did not work. As vigorously as we tried to row, we could not move away from *Rhiannon*. Then Clark and I each tried paddling with one oar, canoe style, instead. This worked. We pulled away little by little while Louis watched us through binoculars and took photos with our camera. Paddling was very tiring. Progress toward shore was painfully slow amidst the wind-driven chop. If we paused paddling for even a moment, we would drift backwards.

Clark and I paddle upwind toward the desolate shore

Nearing exhaustion, Clark and I eventually found ourselves just outside the line of breakers. Further complicating matters, a one- to two-knot current was setting us westward parallel to shore. Surveying the beach, we adjusted our position laterally to the zone least covered by the ominous craggy rocks. We were not surfers. We had no experience whatsoever picking the right wave. For several minutes we continued to paddle, holding our position. We counted waves. We thought that after every seventh wave, there appeared to be a lull.

Sticking to our theory, immediately following the seventh wave in one set, I shouted to Clark, "Let's go!" We paddled furiously. Looking back, I saw a wave towering above me, its top beginning to curl overhead. The stern of the dinghy rose as the wave crest lifted us from behind. We were surfing. Our wave counting system had failed. It was one of the biggest waves yet! The terrifying ride lasted mere seconds. Almost instantly, we were spun sideways and launched from the capsizing dinghy by the breaking crest. I grabbed my glasses and held my breath. I did not know if the bottom would be black lava sand or razor-sharp rocks. After tumbling several times in the cold water, I popped to the surface behind the wave. I saw Clark farther inshore near the inverted dinghy.

I grabbed one of the wooden paddles floating near me. After being knocked down by yet a second wave, I was finally able to stand on the bottom and scramble ashore. Clark managed to pull the dinghy up onto the beach. My pockets and my hair were filled with black sand. We managed to recover three of the four paddles. Other than some scrapes, both of us had reached shore intact.

Using a paddle, I carved large letters into the black sand of the steeply sloped beach, signaling Louis that we were "OK." I surveyed the area. At first, I saw no signs of life, only a barren landscape. However, as my eyes accommodated to the bright sunlight, a wondrous alien world began to emerge.

Two beautiful Galapagos hawks hovered above and then landed about 10 feet from me. They began examining the carcass of a bird atop a jagged lava rock. Small lizards scurried in the sand below. Bright orange Sally Lightfoot crabs clung in groups onto the black lava boulders at water's edge. The dazzling crabs and the white seafoam set against the jet-black rocks produced a striking contrast.

The beach at Isla Marchena

Sally Lightfoot crabs clinging to the lava rocks. *Rhiannon* is anchored in the distance

Scores of perfectly camouflaged marine iguanas basked on rocks, ejecting spray from their salt glands through their nostrils with a sneeze. I sat, virtually unnoticed, amid a cluster of these prehistoric-looking marine iguanas. Their rough, thorny-scaled heads and spine-covered backs and tails blended seamlessly with their surroundings. Amazingly, most of the animals on the beach ignored me as I approached.

Sitting among a group of marine iguanas

At one end of the cove, a group of sea lions, of various size and coloration, lazily soaked in the sunshine. Unlike the other animals, the sea lions disapproved of my encroachment. One sleeping sea lion awoke with a start and hastily lumbered into the water. On the beach, I was drawn to a pile of sun-bleached dry bones on the coal-black sand. Intrigued by what animal it might have been, I began assembling the bones until I could recognize the forelimb of a sea lion.

Clark and I spent about one hour ashore. During that time, the waves subsided considerably. We found a spot on one end of the beach where the break of the waves did not appear too dangerous. From that spot we launched the slightly deflated dinghy, which had sprung a small leak during our landing. Once we passed the breaking waves, the wind swiftly carried us the one-half NM back to *Rhiannon*. Despite my bruises and scrapes, I remained pumped after our amazing excursion.

A sea lion on the beach

Assembling bones of a sea lion limb.

Naturally, Louis wanted to go ashore. I was stoked for another adventure. Later in the afternoon Louis and I launched a second expedition to the beach. Luckily, both the surf and the wind had died down since the morning. I tumbled from the dinghy once more; and was again uninjured. On this trip, we brought our camera ashore, sealed inside its immense underwater housing.

The animals on shore looked as though they had not moved since the morning. At one point, Louis climbed over some jagged lava rocks for me to take his picture near some sleeping sea lions. Suddenly, one sea lion awoke with a start and began to bark loudly. Louis and the sea lion scrambled in opposite directions. I am not sure who was more frightened. We left the island as we had found it, leaving no human trace of our momentous escapade ashore.

Back aboard *Rhiannon*, we patched the dinghy, and each caught a few hours of sleep. We weighed anchor just after midnight for the 45 NM sail to another uninhabited island, Isla Santiago.

Isla Santiago

Once we rounded the west side of Isla Marchena, we turned south through what I noted to be "a most unpleasant chop." We continued sailing through the night and the better part of the next day. En route, we passed alongside Isla Isabela, the largest of the Galapagos Islands. The majestic volcanos with their broad flat crater rims soared above us as we surged on through the waves, heeled well over.

Mid-morning, on Sunday, November 21, 1976, *Rhiannon* crossed the equator into the Southern Hemisphere. We simply snapped a photo of Wolf volcano on Isla Isabela as we passed, to document this major milestone. We were oblivious to the traditional equator-crossing ceremonies and rituals practiced aboard most vessels.

Wolf Volcano, Isla Isabela as we crossed the equator

As we neared Isla Santiago, we headed toward James Bay on the island's west side. In the lee of the island, the waves and wind calmed. One corner of James Bay was marked on our chart as "Buccaneer Cove." Indeed, it appeared exactly as one would envision a pirate's retreat. We attempted to start the engine to enter the anchorage. Once again, the engine failed to start. Sailing rather than motoring into anchorages had become our established routine. We sailed *Rhiannon* to a prime spot in the bay, where we set the CQR anchor in five and a half fathoms.

Approaching James Bay, Isla Santiago

It had been three days since we first entered Ecuadorian waters. We still had not seen any other people, boats, or lights on shore. The last people we had seen were the men aboard the Japanese vessel that had passed in the rain, two weeks earlier.

While we were anchored alone in James Bay, the view from *Rhiannon's* cockpit was magnificently picturesque. To the north, eroded cliff faces revealed arched flowing layers of multicolored rocks. Rolling hills covered by scrub towered behind the cliffs. To the east, the shore was comprised of a yellow sand beach and low mangroves. To the south, a vast, almost infinite, expanse of desolate black lava stretched into the distance toward a volcano. Rough porous boulders were mixed with swirls of congealed magma. Random patches of new growth sprouted from the broad lava field.

Throughout the day, frigate birds, pelicans, blue footed boobies, and lava gulls dived for fish around us. I became so amused by the pelicans begging for food that I had trouble finding time to perform my chores. The late afternoon sun created a surreal landscape, painting the colorful cliff face and small surrounding islets with pink and orange hues.

Buccaneer Cove, James Bay

Concerned that an Ecuadorian patrol boat might arrive, we once again took turns going ashore. Landing here seemed trivial, as only small waves lapped the smooth beach. Although completely different from Marchena, James Bay was equally remarkable. Once ashore, I walked across the sandy beach that lined most of the bay. I continued through the heavy brush and mangroves toward the interior.

Approximately 40 meters inland, I encountered two beautiful placid lagoons. In one of them, I was surprised to find a flock of several hundred pink flamingos, marching and leaping along the margins of the lagoon. Several other long-legged waterfowl stood congregated in smaller groups elsewhere in the brackish water.

I then found a trail, which I followed further inland and up the hill. I followed a ridge for another 400 meters. My walk was astonishing. Attractive red and gray speckled lizards darted off the path, while small black and scarlet birds fearlessly landed on bushes, just one meter away from me. As I climbed higher, I saw six long-horned goats with black, white, and brown fur. As I drew near, they trotted nimbly down the rock-strewn slope into a scrub-covered gully. The black lava rocks rising beyond the gully were completely capped by white bird guano.

I turned around to take in the vista. From this vantage point, I clearly saw the two lagoons and the expansive bay beyond, where *Rhiannon* lay peacefully alone at anchor. The pink flamingos in the foreground appeared artificial, like a Walt Disney fantasy creation. I hiked back down where I found Clark, wandering far out onto a great lava field.

Clark on a lava field, Isla Santiago

We contemplated staying longer but decided that it was time to go to Wreck Bay. Our engine issues were weighing upon us once again. We hoped that in Wreck Bay we could definitively solve the problem. The engine had last worked at Isla Marchena. There we had run the engine to charge the batteries. The sail to Isla Santiago had been a bit rough, and we were frequently heeled far over. Our hunch was that saltwater was somehow intruding through the exhaust system. Waves striking the exhaust outlet on the transom were likely causing sea water to get all the way to the engine. The exhaust riser that should prevent this backflow was probably insufficient, especially when *Rhiannon* was heeled over. We knew that we would need to work on the cylinders and valves once again to repair the damage. We would also have to find a way to stop the ingress of seawater.

Louis, Clark, and I planned to set sail for Wreck Bay at dawn. Much to our chagrin, just as we got ready to turn in for the night, a light appeared off Isla Albany, the large rock at the north end of James Bay. It was a powerboat approaching our anchorage. We prepared to be boarded by Ecuadorian officials.

The arriving vessel simply anchored quietly in the bay, some distance away from us. We never made any contact.

We sailed north out of James Bay the next morning, with barely a zephyr of wind driving our engineless craft. By 9:00 a.m. as we turned eastward along the north shore of Isla Santiago, the wind came up on the nose, requiring us once again to beat to windward toward Wreck Bay. The north shore of Santiago was barren. Small lava islets covered in guano punctuated the shoreline.

As we reached the northeast corner of the island, the wind abruptly died. A miserable current was running against the prevailing waves. Simultaneously, additional wave trains seemed to be coming from several other directions. We were nearly becalmed, drifting with the current near a rocky coast. The churning slop felt like the agitation cycle of a giant washing machine. In these conditions, we would have motored. However, that was no longer an option. In the violent rolling and pitching, we incurred yet more damage on board. Our gooseneck fitting sheared off, our sumlog cable snapped, and everything in the cabin went flying.

While becalmed amid the nasty bobbing, we witnessed the most unusual, fascinating behavior of a group of sea lions. They apparently were playing a game in the ocean. Several of them were in a circle, facing the center, with their doglike heads held up out of the water. These sea lions were all watching a particular sea lion who was swimming on its side, holding only its flippers above the water, imitating a shark. After several seconds of this shark mimicry, the observers would dive at the sea lion in the center in a playful attack. This cycle was repeated several times. The sea lions appeared to be very amused. A few minutes after the group of sea lions disappeared, a large shark coincidentally appeared on the surface near *Rhiannon*, swimming almost exactly as the sea lion had.

When the wind finally returned, it was nearing nightfall. It was raining. We were unsure of our position or the distance we had sailed. Between the strong variable currents and the broken sumlog, all we could do was guess. George faithfully guided us south during the night. Blindly, we passed Islas Seymour and Baltra. At dawn, on November 24, I sighted Rocas Gordon, a distinctive cluster of rocky islets, signaling that it was time to tack eastward toward Wreck Bay on Isla San Cristobal.

Navigating through the Galapagos was confusing. The English-speaking explorers had given the islands one set of names. The Spanish-speaking people who ultimately settled in the Galapagos had given the islands, bays, and landmarks completely different names. In some cases, there was a third set of names, as well. It was worthwhile to learn all the different names to understand cruising guides, historical references, charts, and local conversations.

By 2:00 p.m. we had reached Rocas Dalrymple, the lone guano-covered rock that signals the northern approach to Wreck Bay. Wreck Bay is also known as Bahia de la Naufragio, Puerto Baquerizo Moreno, Puerto Chico, and San Cristobal (which is also one of the names for the island itself). Technically, some of these names refer to the body of water facing the port, and others refer to the village. However, they all are used interchangeably to designate the same place.

Entering this harbor challenged our skills. Under reefed main and working jib, we were making six knots in the strong wind. We tacked back and forth about 10 times in order to sail up the center of the bay, between Arrecife Schiavoni and Punta Lido. Arrecife Schiavoni is the hazardous unmarked reef that gave Wreck Bay its name. With our final few tacks, we threaded our way through the crowded anchorage of work boats, fishing boats, and excursion boats to our selected anchorage, close to the main concrete pier. Although the three of us were concentrating on avoiding obstacles in the cramped harbor we all recognized one anchored vessel. Our friends the Whitings from New Zealand aboard their blue sloop, *Tequila*, were moored in the bay. Louis, Clark, and I were all thrilled to see familiar faces after over two weeks and 1000 NM.

We put on quite a show as we deftly tacked through the anchorage and dropped our anchor under full sail. Inadvertently, we snagged our jib sheet just after snubbing the anchor. The jib filled in a strong puff, and *Rhiannon* momentarily began to sail. Although unintended, this effectively set the anchor quite well. Later, when D'Arcy Whiting asked us about this unorthodox maneuver, we explained that it was a deliberate "trick" we had devised to firmly set the anchor under sail aboard our engineless boat. Knowingly, he winked … and smiled.

Wreck Bay

We hoisted the "Q" flag that afternoon. It was already late in the day. No officials came out to our boat. Although it was illegal for us to interact with the local people or leave *Rhiannon* prior to receiving clearance, we reluctantly spoke with the old local fruit vendor, Luis, who had rowed out to us in a wooden skiff. He offered to bring us bananas and oranges for $4.00 U.S. Fresh fruit sounded quite appealing. We quickly agreed. He promised to bring the fruit in the morning.

As it got darker, we realized that we would not be cleared-in until the next day. We silently rowed over to *Tequila*. Debbie and Annie prepared us a wonderful dinner. They also very graciously sewed us an Ecuadorian courtesy flag that we could fly to avoid being fined. It had only taken *Tequila* six days to sail from Panama to Wreck Bay. They intended to stop briefly at Bahia de la Academia (Puerto Arroyo) before continuing directly from there to Tahiti.

Clark lifting the bananas from the fruit vendor Luis

The next morning, Luis arrived early in his rowboat wearing a red baseball cap. As promised, he delivered a huge stalk of green bananas and a large sack of oranges. We still had not cleared-in. Just as Luis was leaving, el Capitán de Puerto, decked out in clean white military attire, boarded *Rhiannon*, along with his assistant and an Ecuadorian customs inspector. We informed him that we had "just arrived" in the Galapagos. Accordingly, we were granted a four-day stay. He told us that normally they allow only three days. But since the third day fell on a Sunday, when we would be unable to check out, we were given one additional day.

When we later explained that our engine was inoperative, we were granted all the additional time needed to complete the essential engine work. However, we were warned that this permission restricted us to Wreck Bay. We also learned from the officials that the two Ecuadorian naval vessels normally patrolling the island waters both had been temporarily out of commission for repairs. We had lucked out!

Louis, Clark, and I finally went ashore. The locals in town felt isolated and longed for contact with visitors. We were welcomed with open arms. Other than *Tequila*, there were no other visiting yachts in Wreck Bay during our stay.

Puerto Baquerizo was a quiet town. All the roads were unpaved, dry, and dusty. Due to the microclimates on each of these islands, some areas were arid and desert-like, while lush fertile forests were located only a few miles away, up in the hills.

The sleepy main street in town, Darwin Boulevard, paralleled the waterfront. Right in the middle of this dusty road, immediately outside of the police station, stood a volleyball net. An assortment of people came out to play three-man volleyball at all hours of the day. Occasionally, workers came out at mid-day to play soccer on the street. At one end of town, also facing the bay, was an Ecuadorian Naval Base. Young conscripts, mostly indigenous teenage Ecuadorians from the mainland, with military crewcuts, busily moved about inside the base.

Volleyball on Darwin Boulevard in front of the police station in Wreck Bay

On our second day in the harbor, Thursday, November 25, we were again invited by the Whitings, this time for a Thanksgiving meal aboard *Tequila*. Though they do not observe that holiday in New Zealand, they feted us with a delicious dinner. The following day, we said goodbye to them once again, as they pulled up their anchor chain en route to Tahiti. They expected to arrive in Papeete in three to four weeks.

Most of the food in town was cheap. Despite all meat having to be shipped to the islands from the mainland, a steak meal was a bargain. We found a restaurant where we could eat a generous meal of steak, potatoes, and vegetables for $1.00 U.S. For the first few days, we returned regularly. Several days later, the beef lost its appeal. From *Rhiannon*'s deck, I witnessed the inhumane local method of unloading cattle from a small freighter in the bay. A crane would hoist the live bulls high into the air, secured only by a noose around their horns. The poor animals suffered needlessly. It was difficult to watch. I could no longer eat beef in the Galapagos.

Louis, Clark, and I remained in Wreck Bay to make repairs and explore San Cristobal as properly documented visitors. Two of our important projects, our engine and our tiller, required resources from people in town. Our tiller had two issues. The fork at the rudder post had broken, and the tiller itself had delaminated. Fortunately, we had a spare tiller fork aboard *Rhiannon*. We also had epoxy, clamps, and varnish to re-laminate and restore the tiller. However, we felt that we should carry a spare tiller for our upcoming long Pacific crossing.

Walking through the village, we encountered a boat builder named Juan, who appeared close to completing a 35-foot frame and plank commercial fishing boat. He was skillfully using hand tools and traditional techniques to construct this impressive vessel. One day, I approached him and asked if he would be able to fashion a new tiller for steering *Rhiannon*. I brought him our freshly repaired tiller as a model. Using an adze, he carved us a sturdy new tiller from local hardwood for $7.00 U.S. This became our primary tiller. We kept the old one as a spare.

Juan the boatbuilder

With Eduardo the postmaster and his family at the Wreck Bay Post Office. I am holding our new tiller.

Fixing the engine proved to be a greater challenge. We were all aware that the seized-up engine would need to be broken down and completely rebuilt to restore it to life. Clark and Louis were almost at the point of throwing the engine overboard. The resources in the Galapagos were so limited that engine repair appeared unlikely.

I told the others that I would go ashore and find a solution. After a few queries of people in the village, I learned that the only mechanics on San Cristobal were at the Ecuadorian Naval base. Determined to find a mechanic, I strode confidently past the armed guards and proceeded right into the base. In my best broken Spanish, I asked where I could find a mechanic. I was directed to a machine shop on the base.

I introduced myself to Moreno, the mechanic, as he worked on an engine. I explained our situation and asked him if he would be able to fix our engine. I spoke with sufficient authority that he did not consult his commanding officer. He simply consented, requesting that I bring the engine to him right away. The first step was complete. I had found someone who could help us.

However, the Atomic-4 engine, weighing 330 pounds, remained fully installed aboard *Rhiannon*. I rowed back out in our leaky inflatable dinghy to give Clark and Louis the good news. Unfortunately, *Rhiannon* was anchored well out in the bay and no docks in Wreck Bay could accommodate her draft. Also, the engine would have sunk our hopelessly inadequate dinghy in a matter of seconds.

Louis and Clark both looked at me skeptically. Then Clark rhetorically said, "Now what?"

I replied, "You guys remove the engine and hoist it on deck. I'll find a boat to get the engine ashore by the time you're ready. Just be looking out for me when I come back with a boat."

Determined to find a solution, I rowed back to shore and tied up the dinghy. I walked up and down the shoreline, but I could not locate any suitable boats. I looked out into the bay where a freighter was anchored farther out than *Rhiannon*. I watched one of the local wooden commercial fishing boats acting as a tugboat, ferrying a lighter barge between the freighter and the naval base. Aboard the barge was a gang of young Ecuadorian naval recruits piling sacks of grain from the freighter onto the barge.

As the fishing boat/tug brought the loaded barge back to the naval base to unload, inspiration struck. Once again, I walked into the naval base, saluting the guards confidently as I passed. This time, I continued quickly to the tall concrete pier located inside the base. By that time, the dozen young sailors had already finished unloading the heavy sacks onto the pier where I stood. They were casting off, ready to return to the freighter for another load.

As the fishing boat began pulling the barge away from the pier, I gestured to the young recruits that I wished to come along with them. The barge was already six feet from the dock and moving away. They beckoned me to jump. I took a running leap from the tall dock, landing with one foot on the back edge of the barge. Two sailors instantly grabbed my arms and hauled me into the barge before I fell backward into the water. I rode along with the sailors aboard the naval barge out to the freighter.

While they were busy unloading more sacks, I walked to the side of the barge to speak with the captain of the tug. I explained that I wanted help bringing the engine from our boat to the pier in the naval base. *Rhiannon* lay at anchor in a direct line between the freighter being unloaded and the naval base. The captain consented to do this with his vessel, provided we could finish in time for him to go back to retrieve the barge, which was still being loaded at the freighter.

I hopped aboard the fishing boat and cast off the lines. Coming from seaward across the bay, we approached *Rhiannon,* where Louis and Clark were lounging in the cockpit alongside the engine. They were looking toward shore trying to locate me. They had no clue that I was nearing them from the opposite direction. I called out to them. With great shock, they turned and spotted me aboard the tugboat that I had commandeered to transport our engine.

The plan worked out very well. Within a few days, the mechanic at the naval base had revived our frozen engine. I offered him money, which he was unable to accept due to naval regulations. The work was done completely free of charge.

Ultimately, we used a leaky abandoned wooden rowboat to float the repaired engine back out to *Rhiannon*. Clark and Louis successfully reinstalled the engine.

To prevent the corrosive seawater from flowing back through the exhaust system into the engine, we devised a simple solution. Whenever the engine was not running, we compulsively plugged the exhaust outlet on the transom with a big tethered cork.

San Cristobal Days

I was delighted that our engine repair took more than a week. The people on San Cristobal were hospitable, kind, and happy. Warm cordial greetings we received on the streets were a far cry from the menacing stares and stabbings we had encountered in Panama. There were virtually no tourists. We were the only outsiders. We came to recognize the faces of almost everyone in town and quickly became members of the community. We shuttled local children in our dinghy to tour *Rhiannon*. We took locals out for drinks and in turn were invited into people's homes. Most everyone went out of their way to greet us and serve us in any way, asking for nothing in return.

After a welcomed shower

One couple even took us into their home so we could shower — our first since Panama. One evening they invited us to a town dance. I love to dance. For me, local culture is often best characterized by the rhythms and melodies of the popular music. My memories of different places are permanently linked to the local music. Dance connects the soul of the people to the beat of their music. At the town dance, I immersed myself in the steps of cumbia rhythms and Ecuadorian ballads.

Sadly, the mood of the villagers was bittersweet on the night of the dance. A young local fisherman, known to everyone, had died in a tragic accident. While free diving, he had been caught underwater between two rocks and drowned. The whole community was in mourning, yet they still attended the dance to uplift their spirits.

Whenever I walked through the streets of San Cristobal, I heard music emanating from the phonographs in the houses. The cumbia song *Casita de Pobres* by Olmedo Torres was being played ubiquitously.

One day, Louis, Clark, and I rode an old school bus out of town, up the winding mountain road to the town of El Progreso. High in the hills, it was cooler and greener. We were amazed by the contrast in scenery after the short drive. Wandering through a coffee plantation in the lush forest, we encountered burros carrying sacks of coffee beans down the trails. A group of young school children at the Carlos Darwin School thronged around us, posing for a picture. In front of the small church in El Progreso, while waiting for the ride back down to Wreck Bay, we set the timer on our camera to snap a memorable self-portrait of all three of us.

A burro transporting coffee beans at El Progresso

Self-portrait at El Progresso

Although, San Cristobal was civilized and populated compared to Marchena and Santiago, there were very few links to the outside. There was a weekly mail flight to Quito from Isla Baltra. And there was the "telephone and telegraph" system. The telephone worked over a small short-wave transmitter operated from a new stucco building on the edge town. Behind this building was a gravel lot that was crisscrossed by antenna wire strung like clotheslines. The telephone operators were local women who worked in alternate shifts, calling Quito or Guayaquil according to a fixed schedule.

While at anchor, on our Sony radio receiver, we could listen in, while the operators attempted to establish contact with the mainland. We heard a distinctive nasal voice calling, "Quito … Quito!" followed by a more rapid staccato, "Quito, Quito, Quito!! Hola!" And then, "Alo! Quito Hola!" Making contact was apparently quite difficult, as this repeating CQ continued throughout much of the day.

As only 10 or 15 brief calls were completed during a workday, attempting to contact our families was challenging. The process went something like this: We would write down the city, state, country, name, and number of the party we would like to reach. After waiting one or two hours we were told to return the next morning. When we were lucky, the call went through. But the connection would be so poor that spoken words were either inaudible or indecipherable. During one phone conversation with my father, I spoke for almost two minutes before realizing that it was actually him on the other end of the line. His voice sounded like Donald Duck speaking through a tin can. My message eventually did get through. My father was planning to join us in the Marquesas. I related our anticipated arrival in Hiva Oa toward the end of December, five weeks away. We agreed upon a meeting date in early January 1977. The success of such an improbable rendezvous depended largely on chance.

On Saturday, December 4, our last day in Wreck Bay, a small launch from a local lobster boat motored up to us in the anchorage. Two Americans greeted us. Lloyd was a young man who had been working in Ecuador and had recently been transferred to Bali, Indonesia. Pam was a young doctor vacationing from California. She had used some connections to arrange, under the table, a week-long sightseeing trip in the Galapagos aboard the lobster boat *Villamil*. As lobster fishing recently had been restricted, the *Villamil* was being converted to be used for light fish hauling and tourism. Lloyd and Pam planned to visit Isla Española and Isla Floreana. This was significant to us, as we were also planning to visit Post Office Bay on Isla Floreana. We bid them adieu hoping to see them two days later at Post Office Bay.

With the motor running again and the batteries fully charged, we were nearly ready for departure. At about 4:00 p.m., Clark and I dinghied ashore to get our passports stamped at the police station and to obtain clearance from el Capitán de Puerto. The Police Chief/ Port Captain was out, so the other policemen fiddled for half an hour trying to set the date on the official passport stamp. After some trial and error, they successfully moved the date stamp from June to December.

Next, we went to look for el Capitán de Puerto. We had been told that he would be in his office all day. He was not. We found him happily playing soccer in the middle of dusty Darwin Boulevard. He promised to be in his office by 7:00 p.m. When he did show up that evening, several work boat captains were also there, waiting to obtain clearance as well. When our turn arrived, I told my friend, the assistant port captain, that I would send him a postcard from French Polynesia. He was so delighted that he waived the $10 departure tax. I carefully wrote down his mailing address.

Post Office Bay

By mid-day Sunday, we set sail for Post Office Bay on Isla Floreana. Post Office Bay is a storied anchorage that for over a century had been virtually a compulsory stop for vessels passing through the Galapagos. There are many legendary versions of its history. The story we knew was that ships sailing to California from the East Coast of the U.S. via Cape Horn during the early 1800s would stop at Post Office Bay mid-journey to obtain fresh water. A barrel had been placed on the beach in which mail was deposited and retrieved. Eastbound vessels would pick up mail left by westbound ships and vice versa. The original barrel had been replaced several times over the years.

During the 20th century, it became customary for visiting yachts to leave mail in the barrel and to pick up any mail corresponding with their boat's destination. Another ritual involved leaving a carved plaque or sign displaying the name of each visiting yacht at the "post office" barrel. While in San Cristobal, we had been denied official clearance to stop at Post Office Bay. However, all three of us had read of its legendary place in sailing history. There was no way that we would bypass Isla Floreana without stopping.

The sail to Isla Floreana was uneventful. As we approached Post Office Bay, we could see one other boat in the anchorage. It was the *Villamil!* We dropped anchor alongside her in the peaceful bay. Almost immediately, some of her men, along with Lloyd and Pam, drew near in their launch.

We went ashore on the perfect horseshoe-shaped beach and found the "post office" barrel mounted on a post. The ground surrounding it was littered with a mix of hastily carved boards and interesting artwork bearing the names of yachts from the preceding decade. Some were names of famous boats that we knew, others were not. There was no mail in the "box." We left some postcards. Then using a pocketknife, I crudely carved the name "*Rhiannon*" into a scrap of wood.

While hiking around the uninhabited bay, we once again saw sea lions at play. For the first time, we also enjoyed watching a group of Galapagos penguins swimming and waddling along the beach.

We were invited aboard the *Villamil*, where their cook prepared us a sumptuous lunch. They treated us to fresh lobster (caught while we were exploring ashore), beef, rice, soup, newly baked bread, and cold Pepsi. After we had finished eating lunch and expressing our sincere gratitude, their launch brought us back to *Rhiannon*.

Villamil then weighed anchor, leaving us all alone with no sign of humanity or civilization in sight. Louis stitched up a little rent in our mainsail. I fixed a small part in the mechanical sumlog. Meanwhile, Clark made the crucial navigation logbook entry documenting our departure for the South Pacific.

By late in the afternoon on Sunday, December 6, 1976, we were mentally and physically prepared to leave on our 3000 NM sail across the Pacific Ocean to Hiva Oa in the Marquesas. We were setting off on a long voyage, unlike anything any of us had previously experienced. We had no ability to communicate with anyone in the outside world. Only the penguins and sea lions were there to see us off. We propped the camera up on deck and used the self-timer to snap a departure self-portrait. For the picture, Clark put on a white captain's cap that he had been given.

The mail barrel at Post Office Bay

Rhiannon in Post Office Bay viewed from the *Villamil*

We next tried to start the engine using the starter motor. That did not work. Fortunately, the hand crank got our recalcitrant motor going. When we pulled up the anchor this time, we lashed it securely to the base of the mast. It would be a long time before we would need it again.

Our departure self-portrait before crossing the Pacific

We were setting sail into the open ocean unwitnessed. Had we been lost at sea, nobody would have known when we had departed or from what location — that is, until the unstamped postcard Clark dropped into the old "post-office" barrel on the deserted beach, somehow arrived at his grandmother's home in Iowa … twenty years later!

CHAPTER 16

The Southeast Trades

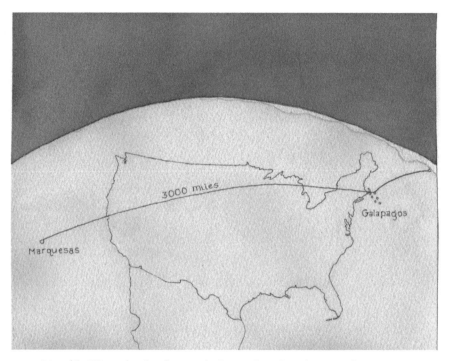

Map of the U.S. overlayed to illustrate the distance from the Galapagos to the Marquesas

Sailing in the Trades

There are two trade wind belts in the eastern Pacific Ocean, between 30° N and 30° S latitudes. (See Map p. 271) The northeast trade winds lie north of the equator, and the southeast trade winds lie south of the equator. The intertropical convergence zone (ITCZ), often known as the "doldrums," is found between the two trade wind belts. The position of these systems, their wind velocities, and their wind directions all vary slightly from month to month and year to year.

Generally, the southeast trade winds blow reliably from the east or southeast at five to 30 knots. On most days, sailors can expect winds in the 12- to 25-knot range. A west-setting current often accompanies these trade winds, while an east-setting equatorial countercurrent can be found in the doldrums, nearer the equator.

Meteorologists did not bring to public attention the widely discussed climatic phenomena of El Niño and La Niña until the major El Niño event of 1982-1983. The trade wind conditions vary considerably between El Niño and La Niña years. However, in 1976, seasonal predictions of trade wind strength and Pacific tropical storm activity only existed in a few scientists' laboratories. There was no seasonal trade wind forecast available to the public.

At the time of our voyage, sailors tended to view all years equally. The only data we had to go on were the monthly average conditions displayed on obsolete pilot charts. Word of mouth and anecdotes in the sailing literature provided us with only minimal additional guidance. None of us had ever spoken with anyone who had made the passage we were about to begin.

Based upon our reading, we planned to be sailing off the wind the entire way with no beating into the wind anticipated. For cruising sailors, an extended downwind sail represents a "dream come true." Due to the consistency of the southeast trade winds, the 3,000 NM trip between the Galapagos and French Polynesia today is commonly called the "Coconut Milk Run."

The doldrums often envelop the Galapagos with calm and fluky winds. Consequently, our goal when leaving those islands was to move south as quickly as possible to find the consistent SE trade winds. Common wisdom held that the trade winds could usually be found approximately 200 NM south of the Galapagos.

On the evening of our departure from Post Office Bay the moon was full, and the wind was blowing steadily at 10 to 15 knots from the SSE. Although this felt to us like trade winds, we decided to stick to our initial plan, sailing south first, just to be certain that we would not end up becalmed in the doldrums. Rather than sail our great circle course WSW, directly toward the Marquesas, we started this passage on a port tack beat toward the south. If we had been privy to any offshore wind information, we might not have done that.

We engaged George and listened to the radio for a while in the moonlight. At about the time that we had lost sight of land, we heard the news that a major volcanic eruption had just begun on Isla Isabela. However, by then, the Galapagos had already dropped below our horizon. There was nothing for us to see. We were making five to six knots, close hauled toward the south. We all went to sleep. Although we did not keep a regular night watch rotation, Clark slept in the cockpit. Several times during the first night, Louis and I each woke up to look around on deck in the bright moonlight.

After two days of beating toward the south, the wind direction remained unchanged. We concluded that we had been in the SE trade winds right from the start. We fell off onto a broad reach, soon averaging over six knots perfectly on course.

On this leg of our journey, we began counting the days since we had left and estimating the days until our arrival. Louis, Clark, and I quickly settled into a routine. This was not the routine of the Caribbean, for we could now depend on George our "fourth crew member," to keep us on track. As the wind generally shifted only a few degrees once or twice a day, we rarely even touched George during the early going. We finally had time on our hands. For once, even the cabin was clean and dry.

As we made tracks away from the Galapagos, the air and water grew steadily warmer. We were in the tropics. We all had fair skin. The significant link between sun exposure and skin cancers was not yet well known. Sunscreen with a sun protection factor (SPF) greater than two was not yet available. At least we did know that sunburn hurt. We spread zinc oxide on our noses, and frequently wore hats.

However, we wore fewer and fewer clothes as the air temperature increased. Clothing became superfluous. Shirts and pants were a nuisance. After a few days at sea, none of us wore any clothing at all. Louis and I did wear our home-made safety harnesses. But Clark rarely used his. Though we tried our best to find shady spots aboard *Rhiannon*, with no spray dodger, bimini, or canopy, we were all deeply suntanned.

At last we began to get a feel for the Pacific Ocean in the SE trades. The color of the water was deep blue. The swells were large and far apart, no matter the wind strength or wave heights. In the troughs, between swells, we were in a valley with no visibility beyond the swell ahead and the one behind. When it was windier, whitecapped waves would tower behind us like hills. As the waves broke noisily, a blanket of white foam would spread out on the surface like a white bridal train on a blue carpet.

The trade wind sky was always slightly hazy. Small puffy cumulus clouds of limited height would march westward all day long. On occasional days, high cirrus clouds obscured all but the yellow disk of the sun. Rain squalls would sometimes interrupt the fair weather, usually arriving in clusters. A few days would pass with no squalls. Then a few days of frequent squalls would follow. The barometer never changed much.

After a few days, the wind direction moved aft. When running dead down-wind, we hanked on and poled out both of our jibs simultaneously. For one of the two sails, we fastened only the lowest three or four hanks to the forestay. That way, if we needed to drop only one jib during a squall, we could easily leave the other jib up. We used the wooden whisker pole that we had made in Panama to pole out the 175% genoa to port and our spinnaker pole for the 100% working jib to starboard. Along with this twin foresail rig, we set a triple-reefed mainsail, sheeted tightly amidships, as a steadying sail.

When a towering sea would advance toward us, it appeared from the deck that we would surely be pooped by its breaking crest. But this never happened. George sometimes veered off to one side as our stern began to lift. Then he would faithfully pull our course back, straight down the face of the long wave, as *Rhiannon* surged with a roar. The transom itself never even got wet. This pattern repeated itself wave after wave, sometimes for a few days at a time.

Our downwind rig with me near the mast

Skittering down a trade wind wave with George steering

We eventually abandoned night watches altogether. I generally stayed up latest in the evening, and Louis woke up first each morning. During the few dark hours in between, each of us usually woke up once or twice to check on our course and look for approaching squalls. Clark generally slept in the cockpit all night, occasionally getting up to look around as well. Though we always checked for ships, we only saw a ship's light on the horizon twice during this entire passage.

Squalls occurred most frequently during the night. On board, each of us became so attuned to the sounds, rhythms, and subtleties of *Rhiannon's* motion that the slightest change would instantly awaken all three of us. If something were squeaking, clicking, or flapping, I would immediately spring from my berth to scramble on deck. A small change in the wave pattern generally signaled an approaching squall. A difference in the angle of heel or sound of the bow wave would alert us as well.

Trade wind sunset with developing squalls

Our "squall drill" quickly evolved into a neatly choreographed routine. The first one awake who saw the approaching squall would awaken the others. He would then go forward on deck to release jib halyards at the mast, dropping one or both jibs as necessary. The second person up would disengage George and take the helm. He would also control the mainsheet as he momentarily rounded the boat up into the wind to help guide the jib onto the foredeck. The third person would go forward to assist in lashing the lowered sail to the stanchions.

The wind was often gusty and shifty for a few minutes during a squall. At times, the cold rain was chilling, especially at night. After 10 minutes or so, the squall would move off. The stars would reappear, and we would reassume our previous configuration. Louis and I were particularly concerned whenever Clark would go forward during a squall without wearing his safety harness. Had Clark fallen overboard, recovering him would have been nearly impossible.

During the day, as the miles ticked off, we passed the time in many ways. On one particularly calm day, Louis and Clark swam for fun behind *Rhiannon*, holding onto a rope as we slowly ghosted along. Usually, the fresh trade winds blew much too hard to consider swimming. Simply gazing out at the ocean from the cockpit was mesmerizing. The kaleidoscopic ever-changing wave and cloud patterns hypnotized me for hours. I regularly witnessed columns of falling rain and bright double rainbows. Every sunset and sunrise provided a spectacle of changing colors and painted clouds worthy of a masterpiece. Most evenings, at sunset, all three of us would sit in the cockpit, often drinking tea, as we watched the technicolor panorama.

Sea life remained a novelty for me. Every new sighting was fascinating. Pelagic birds roamed the ocean, thousands of miles from shore. Petrels skimmed the waves. Frigate birds soared overhead. Boobies wheeled and circled in our wake. The most amusing bird of all was the snow-white tropic bird, with its long trailing plume. The tropic birds would consistently attempt to land on the masthead. The VHF antenna at the top of the mast would generally thwart even their best efforts to plant their feet and fold their wings. Rarely, a tropic bird would successfully perch for brief a moment atop the rotating wind indicator.

Down below, the most visible animals living in the water were the flying fish. In reality, they were only visible when they were airborne above the water's surface. Solitary flying fish or schools of hundreds appeared every day. We saw several species of flying fish. The tiny fingerlings would often strand themselves on deck, as would the three- to four-inch mid-sized flying fish. The big ones, often eight inches long, frequently travelled alone. I was always amazed whenever I watched a school of dozens of flying fish shoot from the face of a wave. Their shiny scales and beating wings would glint magically in the sunlight. After coasting above the water, they would disappear back into the sea, up to several hundred yards away from where they had emerged. I never knew if these fish were being chased by predators or if *Rhiannon's* approach had provoked their flight.

Twice while in the trade winds, we spotted whales spouting a fair distance off. I wrote in my personal log:

> *The awesome beasts were probably a good deal larger than our frail craft. So, we respected their right of way and stayed well clear.*

Chafe is the biggest enemy of long-distance sailors. Wherever a sail rubs gently against a spreader tip or a jib sheet glides back and forth over a stanchion, chafe is insidiously at work destroying important gear. On a daysail, nothing remains in the same position for a prolonged period of time. However, in the trade winds, a small point of contact became a relentless saw, slowly gnawing through cloth, rope, wood, plastic, or even metal.

In Panama, we mounted baggywrinkles that we had made on potential trouble spots in the standing rigging. While running down the trades, each of us made daily inspection rounds to hunt down and stop any chafe. We added protective tape and leather or rerouted lines wherever necessary. We lubricated moving parts regularly. Fortunately, we were always able to stay one step ahead in this ongoing battle.

Fishing and Eating

As the days passed, we were nearly halfway to the Marquesas and still had not caught a fish to eat, other than the tiny flying fish that we found on deck in the morning. In Panama, this had been an embarrassment. We had spoken with the other cruising sailors and listened carefully to their techniques and tips. On the way to the Galapagos, we had tried. But our attempts had been thwarted by thieving fish and bad weather.

Some sailors had told us of their surefire lures. We had them all in our big tackle box. Some people we had met even bragged that they had hooked several large yellowfin tunas simply by using a white rag as bait. Others had slid a section of a plastic drinking straw over the top of a fishhook, enabling them to catch a mahi-mahi or wahoo with ease.

In the trade winds where we were sailing, birds had flown thousands of miles from shore for the abundant fish. Several times we had seen huge shoals of leaping tuna. We had no excuse. We began regularly putting out properly weighted heavy-duty lines with steel leaders and a variety of lures. Our trolling speed was optimal for fishing. A couple of our hooks were sheared off by a large fish of some kind. Each evening before dark we would reel in the bare hook, once again disappointed by our failure.

Out of frustration, by mid-ocean we decided to try leaving a line out at night. With a shock cord attached to the fishing line, we suspended a dinner fork, rigged to clang noisily against the stern railing if something had been caught. On the first moonless evening that we trolled, Louis was sound asleep in his quarter berth. Clark was awake in the cabin. I was the last one up, on deck, watching the stars. As we rushed through the night, with George steering perfectly, our fish alarm abruptly sounded. I was skeptical that we had caught anything. I checked the line. There was a serious tug. I thought to myself: "We're not in a pond. This isn't likely to be a leather boot or an old truck tire."

I eagerly reeled in the line. There was something significant on the hook. As I brought it in, I called Clark up on deck. I asked him to bring the net and the gaff with him. As I lifted my catch from the water, I saw a writhing mass—a blob. It did not look like a fish. Clark filled a bucket with sea water and grabbed a flashlight. It appeared to be a dark grey squid, about a foot in length, not counting the long tentacles. The hook was still in its beak as I dropped the squid into a bucket and carried it into the cabin where we had a better light. I set the bucket on the floor at the base of the companionway steps near Louis's head, as he slept in the starboard quarter berth.

Suddenly, to my shock and horror, the squid began forcefully pumping inky sea water from the bucket onto my naked torso and face. Some liquid squirted directly into my mouth. At that moment, I thought to myself: "This ink is the desperate squid's defense mechanism. And it's probably poisonous or caustic." Being weeks away from any medical assistance, I immediately began spitting, wiping my chest … and swearing. At that moment, Louis woke up and rolled over in time to see me jumping up and down, frantically spitting and swearing. He then saw the inky water shooting from the bucket on the cabin sole toward my face in rapid pulsations. He thought he must be dreaming. He had no idea what was going on. Fortunately, the squid soon died, and the ink was not toxic.

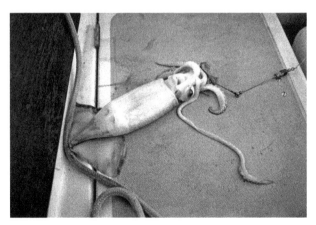

The squid

The next day, we tried to fish again. Instead of wasting our stove alcohol to cook the tough squid meat, we cut it up as bait. By evening, we still had not caught anything. Once again, we decided to try our luck at night. I was in the cockpit just after dark when the fish alarm sounded once more. I could not believe that we had hooked another squid, but just like the evening before, there definitely was something on the line. I anxiously reeled it in, this time fully prepared to deal with another living water pump.

The snake mackerel

As I lifted it from the water, I saw the antithesis of what I had seen the night before. A long wriggling snake-like animal was hanging from the hook. As I examined it, I could see that it was not an eel but rather a long narrow fish with strange big eyes and a mouth full of sharp needle-like teeth. Coincidentally, I had just been reading Thor Heyerdahl's book, *Kon-Tiki*. In the exact same stretch of the Pacific where we were that night, an identical fish had jumped into a sleeping bag aboard the famous raft 29 years earlier. In the book, there was a photo of that fish, which they identified as a rare "snake mackerel," *Gempylus serpens*. Once again, we had not caught an edible fish but instead had hooked a rarely seen creature from the deep.

Although we caught no fish to eat, Louis, Clark, and I survived on macaroni and cheese, tuna casseroles, and canned food. Louis and I sometimes fried the stranded flying fish collected from our deck for breakfast. But Clark stuck to pancakes, oatmeal, and orange Tang. A few times we attempted baking. Louis once made a huge loaf of whole wheat bread in a pot. The outside was delicious. The inside was a bit underdone. We scooped some of the raw dough out and made a pizza with it. By and large, we ate well.

Freshly baked bread

During rain squalls, we collected fresh water for our tanks, easily keeping them topped off. A clean bucket strategically hung at the gooseneck could fill multiple times in 10 minutes. Our biggest complaint was the lack of anything even slightly cool to drink when the sun was out. It was hot. It was humid. We were always thirsty. Our drinking water perpetually remained the same temperature as the air and the ocean, about 82° F.

On one occasion Louis and I tried to invent an evaporative cooler out of a tea kettle and some wet rags. We also tried to improve this cooling device by pumping air through hoses using our dinghy foot pump. We only succeeded in getting sweatier and thirstier. At least we had amused ourselves for a few hours while passing another day at sea.

Navigation

Before GPS existed, sailors used the sun, moon, stars, and planets to find small islands in the vast ocean. This celestial navigation required accurate timekeeping, precise sextant observations, and careful sight reduction calculations. We used Louis's chronometer for recording the exact times of our sextant sights. The chronometer would lose approximately 2.5 seconds each day. We knew this by comparing our timepiece to the signals received on our short-wave radio from station WWVH. It was important for us to know this rate of time loss, so that we could record our celestial sights precisely to the second even if we could not pick up a radio signal.

Our navigation thus remained totally independent of any external man-made source. Aboard *Rhiannon*, we carried my brass Heath sextant, as well as a plastic EBBCO sextant for backup. A sextant is a simple instrument that accurately measures the angle or "altitude" of a celestial body from the horizon. Using arithmetic calculations and referring to published tables, we reduced our sextant sights into lines of position that we plotted on nautical charts.

Of necessity, I devised a technique to securely brace myself whenever I was using the sextant to make observations aboard our rolling sailboat. I had ample opportunity to refine my procedures and develop "tricks" in order to take these sights. I found a position of known eye height, standing in the companionway while bracing my back and my right knee firmly against the hatchway frame. I timed each sight to coincide with *Rhiannon*'s heave, midway between the peak and trough of a Pacific swell. It was important always to visualize the true horizon rather than the false horizon of a wave crest. For accuracy, I would average at least three readings taken in succession to derive a single value to use in the definitive reduction.

While crossing to the Marquesas, one fix (true position) daily proved sufficient to monitor our progress across the open ocean. Most cruising sailors at that time followed a practice similar to ours. When making a difficult landfall, we took additional sights. We usually obtained our daily fix by combining two observations, one at around 10:00 a.m. local and the second at local noon. One sun sight could not produce a definitive "point" as a fix. It only yielded a "line of position" that could be plotted on the chart. The line obtained was always perpendicular to the sun's azimuth (bearing toward the sun) at the time of the sight. The plotted line only indicated that the boat was positioned somewhere along that line. At least one additional line was needed, to cross with the first line, in order to obtain a fix at a single point. Since the sun's azimuth changes throughout the day, the mid-morning line of position ran in a different direction than the noon line of position.

We also needed to account for our boat's movement between the times of the 10:00 a.m. and noon sun sights. On *Rhiannon*'s chart, we simply moved the morning line forward, advancing that line of position by the distance and direction of our travel between 10:00 a.m. and noon. We determined this distance and direction by dead reckoning. Thus, we obtained a noon fix each day, from which we could calculate our daily progress. With many days to practice celestial navigation, we occasionally varied our routine by employing moon sights and, more rarely, star or planet sights. I occasionally experimented with novel techniques of my own. (See Appendix 5.)

The Rhythm of the Sea

It was December 25, 1976. Clark wrote in the ship's log:

Merry Christmas! A strange night last night of squalls coming through frequently. Dropped the 175 and George was having trouble steering. Up quite late, of course. Thought much of home and what everyone was doing. Today, our calculations show us 700 miles from our goal! It's funny, but that seems such a trifling ... Whereas our 500 mile trip across the Gulf of Mexico loomed so ominously. It is quite amazing that we have spent 19 days on the water with only two ships and two whales as our company. The wind, water and sky seem such an integral part. Land is a somewhat blurred but not forgotten concept. If we're lucky, New Year's Eve shall be spent at anchor.

Rhiannon, Louis, Clark, George, and I had become a well-integrated unit, at one with the sea. It is strange how the three of us each became accustomed to both the isolation and the seemingly infinite expanse of the ocean. As one day melted into the next, routines became increasingly comfortable. Voyaging became less a mystery and more a natural routine. There were fewer unknowns than at the outset. The consistent winds, continuous waves, and marching trade wind clouds created a sense of perpetuity. Even astronauts in space maintain voice communication with the earth. We had lost all contact with our former homes. Our home had become the sea.

Sailing toward the sunset

Early in the evening, we would make tea and sit out in the cockpit together to watch the sky. Often, we listened to the radio as we admired yet another spectacular sunset. By Christmas, we clearly received the short-wave broadcasts of Radio Tahiti. The French and Tahitian spoken on the air began to prepare us for French Polynesia. After the news in Tahitian, we enjoyed the continuous program of Tahitian music.

I quickly became intoxicated by the traditional Tahitian songs and tamure drumbeats. The melodies and the sounds of the spoken language itself transported me back to my childhood stay in Tahiti. I remained up on deck late at night, watching the Southern Cross and the night sky as I fell in love with the sounds on the radio. By the time we neared the Marquesas, the distinctive Polynesian voices and rhythms seamlessly blended with the natural sounds of the sea.

On December 28, Clark again made an entry into the ship's log:

Well, we should be 3-4 days from Hiva Oa. Presently at 133° W, 9° S (Hiva Oa is at 139° W 9°50' S). The trip has been a very pleasant one and part of me says we should forever sail the ocean. The easy rhythm of the trades has become part and parcel of our existence. The constant gurgle of the seas as we push ever onward is a sweet lullaby. The 25 days have melted into one continuous frame of happy sailing. Soon every nerve will be taut as our eyes strain for that wave, which does not disappear. Here is hoping our 5-knot average holds.

Landfall

Before we left Chicago, my father had expressed a strong interest in visiting the Marquesas Islands. I had told him that if we ever got that far, he was welcome to join us for a week or two of cruising there. While we were in the Galapagos, I sent a telegram to my father projecting our arrival in the Marquesas sometime toward the end of December 1976. Accordingly, he planned a vacation in Tahiti with my mother during the month of December, with the intention of traveling to the Marquesas on his own afterward to meet us. My mother, who was prone to severe seasickness, would fly home from Tahiti by herself after their vacation.

Over an exceptionally poor telephone connection on San Cristobal, shortly before our departure from the Galapagos, I understood that my father had arranged to meet us on the island of Hiva Oa on January 3, 1977. If he did not find us, his intention was to explore the Marquesas alone. As we neared Hiva Oa, it became apparent that the timing of this rendezvous just might work. Although we had experienced several days of lighter wind in the southeast trades, we were still on track to arrive on December 31, New Year's Eve.

Although our celestial navigation calculations appeared internally consistent, we had no way of verifying our accuracy based upon any type of landmark or definitive visual fix. We steered by periodically adjusting George. Our goal was to maintain a course to within approximately 5° of a selected compass heading.

Theoretically, if we were to steer a course based upon a celestial fix obtained 100 NM from our destination and were off course by only 10°, we would miss the goal by over 17 NM. We did not want to arrive at night. Standing off in the boisterous trade winds would be unpleasant.

Consequently, on December 30 we plotted our standard running fix at noon and for good measure obtained a star fix at dusk. We were trying to reach land during the morning. We decided that with the west-setting current, we needed to slow from six to five knots through the night. We set the 100% working jib, poled out, along with the deeply reefed mainsail. The outboard end of the whisker pole was stabilized with a lift, an afterguy, and a foreguy. We routinely stabilized the pole in this manner, so that the whisker pole would remain stationary even if we dropped the jib. We were sailing wing-on-wing. Before dark, we scanned the western horizon ahead of us to look for mountains. There was no sign of land. All three of us went to sleep for the night.

None of us slept well. We all awoke at least an hour before the first light broke on the eastern horizon. It was a bit chilly at that hour. Louis boiled a kettle of water. We brought our mugs of tea into the cockpit to wait for dawn. The stars and planets were still bright. Despite the shortened sail, we were flying along at six knots. The roar and hiss of our bow wave and the breaking whitecaps around us broke the silence.

I was nervous. I am certain that Louis and Clark were, as well. Would we spot land as the sun rose? Would we be on target to strike the narrow end of a small island after travelling 3000 NM in the open ocean? The sea state was adding to the tension. The waves were as tall as we had yet experienced but closer together, steeper, and breaking more heavily.

With the first light of dawn, a cloud became visible directly ahead. It was the dark shadow of a tall round cloud, not yet fully visible in the early light. The cloud seemed to loom up in front of us. As we slowly sipped our tea, we unanimously concluded that this must be a cloud capping Hiva Oa in the distance ahead. The waves steepened to the point that George was having some difficulty, almost broaching as we surged down the growing waves. The cloud looked funny. It was the only one in the sky, and it was not moving.

Just before the sun peeked over the horizon behind us, the sun's orange rays illuminated this "cloud" on our bow. We each were straining our eyes to be the first to spot a distant island, beneath the strange cloud. Simultaneously, we all jumped up. Clark broke the silence, "Wait a second. That's not a cloud! That's land!"

Within moments, it became clear that we were looking at the face of a cliff and were only minutes from running headlong into the crashing surf at its base. We were about one or two NM from the narrow eastern point on Hiva Oa, called Cap Balguerie. In fact, we were so close that the rest of this mountainous island was completely obscured from our view by the sheer cliff that rose above us.

The eastern tip of Hiva Oa

The topography of the island was not as we had anticipated. We were so confused by the appearance of Hiva Oa from this close perspective that we considered the possibility of having reached a completely different island. George was about to run us onto the rocks. We threw our mugs into the sink. We began a frantic fire drill to lower the whisker pole, jibe the jib, and release the main preventer in order to head up 45° to reach along the south coast of the island.

At about this time, a group of several hundred Fraser's dolphins joined us immediately to starboard, leaping en masse out of the faces of the waves. I had never seen these blunt-nosed dolphins before. Nor had I ever seen such a huge number of cetaceans swimming together. It was as if someone had arranged a welcoming party to accompany us upon our arrival to French Polynesia. As the Polynesian people in their outrigger pirogues had approached the first European ships hundreds of years earlier, these playful animals had come out to greet us.

Hiva Oa, situated over 750 NM northeast of Tahiti, is one of the two most populated islands in the Marquesas. We sailed along the south shore of Hiva Oa and readied the anchor. We had no trouble recognizing Taha'uku Bay based upon the chart and the *Sailing Directions*. On this occasion, almost surprisingly, our motor started as we rounded the headland to enter the protected waters of the bay. When we arrived, mid-morning on New Year's Eve, there were no other transients anchored there. We tucked *Rhiannon* well up inside the bay and set the anchor. We had arrived intact.

The south coast of Hiva Oa

The sight and smell of land were overwhelming. The jagged storybook mountains, lush green valleys, and black sand beaches of Hiva Oa were striking. Seeing them after over three weeks at sea bordered on unbelievable. Thatched-roof huts beneath the coconut palms at the head of the bay signaled our arrival in the South Pacific.

Louis brought out three cans of Point Beer from a small brewery in Wisconsin that a friend had given him, to be consumed on a special occasion. We never drank alcoholic beverages while sailing. Here in Hiva Oa at last, we celebrated on deck. With the camera perched on the coachroof, we snapped a self-portrait of the three of us. It was a bookend to the departure photo we had taken at Post Office Bay 24½ days earlier.

Our arrival self-portrait in Taha'uku Bay, Hiva Oa

CHAPTER 17

The Marquesas

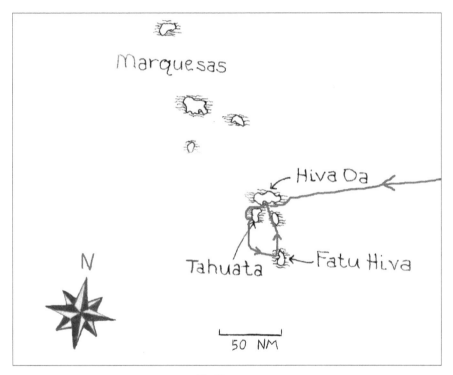

The Marquesas

La Bonne Année

CLARK RAISED THE code "Q" flag. I inflated one of the two dinghies. Louis, Clark, and I rowed ashore together with our documents. We could not fathom that we had arrived in French Polynesia. Somehow, we had managed to navigate *Rhiannon* from New Orleans to Hiva Oa, intact, taken only by the wind. Looking back at her, peacefully anchored in the bay with the towering peak of Mt. Temetiu in the background, stirred our souls.

The three of us walked from Taha'uku Bay along the dusty road. We proceeded around the point and down the hill into Atuona, the biggest village on the island. We checked in easily at the gendarmerie, obtaining permission for a six-month stay in French Polynesia. Next, we managed to convert some traveler's cheques into local currency.

Mt. Temetiu at Atuona viewed from the anchorage in Taha'uku Bay

Initially, everything about this remote landfall felt strange. We were wearing clothes for the first time in weeks. The physical sensation alone was odd. We were unsteady on our feet, occasionally staggering, anticipating the land to shift and roll like the ocean with each step.

With Louis and Clark in Hiva Oa

The scenery was breathtakingly gorgeous. Dramatic mountains towered over the lush Atuona valley. Brightly colored flowers and heavily laden fruit trees grew everywhere. The raucous local children played cheerfully along our path. We had not seen any other people for 25 days. A great mango tree near the center of town cast its broad welcoming shadow across the road. Climbing in the shady tree were a dozen young children. Some were perched on the immense tree limbs, eating fresh mangos. We simply walked around town, in a trance, taking it all in.

A man on the roadside with a neat stack of green coconuts and a machete sold each of us a coconut filled with sweet refreshing coconut water to drink. A yellow two-story colonial-style, wooden-frame building bustled with activity. This was one of the main stores in Atuona. Built in the 19th century, this edifice had stood when Paul Gauguin had lived here during the final years of his life.

Walking in, we were introduced to the Marquesan proprietor's family. One of them, Ozanne, a young man of about our age, eagerly offered to take us on a fishing excursion. He also graciously invited us to sail to Hana Menu, on the other side of the island, where his family owned land. We shared a cold drink with him in a small back room behind the general store.

As we walked through town, many people asked us if we had planned to attend the fête that night for "la bonne année." This unconventional French wording was universally used by the local people to describe the impending New Year's celebration. They also used the same term, "la bonne année," to refer to New Year's Day itself.

By afternoon, the weather was looking iffy, with dark rain clouds gathering in the mountains. Louis felt obliged to return to *Rhiannon*. He had not yet spent a night off the boat during our entire trip. Clark and I wanted to stay ashore. We had no idea where we would spend the night. Nonetheless, we told Louis to return to *Rhiannon*, and asked him to come back for us in the morning.

"La bonne année" was festive in Atuona. An open-air platform covered by a thatched roof, located at the center of town, served as a public dance floor. Clark and I stayed up late dancing with the young women and absorbing the Polynesian music played on a phonograph. This was the same intoxicating music that I had stayed up late to hear on our radio as we were surging through the trade winds approaching the Marquesas.

Many songs were similar, but occasionally a song would crescendo into the distinctive rapid rhythm of the Tamure Tahiti. The men would grin. The girls would giggle. And everyone would jump up to dance. The women all displayed impossibly rapid hip movements while the men danced on their toes, scissoring their bent knees, just as the song would reach its dramatic climax. I tried my best to match the men's moves, much to the amusement and delight of the Marquesans. The dance was a perfect yet surreal celebration of our arrival following the long ocean crossing. The "bonne année" also heralded the beginning of a new year of sailing through the tropical South Pacific.

As the party ended, a few heavy rain showers passed through. Ozanne let Clark and me into the store, where we drank some Manuia beer. By the time the rain had stopped, everyone had gone to bed. Clark and I remained behind on some uncomfortable wooden chairs at the back of the store. We eventually headed out and wandered by the light of the gibbous moon to find a more comfortable place to sleep. We ended up at the black sand beach that stretched across Atuona Bay where we both slept on the sand until daybreak.

Atuona

Clark and I returned to *Rhiannon* in the morning. For the next two days the three of us did laundry, showered at a fresh-water spigot on the beach at Taha'uku Bay, and explored Atuona. Checking out the available food was a priority. Fruit was abundant. Singularly unappealing canned food imported from China lined the shelves in several tiny stores. There was boiled chicken consisting mostly of pieces of bones, fat, and skin. At least the canned corned beef was a bit more palatable. However, the warm freshly baked bread was extremely appealing.

Loaves of French bread were baked daily in two places in Atuona. There was a small bakery with a glass storefront near the center of town. Additionally, there was the octogenarian Chinese boulanger in his unpainted wooden cabin, hidden among a grove of coconut palms located between town and the beach. For several years, Paul Gauguin had lived near the same spot. This baker had come from Canton, China, in the 1920s as a young man. In almost unintelligible French, mottled with Cantonese, he related stories referencing Paul Gauguin's daughter whom he knew. In 1976, she was in her 70s, still living in the mountains of Hiva Oa, reportedly suffering from elephantiasis.

This diminutive man wielded a broad wooden peel to draw his charred bread from the ancient wood-fired stone oven tucked inside the dimly lit cabin. Although neither Atuona bakery was expensive, the old baker's loaves were a bit cheaper. We tried them first. Unfortunately, his bread was as hard as stone, better suited for construction than consumption.

Over the next two days, several other cruising sailboats arrived at Taha'uku Bay. Many of these boats had congregated in another bay to celebrate New Year's. This explained the absence of boats in the anchorage. From several of them, we learned that one week earlier, on Christmas Eve, exceptional storms had pummeled the anchorages of the Marquesas. All the boats that had been anchored at Hana Vave in Fatu Hiva had either dragged anchor or been otherwise forced to leave the untenable anchorage. This was clearly the same weather system that we had encountered during our night of unusual squalls offshore, which Clark had noted in his logbook entry.

The old Chinese baker in Atuona

With the arrival of other boats at Taha'uku, we quickly met many cruising sailors. For example, we met four young Norwegians aboard their homemade aluminum ketch *Preciosa*. Their skipper was about 30 years old, and the other crew members were closer in age to us. They had sailed from Scandinavia around Cape Horn and up the coast of Chile before touching at Easter Island. They had intentionally built their boat with short masts in anticipation of gale winds in the Southern Ocean. Instead, they had rounded Cape Horn in a rare calm and had not encountered any severe weather at all. Most of the other boats in Hiva Oa were crewed by family groups from Europe or Canada.

Unlike today, there was no pier or breakwater restricting space within the anchorage in Taha'uku Bay. At most eight or nine sailboats would be anchored there at any one time. The great crowds of sailboats did not arrive in the Marquesas until a few years later. Many cruisers we met in Hiva Oa talked about a gregarious sailor named Earl Hinz, who was anchored in Nuku Hiva in the northern Marquesas. Earl was beginning to write the first cruising guide-book for this region, which later became the bible for South Pacific cruising sailors. His guidebook facilitated the flood of boats that arrived during the following decades.

Ashore, I heard stories from many of the residents. I wrote the following description in a letter to my relatives back in the U.S.:

> *I was struck by the strange symbiosis that had evolved between the Marquesans and the French. The church was the primary cultural influence of the Europeans. Atuona was the site of the only Catholic girls' boarding school in the Marquesas. About 400 girls are virtually locked up in this little school with the nuns, being indoctrinated into a world which is strict in its notions of goodness and evil. These imposed rights and wrongs restrict the conduct of their lives and the lives of their families.*
>
> *The Polynesian culture cannot survive when the people must give the fruits of their labor to the church. Contrary to outside appearances, the Marquesans are not lazy. They work very hard at harvesting copra and any construction projects they undertake. The men go hunting (for free-roaming goats and cows) and fishing (for spiny lobsters or tuna.) They manage to feed families of 15 children.*
>
> *The sad aspect of this is that the younger generation, which now goes to school until age 14, does not learn the skills necessary to continue the former lifestyle. The subjects learned in school are irrelevant and useless for their day to day life. The Polynesians do not seem to see this because they rarely look toward the future. They do not worry. They do not plan. -- They never needed to do so.*
>
> *We are accustomed to seeing the squirrels store up nuts for the winter. Here, in the Marquesas, the grapefruit and mangoes hang copiously from trees, which are almost collapsing from the weight. A three-hour fishing expedition can bring back enough food for a week. Planting seeds intentionally and saving money remain foreign concepts. Over the years, the skill of sailing outrigger canoes has been lost. The skill of carving stone and wood has been lost. And the feeling of a unified people has been lost.*

I heard of one French couple, the Rauzys, who had settled in Hiva Oa around 1930. Shrewdly, they had acquired much of the valuable land on the island. Their children were educated in Papeete and in Paris. In 1977, the younger generation of the Rauzy family seemed to control everything on Hiva Oa.

Guy Rauzy, who was married to a Marquesan woman, was the mayor of Atuona. Another brother worked as an administrator in the local government. Christian Rauzy was a doctor's assistant at the medical clinic. Yet another brother was a pilot. The Rauzy family members were also the Air Polynesie representatives in the Marquesas. That airline controlled the only commercial air link to the Marquesas, operating one flight weekly to and from Tahiti.

Two or three times each month copra boats arrived on Hiva Oa. These small inter-island freighters, formerly called copra schooners, supplied the islands and often brought copra from the outlying islands to Tahiti. Besides the missionaries, the doctors, and the Rauzy family, there were many other French people on Hiva Oa. School teachers and government workers from France had settled there. Many of them had married local Marquesans.

In January 1977, Jacques Brel, the world-renowned Belgian singer, composer, and poet was living on Hiva Oa, just outside Atuona. His wife was originally from Martinique. He had undergone a pneumonectomy in France and had retired to the Marquesas, knowing that he had terminal lung cancer. He had previously owned a sailboat, which he had already sold by the time we were there. He also owned the only noncommercial airplane in the Marquesas. He kept his twin-engine Beechcraft named *JoJo* at the airport on Hiva Oa. He drove a 4x4, one of only a handful of cars on the entire island.

Jacques Brel led a private life on Hiva Oa, spending most of his time in his home or at the airport. On more than one occasion, he stopped his car on the road to pick me up as I walked from the anchorage at Taha'uku into Atuona. I once saw him buying caseloads of Manuia and Hinano beer at the general store in town. His heavy drinking and wealth provoked some of the local people in the store to laugh at him behind his back.

However, it was well known that if someone had a medical emergency, Jacques Brel would voluntarily transport them in his plane to Tahiti. It was a lifeline that did not last long for the island. Ultimately, he returned to France to die in 1978. He was later buried in Atuona, in the same hillside cemetery as Paul Gauguin.

January 2, 1977 was my 23rd birthday. Louis, Clark, and I walked together into Atuona that evening. There was considerable noise emanating from one of the buildings at the school next to the church. A movie was being shown free to the public. Apparently, the same obscure black and white western film was shown there on a regular basis. The movie provided an excuse for an evening social gathering of the young people in Atuona.

As we sat among the people in the dark room with large open windows, the film suddenly stopped running. Someone had turned off the projector just as the entire audience jumped up to look out one of the windows. Two young men were fighting one another outside. Members of the crowd all seem to be cheering one or the other of the two brawlers. Nobody tried to break it up. When the fight ended a few minutes later, everyone calmly returned to their seats. The movie then resumed, as if nothing had happened.

My Father Arrives

On January 3, we awaited my father's arrival. I expected him on that day solely based upon our brief garbled telephone call one month earlier. While waiting, we baked a cake in honor of my birthday and Louis's 23rd birthday two weeks later. We sat on *Rhiannon*'s deck, anchored in Taha'uku Bay. The whine of turboprop engines from the De Havilland Twin Otter echoed off the hills as the plane passed overhead. The airport on Hiva Oa was built upon a narrow, graded plateau amid the mountains at the center of the island. The only road between Atuona and the airport passed around the shore of Taha'uku Bay.

I knew that if my father actually had arrived aboard the plane from Tahiti, he would need to ride past the bay on his way down from the airport. As soon as we saw a few vehicles heading down the road from the airport, we rowed the dinghy ashore. If my father were in a car or truck, he would see us standing on the road. Five minutes later, a car stopped. He had spotted us. He climbed out with his duffle and a broad smile. We embraced. It was great to see him. This was an improbable rendezvous. But it had succeeded.

His harrowing journey had rivaled our own. My father's Air Polynesie flight from Tahiti stopped in Ua Pou, another Marquesas island, before continuing to Hiva Oa. His flight was the first airplane ever to land at the newly constructed Ua Pou airport. The runway there ran slightly uphill into a steep-sided valley. Landing aircraft had to fly into the valley toward the mountains, and departures needed to fly in the opposite direction, toward the sea.

As the pilot had begun to flare for touch down at Ua Pou, he spotted a large fire extinguisher on a cart sitting right in the middle of the runway. He was able to apply power, hop over the obstacle, and then land on the remaining pavement. My father said that the passenger seated next to him on the plane happened to be a Pan Am pilot. The Pan Am pilot had been quite anxious during the landing and commended the Air Polynesie pilot on his skillful flying.

My father had received one of my letters from the Galapagos telling him about our Kiwi friends, the Whitings aboard *Tequila*, who were headed directly to Tahiti. In my letter I suggested that he might look for them at the waterfront in Papeete and say hello. Indeed, he and my mother had found them in Papeete. My father and mother took Debbie Whiting and Annie on a tour around Tahiti for an entire day in his rented car. My father also told us that D'Arcy Whiting had reassured him that we would make it safely to the Marquesas before his arrival. Even without the Internet, "small world" connections were possible in 1976.

My father immediately adapted to the sparse accommodations and tight quarters aboard *Rhiannon*. He paddled ashore by himself in a dinghy and bathed himself with fresh water from the spigot at the beach. After a quick tour of Atuona together, we celebrated Louis' and my birthdays aboard our boat, using wooden matchsticks as candles on the chocolate cake we had baked in our alcohol oven.

With my father at the old general store in Atuona

Our birthday cake

Tahuata

Though it was an exceptionally windy day, we set sail from Taha'uku Bay to Tahuata the day after my father joined us. Tahuata, our destination, was the neighboring island, immediately to the south of the western end of Hiva Oa. As we departed, our view looking seaward was dominated by the dramatic steep wall of an ancient volcano. Leaving Taha'uku Bay was like sailing out of a volcano's crater.

We reached out of the bay in the brisk breeze carrying the working jib and a reefed main as we flew along. We rode the wind and current down the Bordelais Strait, a short channel between Hiva Oa and Tahuata. We then turned south, in the lee of Tahuata to parallel its western shore. The water became calm and the wind died off as we gently slid passed the white sand beach at Hanamoenoa.

Suddenly, with little warning, a fierce williwaw kicked up a curling cloud of spray as it headed toward us. Though we reflexively let the main and jib sheets fly to luff the sails, the katabatic gust laid us completely on our beam ends. We sustained a nearly complete knockdown. All four of us hung on tightly so as not to fall from the cockpit into the water before *Rhiannon* could right herself after the gust had passed.

Sailing to Tahuata

We sailed on past the principal village of Vaitahu to the small bay at Hapatoni, where a family from Vancouver aboard *Starduster*, a beautiful CT 54, had already anchored. A small underwater ledge just off the village afforded the only viable anchorage, providing swinging room for at most two boats. We thought that we would go ashore for a quick look and then continue sailing.

Clark, my father, and I paddled ashore in the moderate surf, while Louis remained aboard, slowly sailing back and forth. When we stayed ashore longer than initially planned, Louis became impatient and angry that he was still on the boat. He anchored *Rhiannon* behind *Starduster* and swam the short distance to shore.

Starduster anchored at Hapatoni, Tahuata

On that day, there were no men in Hapatoni. The men were all working off the island, leaving the 20 or so women and children behind in the village. The only connection to the outside world besides the beach was a footpath to Vaitahu, the next village. The women of Hapatoni were exceptionally hospitable toward the crews of *Rhiannon* and *Starduster*. The women prepared two dishes for us, poisson cru and fish cooked in coconut milk. The local children spent the afternoon swimming and surfing on plain wooden planks. As they had no radio, the local women were extremely interested in getting news from the outside.

With the women and children of Hapatoni

Clark opening a drinking coconut with the women at Hapatoni

Children surfing at Hapatoni, Tahuata

Although they were without a radio, the women did have an old tape recorder, which they asked me to fix for them. I obligingly took it apart, with springs, belts, and small pieces falling off as I proceeded. A group of women and children eagerly watched as I tried my best to restore their only source of recorded music. Unfortunately, I was unable to resurrect it. At least I was eventually able to return it to its intermittently functional state and save face. I learned a lesson: don't get in over my head, especially when there is a likelihood of doing more harm than good.

At dusk, we returned to *Rhiannon* for the night, hoping for another day of hiking on Tahuata. But a wind shift at midnight left us swinging too close to *Starduster*. We pulled up the anchor and headed offshore, bound for Fatu Hiva.

Fatu Hiva

The wind was light, and the seas remained docile as we tacked upwind toward Hana Vave on Fatu Hiva. Fatu Hiva lies southeast of all the other Marquesas islands. By early afternoon, we found ourselves about five NM west of Hana Vave, in the lee of the island, with a dying breeze. Through binoculars, we could see that there was one other sailboat anchored in the bay. Forewarned by the sailors who had dragged anchor during the Christmas Eve squalls there, we had planned to anchor in a secure spot well inside the bay. In the dying breeze, we attempted to startup our Atomic-4. Almost predictably, the engine would not run, precisely at a time when we needed to progress upwind into an anchorage. This had become a routine pattern for us. Entering anchorages under sail seemed inevitable.

All afternoon we tacked back and forth. An adverse current impeded our progress. Each tack seemed to bring us back to the spot where we had been a half hour earlier. I felt great sympathy for the crews of the old square-rigged ships that could only point 20 degrees higher than a beam reach.

Throughout our afternoon of zig zag sailing, the sun illuminated the unbelievable fairy-tale rock formations at the imposing entrance to Hana Vave. I had read descriptions of this bay, but I had never seen a color photo. Old sketches and black and white photos had not done justice to the panorama. The changing tones of the black basalt were offset by scattered patches of lush green vegetation on the pillar-like formations that frame the bay's mouth. Hana Vave was by far the most spectacularly picturesque place I had ever seen.

As we sailed toward the head of the bay, the towering walls capped by fantastic pinnacles closed in around us. Sounds of splashing waves echoed off the sheer rock walls, as in a cave. Two precariously perched white goats, glowing in the pink late-day sun, grazed high above us on a narrow ledge. At the head of the bay, shiny black stones lined the beach. Behind the beach stood a thick grove of coconut palms. The steeple of a small white church protruded from the trees as the sole indication of an otherwise obscured village.

Sailing into Hana Vave

Goats on a ledge, Hana Vave

Beyond the trees, the valley entrance was narrowed by cliff walls, creating a gateway to an immense green valley that lay beyond. It reminded me of the island in the original film of *King Kong*. As our boat drifted slowly, a short distance off the beach, I rowed ashore with our long half-inch nylon line. I secured it to a sturdy coconut palm. Although the wind consistently blew out of the bay, we dropped a stern anchor to prevent *Rhiannon* from swinging into the nearby cliff face.

Looking into the valley of Hana Vave from *Rhiannon*

In French, Hana Vave is named "Baie des Vierges," meaning "Bay of Virgins." The original French who arrived in the Marquesas named it "Baie des Verges," which means "Bay of Penises," due to the phallic appearance of the prominent rock formations surrounding the bay. That name was quite distasteful to the missionaries who arrived later. Accordingly, the "i" was added to the name, completely altering its meaning.

The only landing spot for our dinghy at Hana Vave was a small concrete ramp tucked into the northeast corner of the bay. Several wooden outrigger canoes sat on the grass above the ramp. Just beyond the ramp was a rectangular single-room white building with a concrete floor and open sides. This served as a school and an all-purpose community center. A path of old basalt stones led from there up through the village.

The landing spot. *Rhiannon* is moored in the bay.

Women resting on a pirogue

A woman, her dog, and her house on an ancient stone *paepae*

As is typical in the Marquesas, houses were constructed upon rectangular platforms made of neatly assembled black lava boulders and smaller stones. The wood-frame homes appeared frail in comparison to these magnificent sturdy foundations. The platforms, known as *paepae*, predated the newer buildings by hundreds of years. They were the sleeping platforms that remained from a time when tens of thousands of people populated the Marquesas. These *paepae*, found throughout the valleys on many of the islands, served as a reminder of the thriving Marquesan culture of the past.

At the time we visited, many of the teenagers and young adults had left Fatu Hiva to study or find work elsewhere. Those who remained expressed their intention to stay. Each day we bought fresh bread from a delightful young woman with a flower in her hair, named Marie Madeleine. She lived with her mother in the only two-story home in the village.

Gardens surrounded most homes. Often these gardens included trees filled with plantains, bananas, limes, and immense grapefruits. Many trees were laden with ripe fruit. The villagers implored us to take bags full of the fruit, as there were only 100 people living there—not nearly enough to eat it all.

We had arrived at a time when Marquesan hospitality was genuine, unspoiled by the commercialization of tourism that would soon arrive. In 1977, tourism in the southern Marquesas was just starting. The only tourists on Fatu Hiva were transient cruising sailors. On Hiva Oa, we had met one solitary, older German

man wandering around Atuona, wearing a straw hat. He appeared to be the only non-sailor visiting for pleasure. Other than staying as a guest in a private home, visitors had few lodging options in the southern Marquesas. In Atuona, one small two-room pension was the only other possibility.

Marie Madeleine with her freshly baked bread

Local craftsmen, at that time, were just beginning to learn woodcarving with traditional patterns, a skill that had been lost for 50 years. A few entrepreneurial young people we met were exploring the possibilities of using these skills to produce items to sell to tourists. In Fatu Hiva there was one young wood carver, about 20 years old, who had a book depicting the intricate traditional patterns of Marquesan war clubs and figurines. My father bought some beautiful carvings as souvenirs. There was also another young man making small pieces of tapa cloth to sell to cruising sailors. He was also self-taught, and his cloth was not very well made. Tattooing based upon ancient Marquesan designs remained a lost art as well, only to achieve resurgence in the years following our visit.

There were no cars on Fatu Hiva. People generally walked. Occasionally, if leaving town to visit Omoa, the other inhabited village on the island, they rode bareback astride small brown horses on over-mountain trails. Dogs roamed freely, while pigs usually had one leg tethered by rope to trees near the houses.

The main road in Hana Vave

Young men and women fished with long bamboo poles either from shore or from outrigger canoes drifting in the bay. Fish were abundant. The young men cleaned the fish or octopus they caught on the concrete ramp at the waterfront.

At night, it was very dark. There was no source of electricity in Hana Vave except a single small Honda generator used primarily to power a movie projector in the open-sided community hall. Just as in Atuona, this village also owned only one movie. They showed it every evening. It was an old black and white French movie about a fictitious queen in her palace.

After dark, the young men dove along the underwater cliffs, hoping to catch spiny lobsters on the rocky cliff walls. Since they did not own any underwater flashlights, they would invite visiting yachtsmen to dive with them, offering lobsters in exchange for the use of waterproof lights. One night, Clark and Louis went diving with them.

Unfortunately, Clark managed to step on a sea urchin, and a spine broke off in his toe. A kind woman showed him the local remedy. Acidic liquids would dissolve the painful urchin spine. She suggested soaking his foot in grapefruit juice or urine. Clark chose grapefruit juice.

Clark at Hana Vave

The next day, while Clark rested, my father sought out Mateus, the old village chief. The chief only spoke Marquesan. My father, who spoke fluent French, apparently spoke to him in French for a considerable time, before realizing that Mateus did not understand a word. Eventually, someone was able to translate so a real conversation could begin.

Meanwhile, Louis went for a hike by himself. On his walk, he located a well-known waterfall. He also found a high lookout on the path to Omoa and photographed *Rhiannon*, tied to shore far below in Hana Vave.

I stayed back and relaxed aboard the boat. I was enjoying watching the activities in the bay and the amusing goats on the ledges above me. With a bit of fiddling and some assistance from another cruiser, I also was able to get *Rhiannon*'s engine running again.

The young Norwegians aboard *Preciosa* arrived in Hana Vave while we were still there. They anchored far out in the bay and came ashore in their red thermoplastic dink to provision. I discussed with them how easy it would be to set up a wind-generated electrical system for the village. But as I thought about it, I realized that the people who remained in Hana Vave were content. They lived in paradise. Plentiful fruit hung from the trees year-round. Fishing was easy.

I could see that introducing electricity would irreversibly alter life on Fatu Hiva. I put aside my schemes. I knew that "progress" such as electricity would be inevitable. However, I did not want to be a catalyst speeding the process.

Rhiannon anchored and tied to shore at Hana Vave

All of us fell into the peaceful pace of life in Hana Vave. Women wearing floral print pareus lounged on the outriggers near the beach. Their barefoot

children played on the smooth black stones near the water. Scenes of life photographed there by my father uncannily mirrored the tranquil subjects painted
by Paul Gauguin 75 years earlier.

Eating pancakes in the cockpit with my father

The extraordinary scenery and picturesque ambiance of Hana Vave morphed continuously with each variation in weather or lighting. When a low gray
cloud moved through the valley, it took on an ominous, somber tone. With the
midday sun, the waters of the bay adopted a blue color, completely brightening
the mood. And most striking of all, the late afternoon sunlight would lend
a mystical, surreal appearance to the towering basalt columns standing their
eternal guard over the verdant valley.

A young girl near a lime tree, Hana Vave

My father on Fatu Hiva

Final Weeks on Hiva Oa

After a few days, our time in this paradise came to a close. We needed to return to Hiva Oa. My father had a plane to catch. The sail back to Atuona was a pleasant reach in fair weather. We passed the uninhabited rocky island of Motane, just south of Hiva Oa. Back in Taha'uku Bay, there were more boats anchored than when we had left. Louis from *Dragon*, who had sold us our windvane parts in Panama, had arrived. We spent the final day with my father in Atuona.

On the day of his departure, I rode up to the airport to see him off. There was no airport terminal at that time, only a tiny thatched-roof shelter supported by wooden columns. My father stood on a rusty balance scale along with his luggage, to ensure that the Twin Otter would conform to weight and balance requirements for safe flight. Jacques Brel was among the dozen or so people at the airport, as well. He was helping the Air Polynesie agent who was organizing the cargo.

A rain squall had just moved off the plateau as the arriving plane touched down. A bright double rainbow arched over the runway, framing the landing aircraft. I said my goodbyes to my father and caught a ride back down to *Rhiannon*.

Hiva Oa airport terminal 1977. (Jacques Brel is visible in the background.)

Air Polynesie staff weighing-in my father for the flight

Seeing my father off at the airport after a rain shower

Not long after that, Clark informed Louis and me of his intention to leave, as well. He had been corresponding with one of his cousins, and they had decided to travel westward around the world together by plane, beginning in Australia. Additionally, he really wanted to be back to the U.S. in time for his sister's May wedding. Clark planned to catch the flight out of Hiva Oa the following week.

Clark had been an integral part of the journey. We would miss him. Louis and I knew that we could and would continue without Clark. It would be a big change after experiencing so much together for six months.

Louis and I deliberated about our ultimate destination. We began investigating the possibilities. Our plan was to sell *Rhiannon* at the end of our journey. We could try to sell the boat in New Zealand or Australia, or we could return to Hawaii in the United States. We started researching the potential market for sailboats in New Zealand and Australia, keeping in mind the cost of import duties and sales tax.

I was still clinging to my fantasy of creating a productive life for myself in the South Pacific. I was ambivalent about my fall back plan to begin medical school in the U.S. in August. We had a visa to remain in French Polynesia until July, with the option of an additional six months if we sailed to another country and returned. We decided to continue to cruise westward through the islands and to defer choosing our final destination.

One week later, Clark boarded the plane for Tahiti. *Rhiannon* seemed spacious and strangely empty. Louis and I sank into depression.

On top of that, I had developed an itchy skin rash on my genitals that I could not identify. I decided to go to the medical clinic in Atuona. The clinic was a new white plaster building with a ceramic tile floor. The outside was neatly landscaped with Bougainvillea and small fruit trees. I waited my turn in the short line in front of the clinic. As was customary, I left my shoes outside before walking barefoot into the building.

The young French doctor examined me and checked the rash. He did not know what it was. He thought it could be syphilis. If it were syphilis, I would require a large dose of penicillin injected into my buttocks every day for 10 days. Intravenous penicillin was not available on Hiva Oa. The alternative was to send a culture to a lab in Tahiti, but it would take two weeks to get the results. If I simply received the penicillin shots, the treatment would be finished before the culture results returned.

I walked back to *Rhiannon* and discussed my options with Louis. Louis's parents were considering meeting us in Tahiti. Accordingly, we did not want to stay in Hiva Oa longer than necessary. I opted for the injections. After the first five days, I was waddling as if I had just gotten off a horse. Unfortunately, my rash was not resolving.

The medical clinic at Atuona

For more than a month, I remained worried that I might have advanced syphilis or an unusual parasitic infection. It was only after visiting a hospital in Tahiti weeks later that I finally learned that the skin lesions were merely eczema caused by sun exposure. A corticosteroid cream cleared it up in no time.

Louis took advantage of our additional days on Hiva Oa to hike in the hills and to join Ozanne on a fishing trip. They rode together out to Motane in a speedboat. Louis got yet another firsthand glimpse of life in the Marquesas.

Louis and I were lonely during the week following Clark's departure. However, we made some new friends among the cruising boats anchored in Taha'uku Bay. One night we saw the lights of a sailboat motoring back and forth outside the bay as if unsure about entering. We turned on the VHF and called. It was the French couple, Paname and Paul Paris, aboard *Sagarmatha*. I had not seen them since we had been in Panama over three months earlier.

By radio, I talked them into the anchorage in the dark. They were just arriving after a 21-day passage from Puerto Arroyo (Academy Bay) in the Galapagos. It was so uplifting for me to reconnect with these old friends and hear about their voyage. Paname told me that they were planning to stop on Ahe to visit Bernard Moitessier, the famous solo circumnavigator whose ketch was the sister ship of *Sagarmatha*.

Two Alaskan families aboard their sailboats, *Rodonis,* a heavy Skookum 47 cutter, and *Desperado,* a Morgan Out Island 41, had sailed to French Polynesia in tandem from Seattle. The skipper aboard *Rodonis,* a gruff, larger-than-life, middle-aged outdoorsman named Dale Sommers, was more comfortable hunting in the wilderness than sailing on the ocean. With no previous offshore experience, these two families had set out to circumnavigate together.

Initially, only one person aboard one of the boats had learned basic celestial navigation. Somehow, they found the Marquesas. They anchored near us in Taha'uku Bay and quickly became our friends. While I stayed behind for my daily injections, Louis went aboard *Rodonis* on a day trip to Hanamoenoa on Tahuata, to collect shells along the beach. This close-knit community of cruisers comprised our family.

Louis received a letter in Atuona, by "poste restante," informing him that his parents wanted to meet us in Tahiti. They were planning a trip to visit most of the Society Islands. They wanted to know when to arrive to coordinate their visit with ours. Clark's father had driven with us to New Orleans, his mother and sister had transited the Panama Canal with us, and my father had joined us to cruise in the Marquesas. It was Louis's father's turn. His father Jim, a lifelong sailor, was excited about sailing with us.

Louis decided to try to call his father from Atuona. We went to the communications office behind the post office to see if this was even possible. We learned that phone calls were routed by short-wave radio to Papeete. The signal was then transmitted via a satellite link to Paris. An overseas operator in Paris would next make a connection through the old underwater trans-Atlantic cable to the U.S., where conventional phone lines carried the signal the rest of the way to Illinois.

It sounded dubious. Nonetheless, I went with Louis to help with the French, in order to complete the call. It turned out that the connection was made, but neither Louis nor Jim could hear one another. The operator in Paris needed to relay what was said. Just as in the old game of "telephone," the final message had a 50-50 chance of being changed as it was passed down the line.

We provided Louis's father with a conservative estimate for our arrival in Tahiti and understood that his parents would get there by February 20. We were both looking forward to seeing them and doing some sailing with Jim.

The time had come again to move on. Between the Marquesas and Tahiti lay the Tuamotus. Our goal was to stop somewhere in the Tuamotus en route to Papeete. When the weather looked favorable, we weighed anchor and set sail once again.

CHAPTER 18

A Green Cloud

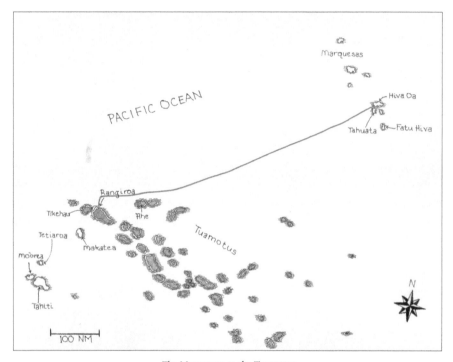

The Marquesas to the Tuamotus

ON FEBRUARY 2, 1977, Louis and I left the Marquesas. We were headed to Tahiti but hoping to stop in the Tuamotus en route if we could get there safely. The Tuamotu Archipelago, sometimes called the Paumotus or the "Dangerous Archipelago," is a group of over 70 atolls spread out over a thousand miles in French Polynesia.

There are several separate island groups within French Polynesia. Each island group possesses a unique cultural heritage. The principal island groups include the Marquesas, the Tuamotus, the Society Islands, and the Gambier Islands. The people of the Marquesas, the Tuamotus, and Tahiti (in the Society Islands) speak three distinctly different Polynesian languages. French is the common language taught in schools throughout French Polynesia.

Geographically, the Tuamotus lie between the Marquesas and Tahiti. Before the advent of GPS, and without radar, the only way to navigate among the

Tuamotus was by celestial navigation. Many highly experienced well-known sailors, such as Nancy and Bob Griffith, had lost their sailboats on Tuamotu reefs. According to insurance statistics from the 1970s, one yacht in ten wrecked in this region. The reasons were simple: uncharted currents of up to eight knots in all directions, low-lying islands and reefs that were not visible more than four miles away during broad daylight, winds that could blow furiously or die off to dead calms at any time, mis-charted islands, the absence of lighthouses, rough turbulent passes to enter the lagoons, a high sun making accurate latitude sights nearly impossible at noon, and treacherous coral reefs that loomed up from nowhere.

Night sailing among the Tuamotus in 1977 was tantamount to suicide. The entire southern portion of the archipelago was off limits due to French nuclear weapons testing on the island of Mururoa. For the first time there were only two of us aboard *Rhiannon*. Louis and I were apprehensive about calling on the Tuamotus. We developed a strategy. We would only visit one or possibly two atolls, and those only if the conditions were favorable. We had to leave a way out, a safety valve, should any doubts ever arise in our minds.

We laid out a battle plan. We would depart the Marquesas one or two days before the full moon so that we could time our initial landfall with more than a half moon for visibility, yet with less tidal current than with a full moon. We would approach the north end of the Tuamotu Archipelago from the north. We would head for a specific point that was well north of an island. From that point we could time a safe approach during daylight without fear of being swept by a current onto a reef during the night.

We chose Ahe as our primary target because we had three charts of the area, including a large-scale chart of the pass into its lagoon. No land lies anywhere north or west of Ahe. Thus, there would be ample sea room to run safely before the southeast trades in the event of a storm or to drift if beset by calms. Additionally, if we ever heard breaking waves to our south during the night, we could turn toward the northwest into the safety of open water.

If conditions for approaching Ahe were questionable, we could try to approach the next island to the west, Rangiroa, in the same manner one or two days later. Should we decide to bypass the Tuamotus altogether, we could travel an extra several hundred miles to the northwest and safely round the entire archipelago.

In the modern era of GPS chartplotters, a navigator can home in on an atoll without ever looking up from an electronic moving map. Navigation has become more like a video game than a true skill. In 1977, out of necessity, we became attuned to various clues that helped us locate a low-lying coral island. This required all our senses.

Expert Polynesian navigators have always relied upon ancient techniques. The reefs surrounding the atolls produce distinctive patterns of swells and crisscrossing waves. Skilled traditional navigators can interpret these waves to fix their location. However, there are signs that an island is just out of view that even an attentive inexperienced sailor can detect. Shore birds often fly home to nest on the islands at dusk. If land is directly to windward, the sailor can often pick out the fragrant perfume of flowers, the earthy smell of soil, or the smokey odor of fires many miles away.

In the tropics, fair weather cumulus clouds form first over land and frequently build to a greater size than the clouds forming at sea. A definitive indication of a coral atoll is the "green cloud." Frequently, the turquoise hue of the water in a lagoon reflects off the flat base of an overlying cumulus cloud, painting the normally grey cloud an unusual distinctive shade of green. Louis and I were always on the lookout for a green cloud signaling the location of an atoll well beyond the horizon.

We set sail from Hiva Oa under a partly cloudy trade wind sky and 10- to 12-knot winds from the southeast. We carried full sail on our planned course toward the island of Ahe, 500 NM away. After experiencing frustrating light winds during the day and a 20-mile drift from current each night for the first three days, we battled violent thundersqualls. Louis and I were on the verge of abandoning our efforts to visit the Tuamotus. We rationalized that these atolls were merely flat rings of hot coral with a few coconut palms and lagoons filled with sharks. Additionally, both our dinghies were leaking air, and our food supply was running low.

However, on the fourth evening, the cloudy sky cleared up just long enough to sneak in a good series of star observations. I reduced the sights. By then we had already passed Ahe. We continued sailing westward. Staying up that night was easy. The moonlit sea was glorious with frigate birds, boobies, and plenty of new constellations. We had shortened sail at dusk so that there would be no need to reef further if an occasional squall passed through. On our fifth morning, the sailing remained ideal. We experienced calm seas accompanied by steady moderate winds. Our celestial fixes told us that we were no longer in the extreme currents.

By noon on the fifth day, still in good weather, our position was 115 NM out of Rangiroa. We decided that we would try for Rangiroa on the sixth day if everything continued to go well. We would need a consistent fresh breeze, a clear sky for celestial fixes at both dusk and dawn, and good visibility under the moonlight during the night. We briefed ourselves for our landfall by reading aloud from the *Sailing Directions* printed by the U.S. Hydrographic Office.

We noted the following information concerning passes in the Tuamotus and the pass at Rangiroa, in particular:

CAUTION-In the Avatoru and Tiputa Passes the tidal currents attain rates of 3 to 6 knots and cause strong rips or eddies, known as "opapé," which are dangerous for boats. During the flood these eddies are found at the inner parts of the passes and during the ebb near the outer parts.

Local schooners… will not attempt the passes against the current …

Concerning tidal currents in Tuamotu lagoons, we read:

The approximate time under normal conditions when the tidal currents change direction may be estimated as follows: three or four hours after moonrise: slack water. Four hours after moonrise: ingoing current begins. One hour before moonset: outgoing current begins. Three or four hours after moonset: slack water. One hour before the moon's lower Meridian passage: ingoing current begins. One hour before moonrise: slack water of very short duration.

Based upon this information, it was critical to enter through the pass at Tiputa, on Rangiroa, during a period of slack water preceding an ingoing (flood) current. Applying the above rule, Louis and I carefully projected the time of the desired conditions to be approximately 12:30 to 1:30 in the afternoon of our sixth day.

Our star sights on the fifth evening placed us 80 NM out of Rangiroa, far enough that we could not possibly reach the reef before dawn, yet close enough to arrive by 11:00 am. Our ideal weather was holding. We decided at least to go and have a look at the atoll, even if we chose not to enter. We reasoned that if we got there by slack water and wanted to brave the narrow channel, we would be able to do it. If it appeared unsafe, we could still sail off.

With this plan, we charged on at six knots under full sail through a light chop toward our morning landfall. At dawn, star and planet sights revealed that we were approximately 25 NM out, with five and half hours remaining until our calculated slack water. By 9:00 a.m. we saw a green cloud. At 10:30 a.m. we sighted the palm trees of Rangiroa while sailing in a dying breeze. We identified Tiputa based on a description of the buildings in the *Sailing Directions*. As per our plan, we arrived off Tiputa at 12:15 p.m. and tried to look for the pass using binoculars. A large swell was running. All we could see was light green water, heavily breaking seas, churning foam, and coral – but no clear pass.

For once, to our delight, the engine obediently started and ran well, with only a small water leak. We dropped both sails. Unfortunately, the main halyard got away, and its shackle flew up to the masthead. At 12:45, Louis climbed the ratlines to con from aloft, while I remained at the helm. Louis shouted to me that the pass was indeed there, as he pointed toward the roiling water. A huge thunderhead moved over us, temporarily blotting out the sun. By 1:00, the wind, rain, and clouds had passed. The sunlight directly overhead was perfect for seeing the coral.

I revved the engine and turned toward the pass. The palm trees grew larger. The swell lifted and dipped us, alternately bringing the shoreline in and out of sight. Before long, whitewater was on all sides. I continued. The engine strained. We were clearly in the pass itself. Land was on both sides with menacing coral heads clearly visible through the waves only a few yards off our beam. I pushed the throttle farther forward and glanced at the knot meter. We were making five knots.

I looked at the water. A swirling cauldron of eddies and whirlpools kicked up mounds of heaving water. I looked at the shore once again, as I fought to keep the boat centered in the channel. The opposing current was faster than our speed through the water. We were moving backwards toward the surf again! The "opapé" were all around us! There was no slack water! The worthless *Sailing Directions* were full of horseshit!

Whenever a high wave would come up from astern, I would square off and slide down the wave at six knots like a Hawaiian surfer. Finally, as we surfed, *Rhiannon* slowly made progress in the channel. It took about 20 minutes to progress 200 yards. But the engine held, and we eventually reached the lighter current and flat waters of Rangiroa's lagoon.

Rangiroa is the largest atoll in the Tuamotus. Entering a lagoon is a bit like entering a harbor. The water of the lagoon is relatively calm, protected by a surrounding ring of coral sand. An atoll and its lagoon are similar to a swimming pool aboard the deck of ship. The lagoon is completely free of the swell that runs on the sea outside the reef. It is a huge placid oasis sitting in the middle of a vast ocean.

At Rangiroa, the lagoon is so wide that the opposite side is not visible at all. The water in most of the lagoon is deep enough for sailing. However, scattered coral heads, often called "bomies," rise up from the bottom in random distribution, creating hazardous obstacles that must be seen and avoided. The ring of coral and coral sand that constitute the atoll opens to the sea in a few places, called passes. Some passes are navigable; others are too narrow or too shallow. In the Tuamotus, some of the islands have no navigable passes, requiring visitors to come ashore from vessels standing offshore in the lee of the atoll. The largest villages in the Tuamotus are generally situated in proximity to navigable passes accessing the lagoons.

Upon entering the lagoon at Rangiroa, we turned to port, immediately arriving at the village of Tiputa. We briefly considered anchoring. However, we had not tied up to a dock since we left the Yacht Club in Cristobal, four months earlier. The large rectangular concrete quay protruding into the lagoon at the center of town beckoned. One side of the quay appeared sheltered from the current. Knowing that our inflatable dinghies were no longer holding air well, the thought of stepping off the boat onto shore was irresistible.

The view looking out the Tiputa, Rangiroa pass with an approaching rainsquall and in fair weather

As soon as we secured our dock lines and fenders, we were greeted by a throng of curious gawking children of all ages. After mooring *Rhiannon*, Louis and I set about retrieving our wayward main halyard from the masthead. Using our spare halyard, I hoisted Louis aloft in the bosun's chair. Louis embellished the acrobatics of mast climbing to the great delight and amusement of the rapt onlookers.

The children are very curious about us

Before long, we checked in with the local gendarme and learned that a supply boat would need our spot on the sheltered side of the quay. Compliantly, we moved the boat to the outside of the pier where a steady current held us a jump-able two feet off the concrete. The water flowing past *Rhiannon*'s hull ran up the mileage on our mechanical sumlog, falsely indicating that we had travelled many miles during the days we remained stationary, tied to the quay.

At the quay in Tiputa. *Rhiannon* is being held off by the current.

Sunset in Tiputa

In Tiputa, people grew bananas and some vegetables, but the coral sand was not conducive to growing the tremendous fruit trees that we had seen in the Marquesas. Several people raised pigs and chickens. Fish represented the primary dietary staple. Though some fishermen ventured offshore to catch tuna, spearfishing in the lagoon provided plenty of fish.

Shark fishing from the pier had not yet been outlawed. A few days each week, sharks were hooked from the quay and mercilessly slaughtered to obtain their teeth and jaws. One man was proud to show the depressed scar in his calf where a shark had bitten him when he was trailing a string of fish from his waist while spearfishing.

Louis and I befriended several young couples who not only welcomed us into their homes but were excited to meet and talk with outsiders. Although Tiputa was one of the biggest and most accessible villages in the Tuamotus, it had been a few months since any other visiting yacht had tied up in town.

One day, Louis and I went spearfishing just inside the pass with a French schoolteacher, Phillipe Gillet. This was my first opportunity to swim among large sharks and a spectacular variety of other colorful reef fish. Had I been the only one fishing, we would never have eaten. What I speared was inedible. However, that evening, we ate a delicious dinner of grilled fish by the edge of the lagoon with Phillipe, his wife Dany, and their one-year old son.

Phillipe, Dany and their son

The gendarme who had checked us in and his wife invited us to their house, and we later brought them aboard *Rhiannon*. It was at Rangiroa that I learned not to complement any items inside of people's homes. It was customary for a host to give a guest any personal possession that the visitor had admired. I found out the hard way how difficult it was to reject such a gift. Eventually, I did graciously accept a straw hat to avoid insulting the gendarme and his wife.

When we were invited as guests into local homes, we usually bought something locally to present as a house gift, for we had little of value aboard *Rhiannon*. We did have a collection of several items that we had brought with us specifically for bartering, including 30 cartons of American cigarettes, about 40 *Playboy* magazines, and a few used t-shirts. But most people we met were more appreciative of synthetic rope than any of those items. Nylon and Dacron line were expensive and difficult to procure in most of French Polynesia outside of Tahiti. We had enough rope aboard that without compromising *Rhiannon* we occasionally could part with a length of line as a token of appreciation.

Sometimes we explored Rangiroa's lagoon aboard *Rhiannon*. It appeared that a tourism boom in the Tuamotus was about to begin. One day we anchored off a new hotel that was just opening on the other side of the pass. The hotel proprietor had just figured out how to provide adequate fresh water for tourists. He wanted us to remain anchored in front of his hotel. He thought it would be good publicity. Although we liked the tranquil lagoon, warm water, infinite coral reef, and quiet seclusion at that site, there was really nothing for us to do there. We returned to the quay at Tiputa.

While in Tiputa, we heard the amazing story of a single-handed sailor who had been unbelievably lucky in avoiding shipwreck on Rangiroa a few months earlier. Louis and I were always particularly interested in learning from the mistakes of others. As several people related the incident to us, a man sailing alone on his 35-foot sailboat had fallen asleep somewhere north of Rangiroa. While he was sleeping, his boat had drifted toward the island in the dark, ultimately entering the Tiputa pass. This in itself is remarkable, as the opening of the pass is only a couple hundred yards wide, along a continuous 40-mile coastline of treacherous coral.

But the story did not end there. On one side of the pass is a tiny beach about 50 feet in length, representing the only patch of sand amid the sharp coral lining both sides of the pass. As this sailor slept, his boat washed ashore, fully intact, onto the tiny beach. Although the story sounds apocryphal, a few people who had themselves helped to free the grounded vessel all corroborated the details.

While *Rhiannon* was tied to the quay, local children would freely come aboard to play. As the children played, I sat on the quay decorating our self-steering vane. I painted a woman's face with hair blowing in the wind onto each side of George's windvane. It was supposed to depict Rhiannon, the witch. However, my attempted artwork was an embarrassing failure. Nonetheless, we never painted over the poorly drawn faces, which thereafter remained prominently displayed for all to see.

A couple of days before leaving Rangiroa, Louis and I picked up three hermit crabs on the reef and brought them into the boat. We left them on the counter in the galley for amusement. We also left a small package of cheese wrapped in aluminum foil sitting out on the counter. The evening before our departure, we noticed some funny gnawing marks on the cheese and a few bits of the foil sitting on the counter. We had trouble explaining it. A hermit crab was right next to the cheese. Naturally, we blamed the hermit crab for raiding our cheese. We removed the crabs before we said farewell to our friends and set sail from Rangiroa toward Tahiti.

CHAPTER 19

The Stowaway

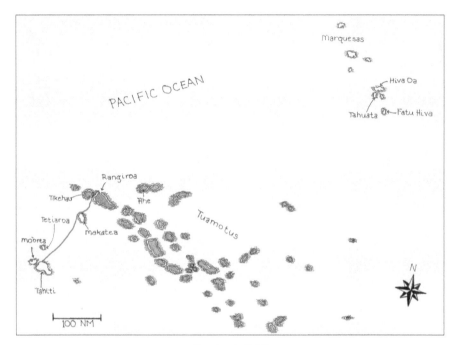

Rangiroa to Tahiti

AT 9:00 A.M. on February 15, 1977, *Rhiannon* shot out the Tiputa pass on an ebbing current near slack water. We set sail in the NNE wind, skirting the reef at Rangiroa and remaining a couple miles offshore. Sailing around the west end of Rangiroa, we turned south onto a pleasant broad reach, entering the seven-NM-wide channel between the islands of Rangiroa and Tikehau. Easily within sight of palm trees on both atolls in the broad daylight, Louis and I remarked to one another how dangerous this channel would be at night. Weeks later, when we discussed this with our friends on *Rodonis* and *Desperado*, we were astonished to learn that they had sailed blindly through the same narrow gap at night—during a squall. Incredibly, they had been navigating solely by dead reckoning based on a fix 50 NM north of the channel. They never saw either island!

Once safely clear of the reefs, Louis and I set a course for the island of Makatea, 70 NM to the south. Makatea greatly intrigued us. Everything we had read about this island was fascinating. Unlike the rest of the Tuamotus, which are atolls, the Marquesas, which are mountainous, and the Society Islands, which are mountainous with surrounding barrier reefs, Makatea is a totally different type of island. It is one of three islands in the entire Pacific originating from a raised coral reef. These are steep-sided islands that appear to rise straight out of the water with sheer cliffs and completely flat central plateaus. Makatea rises 300-400 feet from the sea.

Makatea

Much superstition and legend surround this bizarre island, which is considered taboo by native Polynesians. Caves in its white cliff walls had been used for burial in the past. Human skeletons were said to remain there. Aside from being taboo, the cave entrances are virtually inaccessible, though easily visible from the sea. Few Polynesians visit Makatea because of the taboo. One prominent cliff is said to have the profile of a human head.

The island had been used for several decades by a large phosphate mining operation that ended about 12 years earlier. The rusting machinery and abandoned buildings of the massive operation continued to stand. Almost all the residents had left. In 1977, only a dozen or so residents were reported to live there. It is the only island considered part of the Tuamotus that has a natural source of fresh water. Plentiful grapefruit trees and other fruit trees were rumored to remain, with far more fruit than any of the few residents could possibly use.

The *Sailing Directions* described a large mooring ball for ships on the western shore, near the old phosphate loading complex. There was no harbor or anchorage, only a small inlet for launches near the mooring ball, most accessible during a SE wind. We did not know if we would be able to stop at Makatea. But we intended to look.

Sailing during the calm night, Louis and I heard strange rustling sounds aboard *Rhiannon* that we had not previously heard. We were fairly certain that only the two of us were aboard. Perhaps our imaginations were playing tricks on us, as we thought about the ghostly island of Makatea. Accordingly, we disregarded the sounds.

At sunrise the next morning, the mysterious island came into view to our southwest, illuminated by the pink rays of dawn. It almost sent chills down my spine as we slowly sailed in calm seas with nothing in view but the strange island. Almost immediately, the human profile on the north cliff appeared. Louis and I burst out laughing. It was a perfect silhouette of President Nixon! We continued toward Makatea, eyeing the cliffside burial caves through binoculars.

As we sailed around the north end of the island to turn south along its western shore, remnants of the phosphate loading facility came into view. A huge rusting mooring ball bobbed in the nearly calm water a couple hundred yards offshore. As we approached, it became clear that securing *Rhiannon* to the ball would be challenging, as well as hazardous. Clearly, no other vessels were at Makatea, making a visit even more enticing.

As much as we wanted to explore the island, meet the residents, and perhaps obtain some fruit, it was just not feasible. Had Clark been with us, one of us might have remained on board standing off, while the others went ashore. But with only two of us, every option was too dangerous. We continued to brainstorm for alternative options as we coasted along the shore. However, a change in the weather quickly sealed the deal. A 20-knot wind came up, and the sky became totally overcast. This was no time for a risky shore expedition.

We took our last close look at Makatea and set a course for Tahiti, 125 NM to the southwest. That afternoon, Louis and I noticed that a few things were amiss on board. When I went to brush my teeth, the edges of the aluminum toothpaste tube appeared to have disintegrated. That seemed unusual. Then I opened our box of Reynold's Wrap to cover a bowl of leftovers. Bits of aluminum foil were scattered throughout the galley drawer. Unrolling the foil, I saw that the entire end of the roll had been chewed away.

I finally realized that we had an uninvited crew member on board! Although we had been held off the quay at Tiputa by current, it was likely that a copra rat had scurried aboard on our dock lines. Clearly, this rat had been responsible for the gnawed cheese on the counter. Additionally, this clever animal had learned to associate its delicious snack with the aluminum wrapping. As a result, the rat had chewed on all the aluminum foil on board *Rhiannon* in search of food.

The abandoned phosphate port at Makatea

I looked beneath the port quarter berth, where the cartons of cigarettes were stowed. Sure enough, the aluminum-craving rodent had chewed into the aluminum foil layer of the cigarette packaging, leaving bits of tobacco strewn all about. Once we reached Tahiti, finding, and eliminating the rat would become one of our top priorities.

Sailing toward Papeete, Tahiti, Louis and I prepared for our return to civilization. We were ready to re-provision, attack a growing list of repairs, buy a new dinghy, and rendezvous with Louis's parents. Papeete would be the first port on our adventure where I had been before.

I had distinct recollections of Tahiti in 1963, as seen through the eyes of a nine-year-old. I knew that many changes had come. Regular airline jet service, cruise ship visits, large hotels, and a container ship port had taken Tahiti far from the Polynesian trading post of the 1960s. I knew not to expect the fabled island paradise of the past. The advent of French nuclear testing had changed the islands forever. The simple waterfront with trading schooners moored to the quay would be gone. I mentally prepared myself to find an unrecognizable, modern Papeete.

On the second night of the passage, Louis had the late-night watch, as the bright light at Pointe Vénus came into view. Down below, in my berth, I could hear rolling thunder and steady rainfall clattering on the deck. When Louis woke me for my watch, it was still raining. Louis told me that we had sailed through the most spectacular electrical storm that he had ever experienced. Apparently, I had slept through it all. It was easy for me to sleep on *Rhiannon*. I trusted Louis completely.

By midday we motored through the pass at Papeete. We anchored in the harbor with our stern tied ashore along Boulevard Pomare, west of the paved part of the quay. After clearing in with the port authorities, we carefully returned our passports and important ship's documents to the top drawer in the galley, tightly sealed within their Ziploc bag. One of the first errands that I ran was to a hardware store to find a rat trap.

A copra rat is the typical variety found in these islands. It is somewhere in size between a mouse and the large city rats that we had back home. Accordingly, the rat trap was midway in size between the mouse traps and the rat traps with which I was quite familiar.

The rain stopped, giving way to a colorful cloudy sunset over Mo'orea. I set the trap on the galley counter, baited with a bit of cheese and, of course, aluminum foil. In our quiet cabin, at 2:00 a.m., I was awakened by a "whack!" We had caught our stowaway. However, it would be over three more weeks before Louis and I would learn how the rat had secretly taken its revenge upon us before meeting its abrupt end.

CHAPTER 20

Tahiti

A Dream Fulfilled

TAHITI HAD ALWAYS represented both a fantasy destination and a concrete goal motivating my journey. When asked about my plans before the voyage began, I would tell people that I was going "to sail to Tahiti." Although this sounds like an unrealistic overly romanticized dream, I knew better. For me, Papeete would be a homecoming and, most likely, an urban culture shock. When Louis and I first arrived in Tahiti, my thoughts initially turned toward repairing *Rhiannon* and finding a cold drink. My next thoughts were sobering. At age 23, I had fulfilled my lifelong dream of "sailing to Tahiti."

I needed to grapple with the question of what I would do next. On one hand, I had deferred admission to two medical schools. Each was awaiting a firm commitment. On the other hand, I loved Polynesia and had been hoping that I would find a way to justify staying there. However, after seven months of travel, I was still looking. Seven months had made it clear that as much as I enjoyed sailing, I was not attracted to a lifetime at sea.

I was realistic enough to know that I needed to support myself and had no source of income. My fallback plan of attending medical school in August was looking increasingly practical. I remember rationalizing to myself that I could always sail back to the South Pacific again after a few years. Perhaps I might return someday with a family of my own.

One afternoon, when we were tied to the quay in Papeete, a middle-aged American tourist was strolling along the dock inspecting the boats. He noticed the diminutive size of *Rhiannon,* as she lay wedged between two 60-foot sailing vessels. He saw our American ensign and asked me, "Where are you from?" When he heard how we had travelled to Tahiti, he was impressed that our boat had made the long voyage. He congratulated me. Then, somewhat wistfully he exclaimed, "This is truly a once-in-a-lifetime experience for you!"

I thought to myself, "What does he know about sailing ... or about me?" With complete conviction, I immediately replied, "Oh, no. I'm sure that sometime in my life I'll be able to do this again."

It took me many years to understand that he was absolutely right.

Le Quai

On our second day in Papeete, we were able to get a berth, Med moored to the concrete quay along Boulevard Pomare. The anchors of the moored boats criss-crossed in a tangled web of abandoned anchor chains and debris that covered the harbor bottom. Docking was relatively easy. However, pulling up an anchor to leave could be a nightmare.

Rhiannon at the quay along boulevard Pomare in Papeete, Tahiti

The variety of characters and boats along the waterfront frequently surprised me. Boats of all descriptions were tied to shore, side by side, with either bows or sterns facing the sidewalk. Transient vessels ranged from stately classic schooners to questionably seaworthy dilapidated wrecks. A few small fiberglass boats with their prominent windvanes, jerry cans, and abundant chafe gear lay shoehorned between weathered steel-hulled giants and thoroughbred ocean racers. Almost all were sailing craft. Motor yachts rarely crossed the Pacific. The local powerboats moored elsewhere.

Across the boulevard paralleling the quay stood several landmark establishments. Gone were the legendary South Seas watering holes of Quinn's Bar and the Whiskey A-Go-Go that had characterized Tahiti in 1963. But others more in line with the times had sprung up to replace them. Papeete had no yacht club or harbor lounge where crew members could congregate. Walking across the gang plank from any boat, a sailor landed directly in the heart of the city itself.

In 1977, the lounge at Hotel Stuart, directly across from the quay, served as a meeting place for cruising sailors. Not far away, a few small bars with crowded discotheques, playing mostly Tahitian music, catered to both locals and visitors. I went dancing several times. Just as in the Marquesas, the Tahitian women would smile and giggle as they enthusiastically moved their hips to the lightning fast Tamure rhythms that culminated many of the songs.

Tahitian girls lounging in the cockpit

A short walk away, in a large parking lot near the harbor, food trucks gathered each evening. This was the best place to score a delicious low-cost meal. Nearby, street performers strummed ukuleles, sang, and drummed, while Tahitians and outsiders mingled in a carnival-like atmosphere. Rarely, a cruise liner, foreign naval vessel, or training ship would dock on a specially reserved section of the quay.

The animated waterfront merely provided a backdrop for the colorful characters and dramas that unfolded daily. In general, boat crews were eager to socialize and assist one another in any way possible. A generous crew aboard a gorgeous new Swan 65 ketch regularly invited other cruisers aboard for a happy hour. Two congenial, gregarious men aboard a neighboring 45-footer entertained frequently aboard their boat. One day, both men were abruptly arrested by the police when the authorities discovered that they had stolen their vessel in California! Everyone was shocked. On another occasion, a man sailed into port with the tragic story of losing his wife overboard on his way to Tahiti. Following some investigation by the police, he, too, was arrested—on suspicion of murder.

As in Panama, the core group of cruisers stuck together and supported one another like family. The spaces at the quay were in high demand. Boats that had waited away from the quay, at anchor, normally would take the next available mooring in an orderly sequence. Late one evening, a 40-foot German sailboat arrived just as another boat that had been patiently waiting was about to move into a newly vacated space. The crew of the boat rightfully entitled to the spot was already well known and liked by many of us on the quay.

The German skipper tried to barge into the open mooring. A shouting match in German, French, and English quickly ensued. Most of the crews at the quay were roused by the commotion and quickly gathered along the shore to see if someone needed assistance. The young Norwegian crew aboard *Preciosa* that we had first met in the Marquesas appeared in force to thwart the obstinate German skipper. Amidst the arguing, someone called the angry captain a Nazi. In response, he brandished a handgun on his foredeck while several of those on shore also produced firearms. Fortunately, the German reluctantly stood down and eventually motored off into the night.

On another occasion, the 375-foot four-masted Spanish training ship, *Juan Sebastián de Elcano,* called at Papeete. The Spanish cadets flooded the city on their shore leave. Many drank heavily and wandered the streets intoxicated. On their second day in port, a fight broke out between some Tahitian men and a couple of the Spanish sailors. This devolved into an all-out riot. Luckily, nobody was killed. Following that, the ship was no longer welcome in Tahiti, and the cadets remained confined to the ship for the duration of their stay.

The quay was also where the cruising gossip spread. It was there that I learned that Dr. Peter Eastman, the author of our medical manual, *Advanced First Aid Afloat* was aground on the reef at Huahine in his Cal Cruising 46. I also learned of the fate of various other cruising boats and crews that we had met along the way.

Juan Sebastian de Elcano at Papeete

A cartoon artist from San Diego had sailed to French Polynesia with his wife and three daughters, aged three, five, and seven, aboard a boat similar in size to *Rhiannon*. He had left his work, and the family had sold their home to make the voyage. We had met them in the Marquesas and again in Tahiti. We learned that in the Tuamotus, the youngest girl had contracted dengue fever. The islanders radioed to Tahiti for medical assistance. But tragically, by the time a helicopter from Tahiti had arrived, the girl had died. Hearing these tragic stories put our annoying engine troubles into perspective.

Although the picturesque Med mooring along Boulevard Pomare had been traditional for more than a century, the system was far from ideal. Great swells generated by distant storms occasionally set up a powerful back-and-forth surge in the harbor. For one 18-hour period, Louis and I needed to adjust chafe gear or change dock lines on *Rhiannon* every 45 minutes. I witnessed one-inch-diameter rope hawsers that secured larger vessels snapping like thread with the shock loads generated by the surge.

If dock lines failed, a boat could not get out quickly. Leaving was too complicated. A departing boat would frequently pull up the entangled anchors and overlying chain of several neighboring vessels. Even after that mess was sorted out, an old cable or heavy chain snagged on the harbor floor might still prevent hauling in the anchor. Divers commonly assisted in this complex, unpredictable process. Despite the inherent dangers of docking along the quay in 1977, it was still the most desirable and exciting place to be moored in Tahiti.

During our stay in the Society Islands, Louis and I returned to the quay in Papeete several times. We easily settled into life along the quay and completed some overdue boat projects. The cheap valves on our cockpit drain thru-hull fittings had frozen due to corrosion. We managed to replace them without hauling the boat by ingeniously shifting heavy gear forward and pulling the bow downward toward the quay with a halyard. This effectively lifted the stern out of the water. We also bought ourselves an inexpensive new inflatable dinghy to back up our two leaky Sevylors, rebuilt our alternator, added anchor chain, and performed many other needed repairs.

While *Rhiannon* was tied to the quay, I corresponded with friends and family, receiving my mail via "Poste Restante." I was excited when I received an enthusiastic letter from my motherly navigation instructor, Dr. Wright. She faithfully kept in touch with her widely scattered "family" of students who were using their navigation skills all around the world. Louis and I sent a postcard to Tex, the man at the Bayou Liberty Marina in Louisiana who was forever preparing his boat for cruising, just to let him know that we had reached Tahiti. We never heard back from him. Reluctantly, I also mailed a letter to Case Western Reserve University, committing myself to start medical school in August.

Tahitian Hosts

Although the tight-knit cruising community was our family, we also got to know several incredibly gracious Tahitian families. When Louis's parents arrived in Tahiti, they stayed at the Hotel Tahara'a overlooking Matavai Bay. One morning, I went to the hotel to see them. While waiting in the lobby, I began speaking with a strikingly beautiful Tahitian woman, Fani Brotherson, who was working at the Avis Rent-a-car counter. She had never been outside of the Society Islands and found the idea that we had arrived by sailboat from the U.S. intriguing.

I invited Fani and her husband Michel, who worked as a bank teller, to visit us down at the quay. They lived in Puna'auia, a heavily populated district to the west of Papeete. They were very observant members of a Seventh Day Adventist congregation in Paea, another neighboring district. After visiting our boat one afternoon, along with their one-year-old son, they invited Louis and me to stay for an entire weekend at their home and to attend church services with them on Saturday. We graciously accepted.

On Friday night, we joined them for their choir practice at church. The singing was mostly in French and Tahitian. We were a novelty. The congregants were eager to meet us. The new pastor and his wife, a young French couple who had recently arrived in Tahiti, invited us for lunch on Saturday at their house.

After choir practice, we went back to Fani and Michel's home. They were living in a very old Tahitian-style house, while their new house was being built. The building was rectangular, constructed with plywood walls, painted green on the outside. The windows, hinged at the top, were always propped open. The leaky roof was made of corrugated tin. The house, a single-room structure, was divided into three rooms separated only by curtains. The kitchen area was located in the back, the guestroom was in the center, and the master bedroom/ living room was at the front. A small outbuilding with a toilet and shower stood in the garden immediately adjacent to the house.

With Fani, Michel, and their son in Papeete

Friday night, we stayed up late discussing religion and life in Tahiti. After eventually going to bed, Louis and I both had trouble sleeping. It was noisy. Small beech nuts would rain down on the tin roof. Then an occasional big mango would land with a tremendous clanging crash. Everyone in the house would wake up and start giggling. With only curtains between the rooms, it felt like a slumber party. After the dogs outside began to bark, the baby started crying. As dawn finally arrived, the roosters were crowing, and we all got up.

After church, we ate lunch at the home of the French pastor and his wife. They had invited some Adventists from another church in Tahiti. When they learned that Louis and I were Jewish, they wanted to know more about us.

On Saturday afternoon, we went back to the church for a few special programs. Following some singing and a Bible quiz, Louis and I were asked to speak to the congregation, as the first Jewish guests ever to visit their church. Louis did not want to speak. So, hesitantly, I got up. I did the best I could to explain Judaism in French. An interpreter translated into Tahitian as I went along. Afterward, several other people came over and invited us into their homes.

On Sunday, Louis and I went with Fani to her mother's home in Papenoo. Fani was one of 14 children, as was her mother. Although Fani was born in Raiatea, it seemed that every second person in Tahiti was a cousin, an uncle, a brother, or a sister. Fani and a cousin then took us to a beautiful waterfall in a lush valley where we swam all afternoon. It was a fascinating weekend. It was my first glimpse into the lives of Tahitians in the Seventh Day Adventist community.

I met another Tahitian family through a connection that my father had made with Jeanette Lohman, the Air Polynesie agent at Faa'a International Airport in Tahiti. One day, I had lunch with Jeanette in her home near Papeete, and she invited Louis and me to spend a day at her parents' house in Teahupo'o on Tahiti Iti, the presqu'ile on the far side of the island.

To reach their house, we had to park the car where the road ended and then walk for half an hour along the water. Jeanette's mother prepared a delicious Tahitian meal of pork, fish, and local fruits. Her father proudly showed us the outrigger pirogue that he had made himself. He suffered from elephantiasis but still managed to do some carpentry around the house. This isolated side of Tahiti had an appealing charm and tranquility that contrasted starkly with the urban congestion of Papeete. I noted at that time:

> We were thinking about moving the boat to the lagoon off their house, but the waves have been so big that the small pass there has become dangerous to navigate.

Indeed, the surf on the reef adjacent to the pass was impressive, with a massive heavy curling wave, unlike any I had ever seen. (In 1985, eight years later, a Tahitian named Thierry Vernaudon became the first person to attempt surfing the now world-famous, but still dangerous, break at Teahupo'o.)

Jeanette Lohman's family in Teahupo'o

Following our meal, instead of walking, we returned to the car by boat, inside the lagoon. Jeanette continued to drive us all the way around Tahiti.

Later, we stopped at the home of some other friends of Jeanette, at a place where the Lohmans were planning to build a small weekend cottage. Her friends had a unique swimming pool that cleverly filled from a cascade running down the side of a mountain. I will always be grateful for the warm hospitality displayed by so many Tahitians.

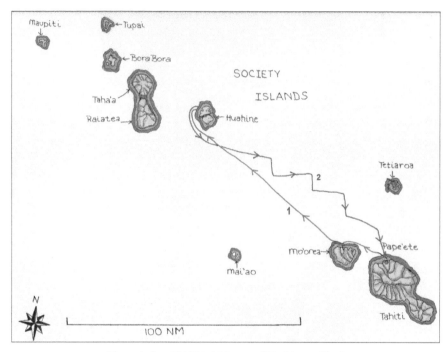

The route from Tahiti to Mo'orea and Huahine, and back

Mo'orea and Huahine

Louis's parents arrived in Papeete just after we had moored *Rhiannon* at the quay along Boulevard Pomare. His parents had pre-arranged short stays on most of the Society Islands. Their first destination after Tahiti was the Club Med on Mo'orea. Louis and I decided to sail there with Louis's father Jim on the same day that his mother flew there by plane.

We cleared the pass at Papeete in the morning and entered the pass at Opunohu Bay on Mo'orea a few hours later. A hot midday sun beat down upon us. Louis, Jim, and I made several unsuccessful attempts to set our anchor in Robinson's Cove, a very picturesque spot within the big bay. The anchor just would not bite. Overheated and tired, we ended up finding another beautiful location in Opunohu Bay where we easily anchored in sheltered water, tying

Rhiannon's stern to two coconut palms on shore. Louis and I spent a couple of days freeloading as "guests" inside the Club Med.

Rhiannon in Opunohu Bay, Mo'orea

When Louis's parents had finished sightseeing and relaxing in Mo'orea, their next destination was Huahine. Once again, we took Louis's father by boat, while his mother flew by Air Polynesie. The three of us left Opunohu Bay shortly before sunset for the 80 NM overnight sail. Jim had never made an ocean

passage at night. He had sailed extensively in the Great Lakes. However, a tropical night at sea was a totally different experience. And this was the perfect
night, with the best conceivable conditions.

The moon was full, with its bright reflection shimmering upon the black
ocean surface. The seas were moderate. The east wind blew steadily at 12 knots
all night, keeping *Rhiannon* on an exhilarating broad reach, occasionally surging down a wave. Even the dolphins joined us for a magical visit at midnight.
Jim was in heaven. George held a stable course. As the perfume fragrance of
land wafted to us through the balmy night air, Jim discovered how glorious
island sailing could be.

Louis and his father Jim sailing from Mo'orea

Louis and I took turns sleeping. Jim stayed up in the cockpit all night. We
anchored off the waterfront between the town of Fare and the Bali Hai Hotel.
Louis's parents spent two nights on Huahine before flying onward to Raiatea
and Bora Bora. After Louis and I bid them bon voyage, we remained in Huahine
for a few more days. Huahine was a delightful place, quite reminiscent of the
Tahiti I had seen in 1963.

In Hiva Oa, Rangiroa, and Huahine, I had many opportunities to watch the
docking, unloading, and loading of the "copra boats," the small inter-island
freighters that were the commercial lifeblood of all the outlying islands. Though
they served as the principal passenger ferries between the islands, they primarily carried cargo of all descriptions on their scheduled runs. In all French
Polynesia, there were only a dozen or so of these vessels in regular service. In
each island group, I would see the same two or three copra boats recurrently, as

they made their weekly or biweekly visits. I came to recognize the captains of the various vessels. When these captains had a few moments free, occasionally I spoke with them about their ships and cargo.

The quays where these boats docked generally were quiet spots for people to sit, fish, or look out on the water. However, when the copra boat arrived, the quays became alive with crowds of animated people. Small trucks and handcarts would arrive at the quay to bring produce or pick up packages. People would sit on deck singing, gossiping, or calling out to friends on shore. The captain would stand conspicuously aboard his vessel or on the quay, notepad and pen in hand, recording the cargo and keeping the books, while simultaneously overseeing the operation.

In the Marquesas, at Taha'uku Bay, before a large dock had been built, unloading a car was a precarious undertaking. I once watched as a vehicle was lowered from an anchored ship onto two small rafts tied side-by-side. The car straddled the rafts as it was slowly pulled to shore.

At Fare, on Huahine, I watched the loading of the seasonal watermelon harvest onto the *Temehani*. The *Temehani* was the stately "grande dame" of the copra boats, the only remaining wooden freighter still making regular rounds in the Society Islands in 1977. Huahine was a major source of watermelons for the market in Tahiti. The round, bowling-ball-sized melons were loaded in a fascinating way. Thousands of watermelons had been harvested at once and stacked on the quay at Fare. Scores of people came to the waterfront to watch and help. Tahitian music blared from a boombox.

Temehani (at Bora Bora)

After the *Temehani* had completely disgorged her deliveries, her captain signaled the loading to begin. A snaking bucket brigade of about 20 barefoot and shirtless men quickly flung the heavy watermelons one by one down the line toward the boat. Several more men on deck received the melons as they were tossed up over the bulwarks and then down into the cargo hold. The captain directed the placement of the green and white melons to properly balance the load. Just when it appeared that the job was complete, several additional small Japanese pickup trucks arrived with dozens more ripe melons.

On another occasion, I witnessed the slightly smaller, steel-hulled *Taporo III* arriving at Bora Bora to pick up eight of the six-man *va'a* outrigger canoes to be transported to Huahine for a major race. Delicately loading and securing the long, narrow craft on the deck of the copra boat took several hours. All the residents displayed great pride in the local racing teams and their meticulously handcrafted canoes.

I wrote the following in a letter, while in Huahine, on March 10, 1977:

Yesterday was one of the two mornings each week that the copra boats come in. Two boats, Taporo III *and* Temehani *were simultaneously unloading construction material and cases of food for the Chinese groceries. The skies were partly cloudy so that the temperature was considerably more pleasant than it had been earlier in the week. As usual, the unloading scene was an animated carnival of action, bringing out fruit vendors, children, workers, and onlookers of all descriptions. The fishermen were selling bunches of fish strung together; and Chinese storekeepers were busy with bookkeeping and restocking—all right on the quay. The painted half-wooden trucks (buses) were mixed in with the whole mess, ready to transport the people and goods to their respective homes around the island.*

I figured that this would be a fine opportunity for me to see the island. I found a truck already filled with women in bright blue and red pareus, barefoot men in straw hats, a few small babies, and a pile of sacks and cartons laden with food. I spoke to the fat shirtless driver who was completing some makeshift repairs on his battery cables. I discovered that the bus would return to Fare later in the day. We agreed upon a price. I got myself a cold coconut to drink during the ride. I climbed over some boxes and sat on the bench between a very heavy woman in a green and white pareu and a toothless old lady whose long white hair hung down out of her brimmed straw hat. The old lady was cackling between sips of orange Fanta (which is imported from Belgium) and eventually she climbed off the truck to get a ride with some other people in a private Land Rover.

As soon as the roof was stacked high, we began to roll. The first stop was in the direction opposite the route of the bus but was necessary so that one woman could purchase some blocks of ice. Finally, we started off with a full load toward Huahine Iti, the smaller part of the island. All the while, Tamure music was piped into the back of the truck and the people were telling jokes in Tahitian. Whenever a vahine would ride past on a bicycle or scooter, one of the men would blurt out something, which everyone found outrageously funny. The truck next stopped in front of the infirmary. More women with babies, a couple of young children with scarred ankles, and an old lady with elephantiasis climbed in. One great big potbellied Tahitian man climbed up onto the roof. I pointed at the sagging ceiling and the people aboard all found this, too, quite humorous. The truck moved along the winding gravel and sand roads through banana plantations and coconut groves, as the riders sang with the music and yelled out to people passing on the road.

This ride reminded me somewhat of a similar trip on a bus in Panama, from Colon to Panama City. That bus was brightly painted with murals and strung with hanging dolls, medallions, and ornaments. It also was loaded to the gills with people who sang along with the Latin rhythms piped through that bus's speaker system. There is probably no more colorful way see the countryside and get a feel for the people than riding on a local bus during a busy part of the day. At one point during yesterday's ride, a man stuffed a piece of fruit into the mouth of a woman who had fallen asleep. She woke up and jokingly wanted me to push the man out of the back of the bus. When I think of a Chicago CTA bus or the New York City subway, it would be difficult to conceive of a similar ride in the U.S.

Who Stole our Passports?

While anchored at Huahine, Louis and I had intended to check-in with the local gendarme. When we looked in the top galley drawer for the Ziploc bag containing our passports and all of *Rhiannon*'s documentation … it was gone! We both seemed to recall putting it there when we arrived in Papeete over three weeks earlier. Slightly panicked, we looked in all the drawers and compartments in the cabin. There was no sign of the essential documents.

Louis and I had planned to continue from Huahine to Raiatea and Taha'a. But now we had no papers. We were depressed, dreading the prospect of obtaining duplicate passports, visas, vessel documentation, and a variety of other official items. We had become undocumented aliens, with nothing to produce for the authorities. Our only hope of beginning the intricate bureaucratic process of verifying our identities and receiving new paperwork was to return to Tahiti. This in itself was unappealing, as we had entered a cycle of heavier trade winds, and Papeete was almost directly upwind.

Feeling great urgency to begin the process, we set sail right away from Huahine. As anticipated, it was a hard beat into steep waves in 15- to 25-knot winds. *Rhiannon* would fly off each wave and slam down with a jarring crash. Steep seas would frequently send green water washing down the deck. With no dodger, Louis and I were constantly doused by buckets of spray. Luckily, George kept us pointing high, optimizing *Rhiannon*'s excellent windward ability.

Besides being wet and blind from the constant salt spray on our glasses, Louis and I were both seasick. We were not vomiting. But we felt far too queasy to go below or to consider eating. On the second day, we forced ourselves to drink some water to prevent dehydration. Following a sleepless night of hanging on to our bucking bronco in the drenched cockpit, we decided that we must eat something. We both were still fighting nausea, and neither of us felt like going into the cabin.

I volunteered to run below quickly to grab the top can of food, regardless of what it was. I handed the large can up to Louis with an opener. Our markings on the mystery label-less can were illegible. We opened it. It was corned beef hash. Just the sight of it was nauseating. As we pitched through the waves, heeled to starboard, I tossed the can through the companionway into the galley sink. Half of the corned beef hash spilled into the sink, already awash with sloshing water. One glance at the sink and one whiff of the greasy brown hash completely erased our appetites.

Since we needed to tack to reach Papeete, the passage took us one and a half days to complete. We eventually sailed through the pass at Papeete in the late afternoon. Our Alaskan friend Dale Sommers and his son Brad, aboard *Rodonis,* helped us moor at the quay. We were suddenly starving. Dale grilled steaks for us on his barbecue. It hit the spot. Afterward, Louis and I showered, dried out the boat, and discarded the remains of the corned beef hash still floating in the sink. We both slept soundly all night.

The next morning, we faced the daunting prospect of reconstituting our documents. We made one more thorough search of every nook aboard *Rhiannon*. While looking beneath the galley drawers, along the bare hull at the turn of the bilge, I spotted a tell-tale trail of aluminum foil leading forward. I followed the bits of foil to the V-berth and began inspecting the deadspace beneath the cabinetry near the bow. Lo and behold, there was a collection of items gathered into a rat's nest ... including the Ziploc bag with all the ship's papers! Yes, on the eve of its demise, the copra rat had emptied the contents of the drawer where we kept our aluminum foil and dragged it all to its nest. Ironically, among the papers it took to its secret lair was our Deratting Exemption Certificate. This rat had subjected us to a miserable, unnecessary passage as its ultimate act of revenge.

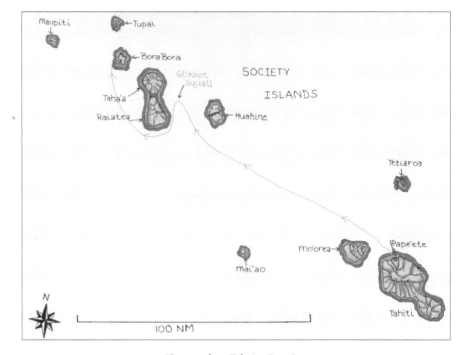

The route from Tahiti to Bora Bora

Windborne

While in the Marquesas, we encountered several of the cruising sailboats that we would later see in Tahiti and the Îles Sous le Vent. Of all the cruisers we met, the Charleson family aboard *Windborne* became our closest friends. Mike, Karol, Kathy, Anne, Clare, Michael, and Mark Charleson had arrived aboard a vessel quite different from all the rest. *Windborne* was a 62-foot Brixham trawler built in 1928 in England as a fishing sloop. After a long career as a working fishing boat, she had been re-rigged as a gaff-rigged topsail schooner. The tired old vessel ended up in Canada, where Mike and Karol Charleson purchased her after selling their house.

Their intention was to sail with their family from Victoria, B.C., through the South Pacific to New Zealand. The five Charleson children ranged in age from 8 to 18 years old. *Windborne* often leaked between her planks. Being a converted workboat, she was a bit roughly finished on deck and down below. Nonetheless, her classic lines — characterized by a plumb bow, a long bowsprit, heavy wooden spars, and a broad fantail — made her stand out along the quay. All the children shared in the work of handling the heavy gaff rig and the huge lever-driven manual windlass. Manually pumping out the bilge was also an ongoing chore.

Windborne

Unfortunately, Mike suffered from diabetes. While in Papeete he needed to be hospitalized. Once he had recovered sufficiently, the Charlesons planned to sail to Bora Bora. Louis and I also decided to head there. Given their large family, *Windborne* had crewmembers to spare. We invited their oldest daughter Kathy to join us on *Rhiannon* for the sail.

Louis and I had been lax in the housekeeping department aboard *Rhiannon*, as one might expect of two male recent college graduates. The stained bed sheets were disgusting, and tropical cockroaches had become well established crewmembers in our cabin. It was not exactly the most welcoming vessel for a guest. Nonetheless, Kathy Charleson was eager for the adventure and cheerfully welcomed the chance to temporarily escape her "oldest child" responsibilities aboard *Windborne*.

We set sail from Papeete earlier than *Windborne*, en route to Bora Bora. The weather remained pleasant during the first night. With George sailing, Kathy took her own shift on watch. Even though we were never able to raise *Windborne* on the VHF radio, we knew that we would eventually rendezvous at Vaitape in Bora Bora.

The following day, while sailing in the channel between Huahine and Taha'a in a calm sea with moderate wind, we saw a squall approaching from the north. There was nothing typical about this squall. The rain shafts were nearly horizontal, and the leading edge of the squall clouds reached low to the water. The squall was moving rapidly. We dropped and furled the jib. I ran below to grab the camera to photograph the unusual, fast-approaching raincloud.

Within minutes, white water appeared near the leading edge of the rain. As the first gust hit, we turned downwind toward the south to run with the squall. The wind overpowered us almost immediately, so we dropped the mainsail as well. Rain began to pelt us with unusual fury as the wind increased to strengths we had never before experienced. We estimated the windspeed at 60 knots.

Rhiannon flew downwind at six knots under bare poles. I was unable to turn my face toward the forcefully driven rain. The waves were never big, but the strong wind continued for 20 minutes.

60 knot squall

Stunned by the experience, we were reluctant to raise our sails again until long after the squall had passed, and steady winds had returned. We realized that we had been blown 10 NM south along the eastern reef of Taha'a and Raiatea and that we could no longer make it to Bora Bora before dark. Louis, Kathy, and I decided instead to continue south, circumnavigating Raiatea and Taha'a clockwise, in order to approach Bora Bora from the south on the following day. We spent a second night at sea.

The next morning, we reached northward along the western reef of Taha'a, enjoying the magnificent scenery. All morning we approached the dramatic towering peaks of Bora Bora. A school of leaping tuna passed near us. We trolled a line. Only one fish bit, but we lost that fish before we could get it on board. Upon clearing the reef, through the expansive Passe Teavanui, we spotted *Windborne,* already in the lagoon, tied to the quay at Vaitape. They had been mildly concerned when they could not find us upon their arrival the previous evening. But they had remained confident that we would eventually show up with their daughter.

Louis and I spent a few weeks in Bora Bora. We spent most of our stay moored at the quay in Vaitape. Occasionally, we needed to reposition *Rhiannon* on the quay to make room for arriving copra boats. After we moved, our keel sometimes bounced gently on the shallow bottom. We explored Bora Bora, visiting the large bays and climbing the hills. We ventured out to the motus on the reef. Once, we rode aboard *Windborne* with the Charlesons to the picturesque, completely uninhabited island of To'opua within Bora Bora's lagoon. We spent the day swimming and picnicking. Today, a luxury mega-resort occupies that island.

At the quay at Vaitape, Bora Bora

There was much to see in Bora Bora. Scattered along the main road were the remains of several sacred Polynesian *maraes*. Interspersed with these ruins were the remnants of the American occupation of Bora Bora, as a naval base, during World War II. Intact concrete bunkers with rusting steel doorways were open for us to explore freely. Tidy houses painted green, white, or a pastel color lined the main road near the villages. Most yards were fenced in, often with dogs or chickens roaming around. Many houses also had white-painted graves in the front yard. Despite the abundance of luxuriant tropical blossoms, Tahitians paradoxically decorated these family tombs with artificial plastic flowers.

A World War II bunker on Bora Bora

On the quay at Vaitape, Louis and I got to know many of the residents who strolled onto the quay in the morning or joined in the beehive of activity whenever a copra boat called. Children loved to play aboard *Rhiannon*. Most afternoons, I would get together with a young man my age, Tefa Rooiti, and his friend Pafe. I tried hard to learn some spoken Tahitian. I gradually picked up a few useful expressions. Once, when I was testing out my language skills among a small group of people, I attempted to use the Tahitian name for the "north wind" and inadvertently said something similar sounding that meant "large penis." My mistake provoked the expected reaction. Louis and I took Tefa and Pafe daysailing on *Rhiannon,* out in the ocean well beyond the pass. And they, in turn, took us spear fishing among the beautiful coral reefs of the lagoon.

Grave with plastic flowers in a front yard

One day, Paname Paris — the French alpinist I had befriended in Panama — and his wife Paul, aboard *Sagarmatha*, anchored in the lagoon. They told me that they had indeed stopped at Ahe in the Tuamotus and spent time with the renowned single-handed circumnavigator and author, Bernard Moitessier. They were still planning to live on Tahiti. I also saw Louis, from *Dragon*. He came aboard *Rhiannon* to inspect his former windvane parts, which we had used to build George. He approved of our installation and asked me how the self-steering had performed at sea. Louis and I calculated that since leaving Panama, George had sailed farther at night while we had slept than we had sailed during the daytimes while awake.

Robert

The Charlesons became pressed to start heading west to the Cook Islands, as they needed to get to New Zealand before the winter season. We bid them an emotional farewell on the day they untied their lines to sail off. We hoped to see them in Rarotonga, in the Cook Islands, our next destination. Two days after their departure, tropical storm Robert developed several hundred miles northwest of Bora Bora and began to drive south. We needed to sit tight in Bora Bora.

We really had not thought much about major cyclones, even though it was the heart of the storm season. Perhaps we had been nonchalant. Due to exceptional luck, our track record had been good. We had somehow managed to avoid hurricanes in the Caribbean in 1976. Tropical storms in French Polynesia were far less common. Nonetheless, everyone on Bora Bora became concerned and visibly anxious when storm warnings were issued for Robert. Robert had been upgraded to a "severe cyclone" and was on a direct course toward Bora Bora. Forecasts projected landfall in approximately 48 hours.

That evening, as the sun was setting, the distinctive silhouette of the wooden copra boat *Temehani* alongside the palm-covered motus on the reef was ominously outlined against a blood-red sky as she entered Passe Teavanui. This was by far the most menacing evening sky that Louis or I had ever seen. Slowly, the barometer began to fall. *Temehani* made a quick turnaround at the quay and departed safely toward the southeast that night.

Temehani entering the pass with an ominous red sky

On the next day, great swells generated by Robert were already crashing upon the reef. Even the wide, deep pass appeared inhospitable. We motored *Rhiannon* to a hurricane hole inside of an abandoned World War II boat docking inlet, within a sheltered bay in the lagoon. Others had the same idea. A few local boats and a tidy yacht, sailed by a retired doctor from New Zealand and his wife, all crammed into the tight inlet with us. The crews cooperated to weave a web of docklines leading from each boat to shore in every direction. As cordial as the New Zealand couple had been toward us, they were understandably reluctant to tie any lines between our two vessels once they learned that *Rhiannon* harbored cockroaches.

The hurricane hole at Bora Bora

That night, everyone nervously kept vigil as the rains came. Most of the 30-knot winds remained aloft, passing above the boats, as this hurricane hole was situated in the lee of a tall bluff. Fortunately, Robert had taken a slight turn to the west and merely glanced by Bora Bora as it passed between the Society Islands and the Cook Islands. We had survived totally unscathed. There was no storm damage on Bora Bora. All the preparation appeared to be for naught. However, given the crude state of cyclone prediction in 1977, safe was better than sorry.

CHAPTER 21

The Cook Islands

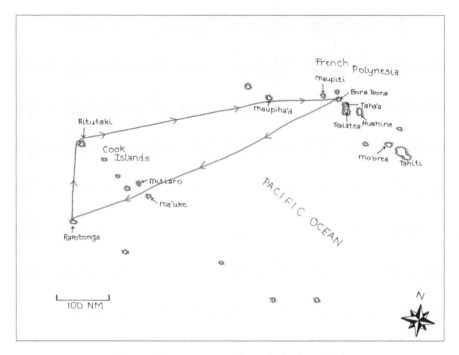

The route from Bora Bora to the Cook Islands and back.

At Sea Again

LOUIS AND I had intended to leave Bora Bora for the Cook Islands in Robert's wake, before another tropical storm had a chance to materialize. However, as soon as the cyclone moved south, only glassy calms remained. We waited several more days, hoping for an easterly wind. On the morning of April 23, 1977, in sunny weather we finally cast off. The trade winds had totally disappeared. Layered clouds uncharacteristic of the typical skies in French Polynesia gradually overtook us, blotting out the sun. The wind shifted from northeast to southwest, then back to the east-northeast. To keep up with the ever-changing wind, we needed to frequently readjust George. Our destination, the island of Rarotonga was 540 NM away.

Between Bora Bora and Rarotonga were two outlying Cook Islands, Mitiaro and Mauke. We had no desire to stop at either of these, as there were no sheltered anchorages or suitable harbors at either one. Our biggest concern was avoiding the reefs that surrounded these two islands. After the first two days, rain fell steadily each day for long stretches rather than during distinct circumscribed squalls. Fortunately, the sun peeked out from time to time, giving us a chance to obtain some sextant sights.

During one of those sunny periods, we finally caught a good-sized wahoo. We were not only elated, we were shocked. We brought out the camera. We needed some proof that we had finally landed a large edible fish. We fried the fillets in margarine and served them very simply with lime juice. It tasted delicious. Louis and I were hoping that the fish was a good omen during the otherwise dreary sail.

We finally caught a fish

On the night of April 25, with barely a half moon in the sky, Louis and I both observed a complete "moonbow" beneath a passing rain squall. It was a dark, colorless arch, composed of multiple shades of grey. It was awesome. Neither of us had known that such a phenomenon even existed. We had no idea how common moonbows were. We needed to convince one another of what we were in fact witnessing. Although we were seven months into our journey, our moonbow discovery reminded us that we were still strangers to the remarkable, mysterious sea.

The weather continued to be unstable. The wind varied frequently in force and direction, often accompanied by rain. We frequently changed sails. During one short-lived light easterly breeze, we tried flying the spinnaker. The wind again shifted before the big red and white sail had sufficient time to do us any good. At one point, the wind strengthened so much that we flew only the triple-reefed main and the storm jib. When the east wind died, a new breeze came up on the nose. We tacked repeatedly to stay on track.

Using navigation protractor triangles, we carefully penciled our zig-zag path onto the chart. We were averaging less than 100 NM each day. By the fourth day, we received the Rarotonga radio beacon on our RDF. Gradually, we homed in on the signal.

Rarotonga

Rarotonga is an oval shaped island, approximately six miles long by four miles wide. It is covered by luxuriant vegetation. Spectacular peaks and craggy cliffs loom up at the center of the island. The Cook Islands, of which Avarua, Rarotonga, is the capital, had been a dependent territory of New Zealand until they were granted a constitution with self-government status in 1965. In 1977, the Cooks remained in free association with New Zealand.

A barrier reef with only a few passes surrounds the island of Rarotonga. It has no completely sheltered harbor. In 1977, the port of entry, Avatiu, was the only small harbor suitable for visiting boats. Fatigued, we finally approached the island in the late afternoon of April 29.

Avatiu harbor, consisted of a small break in the fringing reef opening into a rectangular basin that was completely exposed to the north. Space for visiting yachts was extremely limited. A seawall lined with rusting steel reinforcements was used for Med mooring. A dinghy was required to get ashore, due to the continual surge entering the harbor through its totally unprotected mouth. We cautiously entered the Avatiu pass flying our code "Q" flag. We anchored *Rhiannon* adjacent to the seawall, and tied off to await official entry clearance, including a critical health department inspection.

Louis and I both looked forward to a good night's rest. However, the health officials did not work after dark. By sunset, they had not yet appeared. The police informed us that we could not stay in the harbor unless we had been cleared. Nothing we said would persuade them to let us stay.

Once again, we were sailing, out of the harbor into the night. Fortunately, the weather remained fair as we took turns at the helm, guiding *Rhiannon* through the water well clear of the fringing reef along the north shore of the island. Under main only, we sailed back and forth all night, in the light wind, listening to the waves breaking steadily on the reef.

After standing off all night, we re-entered the harbor and moored in the morning. Local officials arrived and began to check us in. There was a mandatory procedure required before we could formally enter the country. *Rhiannon* needed to undergo a complete fumigation. Rarotonga exported oranges and other citrus fruit as an essential part of its limited economy. A small invasive beetle originating in Australia posed a threat to the oranges and, consequently, to the entire Cook Island economy. Visiting yachts represented a potential threat. I was surprised that non-essential vessels were permitted to visit at all.

Fumigation meant that any fresh food and other items not in sealed containers aboard our sailboat would be poisoned. While the fumigation took place, we needed to remain on shore, at a safe distance. We could not return for several hours. On deck, a prominently mounted sign, written both in English and the local Polynesian language, warned of the dangerous poison. Men in gasmasks boarded *Rhiannon* to fumigate. We stood far back, as clouds of the toxic insecticide billowed out of the hatches. Although Louis and I were somewhat concerned about our food provisions and the prospect of lingering fumes, we were grateful for one fortuitous benefit of the gassing: Our resident cockroaches would be exterminated—at least for a while.

Fumigation in Avatiu Harbor, Rangiroa

Moderate-sized inter-island freighters regularly called at Avatiu, often passing perilously close to any yachts moored in the harbor. We moored *Rhiannon* facing north, into the swell, parallel to the deteriorating eastern basin wall. We used two anchors off our port side in the poor holding ground of the shallow harbor. Several lines to starboard maintained our position relative to the treacherous wall. We also devised a continuous loop system between *Rhiannon* and the shore to shuttle our dinghy back and forth as needed. Whenever a freighter departed, we would momentarily ease our anchor rodes to be certain that they would not be overrun by the ship as it passed only a few feet away.

Inter-island freighter *Manuvai* in Avatiu Harbor

The commercial and government center of Rarotonga is the Avarua District, only a short walk from Avatiu harbor. It rained most nights. In the mornings, an ethereal patchy fog cloaked the green trees lining the road to Avarua. In Avarua we found a hardware store to purchase some parts for the boat. We also located some retail food warehouses where we could buy canned food for the next three months. Louis and I sampled the available selection. Our favorite bargains included canned corned beef from Fiji and canned sheep's tongues from New Zealand. We bought dozens of cans.

The people we met were all exceptionally helpful and friendly. Several of the government workers and store clerks became our friends. Even strangers on the road would greet us as we passed with a heartfelt, "kia orana." The Cook

Islanders seemed to get along much better with the Kiwis, than the Tahitians did with the French. I never sensed any colonial resentment by the locals.

The road to Avarua after a morning rainshower

The commercial center in Avarua

In 1977, the government of the Cook Islands was controlled by the long-time Premier, Sir Albert Henry. Nepotism seemed to prevail in local politics. Virtually all the high officials or influential people in charge of the islands were nieces or nephews of Sir Albert. While we were in Rarotonga, the Premier's 50th wedding anniversary was observed as a two-day school holiday, a bank holiday, and a government office holiday.

Louis and I spent two weeks in Rarotonga. On one weekend, we were invited to watch a rugby match. This event drew a huge crowd. The game was played on a muddy field in a picturesque valley filled with banana trees and coconut palms. The spectators enjoyed themselves immensely, laughing and shouting as the players rolled around in the big puddles on the field.

One day, we rode all the way around the island on rented Honda 50 motor-cycles. The scenery changed unexpectedly with each turn in the road. Other than in Avatiu and Avarua, the compact island, dominated by its fantasy island green peaks, appeared tranquil and uncrowded. During our island tour, we were on the lookout for a small mangrove inlet on the eastern side of the island. Local fishermen told us that the sheltered spot was used as a hurricane hole for small local vessels. We remained acutely aware that the threat of cyclones had not yet passed.

On another day, I went dinghy sailing with members of a small boat club. While there, I met some local drummers practicing on the lawn of their house. These drummers were preparing for a gig accompanying a dance troop in Avarua later that day. Dance was a major source of entertainment, community participation, and pride on all the islands we visited in both French Polynesia and the Cooks.

Over the years, many sailboats heading west from French Polynesia have stopped at Rarotonga, despite its poor harbor. For decades, a local priest named Father George kept a book recording the names of visiting yachts and their crews. Unfortunately, he was in the hospital at the time of our visit. A friend of Father George's brought us the fascinating voluminous record. We were able to enter *Rhiannon* into the tome. We learned that we had just missed our friends the Charlesons, aboard *Windborne*. They had moved on shortly before our arrival.

Three or four other cruising sailboats passed through Avatiu harbor during our stay. The graceful double-ender *Svea* arrived as she continued her circum-navigation. It was great to see Don and Sue Mosely once again. In Avatiu, we also encountered a most unique wooden boat, named *Duen,* with a fascinat-ing history. A young couple, Dottie and Albert Fletcher had painstakingly and lovingly restored and repurposed a 50-foot Colin Archer-designed Norwegian fishing boat into a magnificent gaff-rigged ketch. Her beamy, double-ended wooden hull sported a dark brown, natural wood finish.

While in Rarotonga, the Fletchers hauled out *Duen* for some bottom work. Propped up by jack stands on the quay, her form resembled a storybook depiction of Noah's ark. After we met them, Dottie and Albert continued a multi-year circumnavigation in their spectacular ketch.

Somehow, all these cruisers managed to find moorings around the periphery of the tiny basin, allowing room for the regular visits of the inter-island freighter *Manuvai*. When in port, this white and blue steel ship berthed at the southern end of the tiny harbor. One Sunday, the *Manuvai* departed for Aitutaki, carrying hundreds of people who had come to Rarotonga for a dance festival the previous week. Aitutaki's dance troops had cleaned up in the competition, winning almost all the prizes.

As the ship left, scores of people stood in the rain to see them off. Bystanders were wearing their crowns of bright flowers, playing guitars, and beating out fast rhythms on traditional wooden drums. Louis and I stood by, on *Rhiannon's* deck, ready to slack our anchor rodes as the ship squeezed past toward the harbor's mouth. A long tenor blast of the ship's horn signaled her departure from the dock. As the freighter accelerated toward the pass, a dozen children, who had climbed up onto the ship while she was moored, all dove off her tall stern rail into the harbor, amid cheers and laughter from the onlooking crowds on the quay.

Often, during my stay on Rarotonga, I would walk into Avarua and sit alone beneath a shady tree, gazing out onto the reef. As the sun shone down on the breaking waves, I watched black clouds with columns of falling rain march past across the distant horizon. Solitary local fishermen would stand on the reef or fish peacefully from their outrigger canoes near the shore.

Prominently perched, high upon the reef laid the wreck of the brigantine schooner, *Yankee*. When she had been owned by Irving and Exy Johnson, she had circumnavigated four times with young crews. Captain Johnson's travelogues at the Field Museum, including his films taken aboard the *Yankee,* had inspired me as a child. This vessel had been sold twice after she was skippered by Johnson. She met her ignominious end on the reef at Avarua in 1964. At that time, she was owned by Mike Burke out of Miami and was one of the ships in his poorly managed Windjammer scheme. It was sad to see the once-magnificent, graceful brigantine transformed into a rusting hulk.

I felt enormous gratitude for the open-hearted hospitality shown to me by so many of the islanders whom I befriended in Rarotonga and throughout the Pacific. Their welcoming reception of visitors was unparalleled. Before we left Rarotonga, some wonderful Cook Islanders generously gave us two sacks filled with oranges and grapefruits. Louis and I were appreciative of this delicious source of vitamin C. Although scurvy was uncommon in 1977, we were concerned about our upcoming long ocean passage. Without refrigeration or access to fresh provisions we could still develop illnesses resulting from vitamin deficiencies during our extended voyage far from land.

Fishing boats at Avarua

The hulk of the *Yankee* on the reef near Avarua

Well stocked with a 60- to 90-day supply of canned food and non-perishable staples, we were anxious to move on. I wished that we had the time to stay longer. But we had decided to sail to Hawaii to sell *Rhiannon* in the United States. Unfortunately, time was becoming a factor. Although I had wanted to continue to Samoa, Fiji, and points west, there was no market there to sell *Rhiannon*. We needed to begin making our way to Hawaii.

Aitutaki

Louis and I were eager to visit another of the Cook Islands. Aitutaki, one of the 15 Cook Islands, is situated 140 NM due north of Rarotonga. We knew exceptionally little about it. Its obscurity was part of its attraction. We knew that Aitutaki had just won the inter-island dance competition. The acclaim of its dancers, its exotic mellifluous name, and its reputation as a picturesque island all beckoned us to check it out. We were able to obtain permission to visit Aitutaki from the Immigration Office in Rarotonga.

Early on the morning of May 11, 1977, we stowed our anchors and set sail just outside the pass at Avatiu. As we escaped the lee of Rarotonga into a rising ESE breeze, George steered us straight north toward Aitutaki. Boosted by following seas, *Rhiannon* averaged six knots on a boisterous broad reach. By sunrise the next morning, the green hills of Aitutaki were in sight, dead ahead. We approached the southern tip of the island's huge barrier reef only 23 hours after leaving Rarotonga.

By the time we arrived, the waves had become uncomfortably large. Louis and I were hoping to find sheltered water. We knew there was a long narrow passage that cut through the broad coral reef and led to the principal town of Arutanga. The *Sailing Directions* indicated that this channel offered a minimum depth of five feet at high tide but should only be attempted with local knowledge. Any vessels drawing over five feet must remain outside of the reef and use small boats to ferry passengers ashore.

We had mentally prepared ourselves to stay outside the reef. However, temporary anchorage was only feasible in calm weather. That day, the seas were far from calm. In fact, Louis and I were both in need of respite from the waves. As *Rhiannon* sailed north along the west side of Aitutaki's reef, we could see the village beyond the foreboding coral barrier. Entry appeared impossible.

Just as we reached the tiny opening to the completely unmarked passage, a local fisherman in a small wooden outrigger greeted us near the entrance. He confidently encouraged us to go in and even offered to guide us through. *Rhiannon* drew five feet, perhaps enough to clear the bottom—or perhaps not. Louis and I were both ready to try.

In the morning light, the channel appeared indistinguishable from the hazardous surrounding coral. Blindly, we motored *Rhiannon* through the long winding passage directly behind the fisherman. Luckily, we never touched the bottom or hit the sides. Once inside the lagoon, we had almost reached the village. A small basin of slightly deeper, placid water opened before us. We tied *Rhiannon* safely to the quay. Other than a few small pirogues, *Rhiannon* was the only boat there.

Aitutaki is similar to Bora Bora, except that the main island is smaller, with low hills and no high mountains. The lagoon formed by the barrier reef at Aitutaki is also much larger than Bora Bora's. Unlike other volcanic islands we visited, this island featured a network of roads that crossed directly over the center of the island. Banana trees, palm trees, and most varieties of tropical fruit grew abundantly.

The people of Aitutaki were outgoing and friendly. They reminded me of the people we had met in the Galapagos. Life on Aitutaki was very leisurely. People readily took time off from work to play rugby and netball on Friday afternoons. As on all the islands that we visited, sports were important. Festivities always followed the inter-district and inter-island competitions that were held throughout the year.

Louis and I stayed in Aitutaki for three days, spending much of our time dancing, eating local dishes, and visiting with the islanders. The traditional drum dances were exceptionally popular there. One evening, some of the dancers invited me to join them. I eventually picked up a few of the moves. Needless to say, I never came close to matching the skillful performances of the local dancers.

Female dancers wore elaborate costumes. Their handmade dried grass skirts were decorated with colorful shell and feather ornaments. The dancers' skirts alternately flowed sinuously or vibrated rapidly with their seductive hip movements. Their torsos, with bare midriffs, were held motionless above their sharply shifting hips. The dancers moved in unison, in perfect synchrony with the staccato beat of the drums. Each dance had its own characteristic hand gestures and arm movements.

In the afternoons, I lounged in *Rhiannon*'s cockpit, absorbing the tranquil scenery surrounding the boat basin and drinking cool coconut water. In Aitutaki's lagoon, old women fished from fragile looking pirogues, waiting silently and patiently, bamboo poles extended over the water. These women usually wore flowers in their hair or woven pandanus leaf hats. They would throw pieces of small fish into the water to attract the desirable bigger fish that were foraging in the lagoon.

The boat basin at Aitutaki

During our short stay in Aitutaki, one other cruising yacht arrived, also managing to tie up inside the lagoon. *Harikoa* was a 33-foot sloop made of kauri wood. Hailing from New Zealand's North Island, she had been designed as a miniature version of the famous Nathaniel Herreshoff-designed ocean racing ketch, *Ticonderoga*. Aboard were a recently separated middle-aged man, Jack, and his young new cruising partner, Karen. They were planning to head for Suvorov Island in the northern Cooks. Suvorov atoll became famous when a self-made castaway and survivalist from New Zealand, named Tom Neale, wrote about his experiences there in a book called *An Island to Oneself*. He had lived on the atoll for over 16 years. This couple was hoping to sail there and meet him.

When I told Jack that we had news that Tom Neale had been hospitalized in Rarotonga with a grave illness, he had second thoughts about sailing to Suvorov. Louis and I suggested that they visit Bora Bora, which we had enjoyed so much. Jack changed his plans in short order and decided that the two of them would sail to Bora Bora instead. I told them that we intended to return to Bora Bora ourselves. Like Louis and me, Jack had grown up racing sailboats. He gamely challenged us to a long-distance match race from Aitutaki to Bora Bora. Louis and I accepted immediately.

Harikoa

The Race

On the morning of our departure, a small outrigger escorted both boats out through the channel to the west side of the island. The wind was blowing about 10 knots from the north. Both crews hoisted their sails almost simultaneously. We each started heading north on opposite tacks and soon re-converged, crossing within less than a boat length of one another. It was an even start for the 480 NM sail to Bora Bora. Throughout the morning, we crossed tacks within a boat length of one another. The wind moved aft gradually, and we each steered our own selected compass course. We had chosen identical courses. The two boats remained side by side as Aitutaki progressively dropped below the horizon astern.

By midday, a dark rainsquall closed in from behind. At that point, *Harikoa* was a hundred yards behind us. Louis and I had been pushing *Rhiannon* as hard as we could, concentrating on optimal sail trim. As we watched the squall getting closer, Louis and I began to reef the mainsail proactively. While we were reefing the sail, the New Zealand sloop shot past us only a few feet away. A minute later, the squall hit with driving rain and 40-knot winds. *Harikoa* was greatly over-canvassed. Immediately, they were laid over and stopped dead-in-the-water by the fierce wind. Our shortened sail was perfect for the violent shrieking gusts, and we quickly surfed past them as they struggled to reef during the blow.

For the next 300 NM, we lost sight of them each evening at dusk but found them sailing nearby once again at dawn. Incredibly, though we were independently calculating our respective routes to Bora Bora by celestial navigation, we remained virtually side by side. One night in a calm, we lost sight of them for good. After that, the weather varied between light wind and no wind whatsoever. We had no idea what had become of *Harikoa*. We could not raise them on our VHF radio.

Nonetheless, Louis and I continued to race. On one evening as the sun was setting, we sighted the outlying French Polynesian atoll of Maupiha'a (Mopelia). The wind was light, and the sea was calm. We could clearly see the waves breaking upon the reef along Maupiha'a's south shore. Our charts indicated a navigable pass on the western side of the atoll. *Sailing Directions* described a village with a small, mostly transient local population. Very few yachts ever stopped there. We really wanted to check it out, but we were in a race. We sailed to within a stone's throw of the reef itself, before prudently tacking away from the island. Had we not been racing, Louis and I surely would have entered the pass. As the stars came out on that moonless night, we spotted the glow from kerosene lanterns in the buildings on Maupiha'a's eastern motu.

The next day, the mountain peaks of Bora Bora came into view as a tiny bump on the horizon. We were becalmed. We started our engine and dropped the sails, completing the final 30 NM to Bora Bora under power. When we entered Passe Teavanui, we saw that our competitors had already anchored off the village of Vaitape. Jack and Karen had begun quarreling and had motored *Harikoa* for over two days. One of my biggest regrets has always been that Louis and I did not drop out of the race to stop at Maupiha'a. My overzealous commitment to the integrity of the sailboat race had unduly influenced my priorities. It was a lesson that I never forgot.

CHAPTER 22

Facing Reality

Bora Bora Homecoming

Being back in Bora Bora was like returning home. Once again, we tied *Rhiannon* to the familiar quay at Vaitape, reclaiming our former secure berth in the heart of town. There was no fee for mooring there, and we were never asked to move. The ability to step on and off the boat at will made visiting the people of Vaitape easy and eliminated the hassle of dinghy trips to shore.

Most cruisers preferred to stay at anchor for privacy and safety. We already had dealt with cockroaches and a rat. Infestations no longer concerned us. We trusted the people and never worried about theft or personal safety. *Rhiannon's* hatches remained open all the time. We did not even have a lock. On the first day of our return, as we walked through Vaitape, we were welcomed by old friends. Louis was offered a refrigerated coconut to drink. After days in the hot sun without a single cool beverage, Louis found the cold coconut water to be exceptionally satisfying. He has subsequently referred to that particular drink as the most refreshing he ever experienced.

Local visitors in the cockpit at Vaitape

After we cleared-in with the gendarmes, I went for a longer walk. Many children recognized me. They called out, "Mike! Mike!" Often, they would shout something that sounded like "Te tianoto!" referring to my eyeglasses or "Huru Huru Ta'a!" meaning beard. At one point, on a whim, I had shaven part of my beard, leaving behind a pair of ridiculous looking bushy mutton chop sideburns and a moustache. The word for sideburns was apparently the same as the word for beard.

I stopped at the Chinese grocery store for some bread and then sauntered down the road to find some of my friends. Tefa, who worked as a woodcarver at his own little tourist stand, invited me to his home for a shower and dinner. We ate octopus in coconut milk, manioc, and some type of fish. His sister had also made a sweet cake with coconut meat and plantains. We listened to Radio Tahiti and talked for hours by the light of kerosene lanterns.

Spearfishing with Tefa on the reef in Bora Bora

Va'a racing in the lagoon, Bora Bora

At Vaitape, *Rhiannon* became a regular playground for younger children who freely climbed around on deck or used her as a dive platform. When Louis and I wanted privacy, I knew how to tell the children in Tahitian to get off the boat and go home. My friends had even taught me some stronger language for those who would not heed my first requests. Louis and I were generally very amused by the kids and enjoyed their company. I was impressed by the ways that children adapted to conditions that we considered disabilities in the U.S. One little boy had the congenital deformity of a bifid thumb, forked at its tip. Back home, this would generally be treated surgically, to prevent stigmatization and to permit glove wear. This young boy was the envy of his friends. He cleverly used the fork in his thumb as a pulley when feeding out and retrieving a fishing line, something none of the others could do. Of course, winter gloves were never an issue in Bora Bora.

In a letter to my sister, I wrote:

Each evening tens of children come out to our boat. They sit on the boat and play Tahitian songs on the guitar and ukulele. Everyone sings along well into the night. There must be about 50 popular songs here which I've heard over and over again since the first night I arrived in the Marquesas for the New Year's Eve dance. Actually, I've heard the songs since we first picked up Radio Tahiti over a week before reaching Hiva Oa. We also heard many of the same songs on the Voice of the Cook Islands radio in Rarotonga. —No matter. I love the music more each time I hear it.

But it would never be the same without the children. Most of Polynesia's population is under the age of 18. The atmosphere would just not be the same without the tens of young Tahitians, Bora Borans, or others that swim and fish at the waterfront of every village at which we've stopped. Most children have 13 or 15 brothers and sisters and a number of half brothers and sisters, too.

This situation arises from several customs which are typically Polynesian. Tahitians often marry unofficially. They live together and refer to each other as husband and wife. But there was never any official ceremony or document. These "marriages" often result in many children, but they don't last a lifetime. This is not unlike the U.S. except that a divorce is not necessary, and usually many more children are involved.

Another custom is informal adoption. If one woman had a baby whom she did not want, she would readily give the baby to someone who wants one, perhaps a cousin, a mother, a grandmother, or a friend. This adoption system, along with the great cultural love for children leaves almost no orphans in the society. Even children of age 6 or 7 years may be given to a different family. Surprisingly, this seems to cause little or no problem.

Although Louis and I found time to relax and explore more of Bora Bora, our primary mission at this stop was to prepare for the passage to Hawaii. We needed to be certain that everything was in working order aboard *Rhiannon*. We scraped barnacles from her badly fouled bottom, still covered by the original antifouling paint that we had applied in Waukegan almost a year earlier. We went aloft to thoroughly inspect the rigging. We finished stocking canned provisions and refilled our water tanks using rainwater treated with chlorine bleach. The engine seemed to be working well. We waited until our departure date was at hand before procuring fresh produce.

The biggest decisions we faced involved planning our route. Honolulu lies 2300 NM north of Bora Bora. However, sailing directly north would involve close reaching or beating into the NE trade winds for the second half of the trip. Sailing upwind into boisterous trade wind seas aboard *Rhiannon* had been exceptionally wet and unpleasant for Louis and me. We reasoned that a longer but easier passage would be kinder to *Rhiannon*'s gear.

No matter what route we chose, sailing to Hawaii would necessitate traversing three major weather zones: the southeast trades, the doldrums (ITCZ), and the northeast trades. We also knew that while in the northeast trades we would need to contend with the eastern Pacific hurricane season. Our plan was to make as much easting as practical while still south of the doldrums before turning north. If we approached Hawaii from the southeast, through the northeast trade winds, *Rhiannon* would be on a beam reach rather than a beat.

Some cruisers with reliable engines would sail north from the Society Islands in the prevailing SE wind until they reached the calms and the eastbound equatorial countercurrent in the doldrums. They would then motor east through the doldrums to a point southeast of Hawaii in order to reach through the NE trades. With our unreliable Atomic-4 engine and limited fuel capacity, this was not an option for us.

While in Bora Bora, several days before our departure, we happened to meet the crew of a 60-foot high-performance sloop on a delivery trip between New Zealand and Hawaii. Aboard was Paul Whiting, the yacht designer son of D'Arcy Whiting. He was engaged to marry Annie, whom we had first met in Panama aboard *Tequila*. We later learned that Paul Whiting's crew were able to complete the sail from Bora Bora to Hilo in under two weeks, with some help from their engine, motoring through the doldrums. (As I mentioned earlier, this was only three years before Paul Whiting and Annie both tragically died at sea following the Sydney to Hobart Race, in 1980.)

Our proposed route to Hawaii would take us close to the northern Tuamotus and perhaps the northern Marquesas. If hard beating to windward were not required, we hoped to call at Ahe in the Tuamotus and Nuku Hiva in the Marquesas, two islands we had not previously visited. If we proceeded non-stop, we anticipated a voyage of 30 to 40 days. We did not carry sufficient fuel to motor through calms. Getting through the doldrums under sail could take days or potentially even weeks. With no available weather forecasting, we simply would need to live with the odds and hope that we would avoid major storms. Although our planned passage coincided exactly with the eastern Pacific hurricane season, (perhaps naively) we deemed the risk of encountering a severe storm to be low.

We were prepared to leave imminently. Unfortunately, there was no wind. We continued to enjoy our time on the island. Although the sun was out, the temperatures stayed moderate. Even the young Mormon missionaries, wearing their long-sleeved white shirts, dark neckties ties, and long pants, appeared comfortable as they rode their bicycles along the road through town.

As we awaited our weather window, I heard that a professional dance troupe from Tahiti was to perform at a small church in Vaitape. This was a travelling company that was on tour, dancing for the residents at a few small churches on several of the islands. As usual the dancing was spectacular. The beguiling sensuality of the dancers' movements electrified the audience. A written program listed the names of the dancers. The family name of one of the female dancers, Robinson, immediately caught my eye.

Following the show, I walked over to speak with the dancers. One of the lead performers, a woman of about my age with flowing black hair, happily spoke with me. She was the youngest Tahitian daughter of William Albert Robinson, the sailor and author who had been so inspirational to me. When I was in Tahiti with my family at the age of nine, we had stopped to visit "Robbie" at his home in Paea. I remember playing outside with his daughters at that time, one of whom, Tumata, went on to pursue a lifelong career in dance. I was delighted that we had met once again.

CHAPTER 23

The Longest Passage

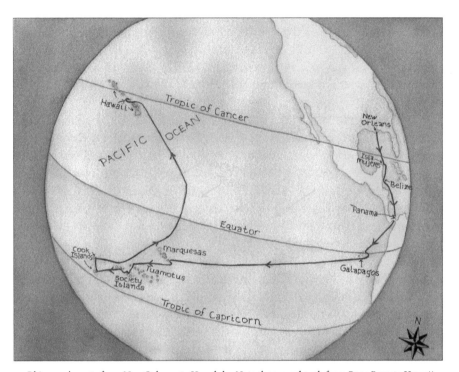

Rhiannon's route from New Orleans to Honolulu. Note the curved path from Bora Bora to Hawaii

ON MAY 29, 1977, Louis and I set sail from Bora Bora beneath a cloudless sky in a light easterly wind. Initially, we could comfortably beat toward the ENE under full sail in the calm deep-blue ocean. We remained silent, each of us separately contemplating our time in French Polynesia while preparing ourselves mentally for the prolonged confinement aboard *Rhiannon*. This extended passage was different. We were no longer headed toward exotic new destinations, but rather we were headed home. I dreaded returning to life as a student. This ocean crossing would be a stark transition period between the outbound voyage and my new life.

I would keep myself occupied with the myriad of more immediate challenges during the trans-Pacific sail. I held on to a slight hope of stopping at Ahe in the Tuamotus or Nuku Hiva in the Marquesas. But deep inside, I realized that getting to Hawaii was our true priority. Besides, to reach these two

271

islands, we would not be able to avoid a miserable beat into strong trade winds. Louis and I had vowed that we would not deliberately subject ourselves to that punishment.

We had chosen this route to be easy on the boat, her equipment, and most importantly her crew. The odds of encountering a major tropical depression were low, even during the eastern Pacific storm season. Though we planned to evade hurricanes, we felt prepared to handle a lesser gale at sea if necessary.

On our second day, we encountered the southeast trade winds, blowing at 10 to 12 knots from the ENE rather than from the SE. Consequently, we needed to alter our course and veer toward the NNE. On this course, we would bypass Ahe. It had been a blessing to start out in tranquil conditions with waves and wind building gradually over the first few days. Our vestibular systems could accommodate progressively, without seasickness. Our biological clocks also habituated effortlessly to the doublehanded watch routine aboard *Rhiannon*.

Over the next day, the wind continued to increase incrementally. Consequently, we shortened sail. The winds grew to a steady 25 to 35 knots, still from the ENE. We fell off onto a close reach and eventually pressed on under a storm jib and triple-reefed main. During the night, fierce squalls developed with wind speeds varying between 20 and 50 knots. One of the mechanical linkages on George broke. Temporarily, we needed to steer by hand.

Given the frequency of squalls throughout the pitch-black night, we finally dropped the storm jib and hove to until dawn. Louis and I were both able to get some rest. By morning, the waves were running at about 12 feet. We repaired George and once again pressed on with the reefed main and working jib.

For the next two days, we experienced unsettled, completely overcast, squally weather. As much as we tried, we could not find a reasonable sail combination. Our working jib would overpower us, while our baggy canvas storm jib would not drive us through the waves.

The barometer fell from 29.64 to 29.52 inches of Hg. We began to run through our storm preparation checklist. (See Appendix 4.) We waited vigilantly to see what Mother Nature would bring us next. But the anticipated storm never materialized. The grey squally weather continued for four days, until a large swell out of the southwest suggested that the storm's center had passed to our south.

On June 3, the barometer finally climbed back to 29.74, and typical trade wind conditions returned. We experienced the SE trade winds for only one day before the winds began to subside. On the morning of June 4, while ghosting along in the light wind 160 NM NNW of Rangiroa, we sighted another vessel.

This was the only time we ever saw another yacht in the open ocean. She was the fishing schooner *Sabrina*, originally from the west coast of the U.S. We spoke with the skipper on the VHF radio. Her crew, Wayne, Deloris, and son

Jeff, were 25 days out of Hawaii en route to Tahiti. They were concerned about their water supply. We suggested that they might stop at Rangiroa.

Later that day, the wind totally died. We had fallen into the tenacious clutch of the doldrums. We ran the engine briefly to charge the batteries that afternoon. But, having no intention of powering through the calms, we shut the engine down after only a few minutes. On June 5, we began to navigate through the doldrums as sailors had for centuries, by patiently enduring the calms and promptly snatching the fickle winds from passing squalls. Shortly after entering the doldrums, we discovered that our 12-volt lead acid batteries were both dead.

Louis and I expectantly cranked the engine by hand. Usually hand-cranking worked instantly. But this time, all efforts proved futile. Barely one week into our month-long passage, *Rhiannon* was yet again without her engine. And this time, she was also without electricity. We no longer had electric lights, a VHF radio, or a depth sounder. Nevertheless, Louis and I carried on routinely, unfazed by the loss of these superfluous devices. Oddly enough, we actually felt relieved by the imposed simplicity of sailing with neither an engine nor batteries.

The doldrums

Nonetheless, the next segment of our voyage, trapped in the doldrums, totally at the mercy of the elements, became an excursion into an alien world. The doldrums lived up to their infamous reputation, unleashing insidious torture upon us for days on end. It might seem to the uninitiated that floating in the tropical sun on a calm day would create a relaxing holiday atmosphere. That could not be any farther from the reality of our experience. First, the blinding intensity of the scorching equatorial sun was magnified by reflections off the ocean's surface from all sides. Secondly, the immense rolling swells, emanating from multiple directions at once, created a vista comparable to drifting dunes in an infinite desert.

But isolation in a virtual desert was not the main issue in the doldrums. As we baked in the sweltering heat, bobbing on the glassy sea, the boat would begin to roll with the swell. At first the amplitude of rolling was small, with minimal movements to port and starboard. Then, with each pendulum swing of the mast, the excursions became greater and more extreme. As the rolling reached a crescendo, the natural period of the boat would resonate with the period of the swells, creating a violent whiplash more powerful than the surge from a gale.

For us, nature's relentless repetitive pattern — minute after minute — hour after hour — day after day — was as agonizing as any punishment devised by man. The rapid rolling would cause any object not securely fastened, lashed, or wedged in place to shift noisily or fly about inside the cabin. Shackles, bolts, and other fittings readily failed from the repetitive shock loading and the insidious chafe while we remained trapped in this evil zone. Internal halyards clanged incessantly.

Louis and I longed to modulate the motion in any way possible. Hoisting the mainsail could dampen the roll. However, unavoidable slatting would flog even the strongest sail to shreds within minutes. With no headway and no steerage, there was no easy escape.

Amid the smooth hills and valleys, continuously undulating in random patterns, we welcomed occasional visitors. As I looked over the side, hanging on with one hand so as not to be flung overboard, I watched various fish finding shelter in *Rhiannon*'s shadow. For two days, I observed one black trigger fish that never ventured more than a foot or two away from the boat. I told Louis that I would catch this fish, using a small hook. He said, "No way!"

I dangled the hook over the side and jiggled it so that the bright sun would glint off the shiny metal. The triggerfish swam out to examine the bare hook many times over the course of an hour. I then put a little piece of canned "Irish stew" onto the hook. The fish bit! I quickly flipped it into the cockpit, much to Louis's surprise.

We filleted the fish, but then decided not to eat it. There was a possibility that the fish could be carrying ciguatera toxin (fish poisoning) picked up at an atoll. We threw the cut-up pieces of fish back over the side, attracting many more fish to entertain us. These mindless, time consuming activities provided amusing diversions for us.

The triggerfish in the doldrums

One day as we wallowed in the doldrums, an exceptionally large pod of dolphins arrived. We had been accustomed to seeing dolphins energetically pacing *Rhiannon* during periods of boisterous sailing. This time their behavior was quite different. This group of about 30 dolphins stopped just off the bow. They slowly drifted in circles, floating on the surface. Next, several of them turned their attention toward one individual dolphin that appeared to need help reaching the surface to breathe.

During this display, they continuously produced eerie, plaintive calls, audible through *Rhiannon*'s hull. We speculated that perhaps one of them was ill or perhaps a newborn dolphin needed assistance. Even through binoculars, we could not see enough to understand what the fascinating behavior represented. It remained an unsolved mystery to us.

While we were becalmed in the doldrums, the equatorial countercurrent fortuitously pushed us eastward at about one knot. We appreciated the easting as one of the few bonuses of being in the ITCZ. Exiting the doldrums farther east would provide us a more comfortable point of sail when we eventually turned toward Hawaii, in the NE trades.

The sky was generally clear with occasional cirrus clouds developing each day. Zephyrs of wind revealed by cats' paws on the surface of the swells would prompt us to scramble to raise some sail. An occasional rain squall would develop, providing cool drinking water and a refreshing shower. Some squalls brought with them light usable wind; others brought temporarily overpowering gusts. Louis and I did our best to milk as much mileage as possible out of every type of wind we encountered.

As we neared the NE trade belt, the swells emanated more uniformly from the east. The light east wind gradually became more consistent. We were finally beginning to escape the doldrums. On June 10, in a moderate NE wind, the mainsail suddenly ripped all the way from the tack to the clew, along the foot, just above the boom. We were loath to keep the mainsail down for the time required to hand-stitch a repair. We tied in the first shallow flattening reef, which we had never used. This minimally shortened mainsail configuration concealed the tear and became our full main for the duration of the passage.

For several days, the wind varied between dead calm and moderate easterlies, sometimes from the NE and sometimes from the SE. We passed through an immense garbage patch of floating debris trapped in a localized gyre. The flotsam extended for miles. Bits of Styrofoam, barnacle-encrusted boat fenders, and colorful glass fishnet floats were scattered about.

Eventually, flying fish, petrels, and friendly cumulus clouds signaled our definitive entry into the NE trade winds. On June 20, after 15 days in the doldrums, Louis noted in the ship's log: "NE trades are here. Waves breaking over side." Our path was never within striking distance of the Marquesas. Though we had reached the longitude of Nuku Hiva before turning northward, by then we were more than 700 NM away. Beam reaching across the NE trades became our new existence. The doldrums had been a trial of one sort. This quickly became another.

Rhiannon stayed on starboard tack, heeled to port, as we sailed primarily under double-reefed main and working jib for days on end. The trade winds blew reliably between 10 and 25 knots day and night. Occasionally, we hanked on the storm jib in preparation for a windier night. No matter what sail combination we chose, *Rhiannon* charged onward. Louis and I just hung on for the ride. With the wind on the beam, each wave would roll the boat vigorously, demanding that we brace ourselves continuously. Every few minutes a breaking wave would crash against the hull, launching a shower of salty spray into the cockpit.

Louis and I rigged a canvas barrier along the starboard lifeline. It only helped a little. The ride was rough. Simply sitting upright required a fatiguing workout of core muscles. It was challenging to take sextant sights with the spray and the vigorous constant motion. Sitting in the cabin to reduce the sights was an even more arduous task. We would complete our calculations as quickly as possible to get back up on deck. Doing arithmetic, while propped behind a severely listing table and juggling the *Nautical Almanac,* required considerable dexterity and concentration.

As George steered *Rhiannon* flawlessly through the NE trades, Louis and I maintained complementary sleep schedules. We were both awake for dinner and for navigation sessions mid-morning and around local noon. Otherwise, we basically kept to ourselves. We were rarely on deck or in the cabin together, except when we both slept at night.

Looking to windward in the Northeast Trades

We did not bother with running lights while far from land. Lighting the kerosene running lights in the cabin and bringing them forward on the heeled rolling deck, in the spray, was hazardous. We did not see the point of doing it. Our tiny boat felt invisible, low in the water, deep within the troughs of the Pacific swells. We always flew a radar reflector high in the rigging. We never saw a ship. However, there certainly might have been a vessel that passed unseen, as I rarely wore my glasses. The salt spray on the lenses would blind me even more than my severe myopia.

I gained considerable weight during this passage. *Rhiannon* had no scale to document it, but I watched my belly grow noticeably larger. Our abundant food stores were highly caloric. Sitting alone, wedged into the leeward corner of the cockpit with my back against the cabin bulkhead, was monotonous. Facing aft seeing the great waves marching toward us while marveling at George's timely mechanical reactions became hypnotic. Eating was often the only other thing to do.

I made myself ultra-rich chocolate milk drinks by mixing sweetened condensed milk with cocoa powder and water. I ate way too many cans of peaches packed in sugary syrup. I frequently used the winch handle or the genoa track to crack open one of the eating coconuts supplied by a friend in Bora Bora. Their dry nutty meat reminded me of the islands.

Louis and I still had abundant reserves of canned New Zealand sheep's tongues and salty Fijian corned beef to eat for dinner. Both these canned meats had flavors very reminiscent of corned beef or tongue sandwiches served at Jewish delicatessens back home. No, I did not have a healthy diet on this sail. But the food I ate was both filling and comforting.

Louis and I followed our incremental progress toward the Hawaiian Islands, plotting our daily positions on the large Pacific Ocean chart. The miles steadily ticked off in the NE trades. On our best days, we managed respectable daily runs of 153 NM, 152 NM, and 133 NM, without any assisting current. Sadly, I realized that I would miss the weddings of two of my best friends from college, as we continued our voyage, far out at sea. The beautiful sunsets took on a melancholy aspect. Though many days of vigilant sailing fraught with unknown obstacles remained, the end of our journey was near.

Louis and I did not openly share our feelings about the imminent conclusion of our cruise. Sitting together in the cockpit eating dinner at dusk, we generally limited discussion to the practical business of managing *Rhiannon*. However, from time to time, novel observations concerning the sea state, the sky, or the pelagic birds would dominate our interchanges as we ate.

Each day, I listened to the Pacific Ocean storm forecast on WWVH. The closer we came to Hawaii, without impending cyclones, the less likely it became that we would face severe weather. By chance, 1977 turned out to be a record quiet year for eastern Pacific hurricanes.

Despite our opposite sleeping schedules, I found that confinement with Louis became tiresome, especially during the hard-driving slog through the windy segment of our passage. We spoke progressively less to one another with each successive day. Although we never quarreled, we kept to ourselves most of the time. On this long passage, time lost meaning. Days seemed to fuse together into a seamless continuum. I have little recollection of individual days. But rather I recall the endless days of constant rolling with the beam seas that defined our passage through time and space.

On June 26, exactly 28 days out of Bora Bora, our celestial fix placed us 100 NM east of the summits of Mauna Loa and Mauna Kea on the big island of Hawaii. It was a gorgeous day. The trade winds had moderated to 10 knots from the SE and the seas were calm. Friendly trade wind cumulus clouds dotted the sky. Gazing westward through the haze (with our glasses on), Louis and I saw the distinctive silhouettes of Hawaii's massive volcanos looming on the western horizon. It was breathtakingly awesome!

Louis on the foredeck with two days to go. The jib and spinnaker are both flying.

Our moods soared. Our spirits were completely renewed. The combination of sighting land and sailing in exceptional conditions was glorious. Dolphins arrived to cheer us on. At that moment, I could easily imagine the elation of the ancient Polynesians who first discovered Hawaii on their incredible ocean voyages.

For the first time during this leg, we were sailing comfortably downwind. We hoisted the red and white spinnaker. We brought out our camera. We had neglected to take any other photographs at all since leaving Bora Bora. Until dusk, *Rhiannon* flew her chute, as George faithfully steered us toward Honolulu, still two days distant.

From then on, we stayed within sight of land. We began again to light the kerosene running lights as the sun went down. We resumed formal night watches. The night was filled with stars, as a gibbous moon hung in the sky. The fair weather continued into the next day, with 15- to 20-knot daytime winds ensuring good progress. We began to plan our approach. At noon on June 26, *Rhiannon* was 105 NM from Ala Wai Boat Harbor in Honolulu.

That day we sailed along the northern coast of Molokai. Kalaupapa boasts the tallest sea cliffs in the world. The spectacular furrowed green cliff faces, which protect the flat peninsula housing a famous leper colony, towered over us. Skirting the coast, we began to see inter-island barges and other shipping traffic.

As the afternoon passed, we fell into the shadow of the mountains. Our wind began to die. The Molokai Channel (Ka'iwi Channel) between Molokai and Oahu has a reputation for steep waves and funneling east winds. Louis and I mentally prepared ourselves for this last boisterous run through potentially tall breaking seas.

We were completely surprised when the wind died off to under 10 knots at dusk, just as we passed the northwest point on Molokai. We raised the 175% genoa and poled it out to sail wing-on-wing down the 25 NM channel. A balmy night breeze, uncharacteristically flat water, and guiding lights on shore produced a fantastic final night at sea. The westbound current smoothly flushed us through the channel toward Oahu.

Louis wrote in the ship's log:

Koko Head about 5 miles ahead—Diamond Head another 7 miles and Ala Wai Yacht Basin 2 miles further. FANTASTIC CURRENT all night going with us! One of the best nights of sailing of the trip under main and 175, wing-on-wing. A great end to the trip of a lifetime.

Still in light wind at dawn on our 30th day at sea, Louis and I sat together in *Rhiannon*'s cockpit as we reached along, past Koko Head and Diamond Head, toward Waikiki. The high-rise buildings, the traffic on shore, and the people on the beach provoked an indescribable culture shock. I was daunted by the prospect of finally stepping off the boat that had been my home and protective cocoon for so long.

Approaching Oahu on the final morning

We had arrived in Honolulu. One final obstacle yet remained. Without an engine, we needed to enter the narrow channel just north of the Waikiki surf to get into Ala Wai Harbor. We raised our code "Q" flag. *Rhiannon* close-reached at a snail's pace into the channel on barely five knots of wind. Louis and I were uncertain whether the breeze would be sufficient to keep us moving without drifting out of the channel. Gradually we inched forward. Eventually, we tied up safely inside the harbor, at the end of the long pier, directly in front of the Hawaii Yacht Club.

Less than two weeks later, the ULDB *Merlin* tied up in the exact same spot, after winning the Transpac Race with a record-shattering time that stood for 20 years. The day after we landed, our friends from *Starduster*, the CT 54 we had met in the Marquesas six months earlier, spotted us. They helped us tow *Rhiannon* to a transient slip in the marina with their dinghy. A few days later, I left Louis in Honolulu and flew back to the Midwest to begin medical school.

Louis felt abandoned. I had left him behind with the arduous tasks of restoring *Rhiannon* to a presentable condition, finding her a safe long-term mooring, and putting her up for sale. I truly felt guilty about leaving him. But I felt that I had no choice. I was now working on a fixed schedule, with timetables and deadlines.

Returning home, I found myself in a prolonged stupor-like daze. I was daunted by the reality of rejoining society and dealing with people. I was filled with regret and mad at myself for simply returning to a predictable life.

A few days later, while wandering alone down Michigan Avenue in downtown Chicago, I encountered Tristan Jones, surrounded by a crowd on the sidewalk. Tristan Jones was a colorful, eccentric, single-handed sailor, who authored several books recounting his exploits. He had come to Chicago to promote his most recent book, about transporting his boat from the sea, over the Andes Mountains, and across South America. I walked up to him on the sidewalk in front of the Wrigley building. Uncharacteristically, I angrily challenged him, "Why are you here, and not 'out there'!?" He appropriately brushed me aside and ignored my question. As I turned to walk away, I realized that, in truth, I was asking that question of myself. To this day, I still search for the answer.

Epilogue

The oceans have always aroused my curiosity. Sailing has always challenged me to harness the raw forces of nature to reach distant shores. Sadly, technology has advanced to the point that complex sailing machines can now navigate autonomously. The era of crossing oceans in simple harmony with the wind, water, and sky, without electronic devices or outside assistance, has passed. The skills of self-sufficiency at sea have largely been lost.

Mankind has polluted the water, depleted marine life, and altered the environment of our planet. However, compared to the continents, the oceans have changed little. We must remember that we will never become masters of the sea. Long after mankind is gone the sea will endure.

The sea is strange and alien to man. It is cruel. It is beautiful. Our relationship to it is in the nature of a contest in which the greatest satisfaction comes with using its winds and forces to the greatest advantage, driving your ship to its maximum ability ... The sea is for action: cresting white foam at the bow, racing wake astern. But the sea only accepts our small audacious craft on sufferance, and at a price. There are times on a long voyage when you swear you will never do it again. You long for port, although at the very end when there is the perverse desire to delay entering the harbor, you are never quite sure whether it is in order to savor to the utmost the delight of landfall, or whether it is regret that the voyage is done: that you are leaving behind the heave and freedom of the open sea, the eddying phosphorescence at night, the dawn watch ... but underneath it all you know, if only subconsciously, that what is troubling you is that your goal has been achieved and is gone. (From *Return to the Sea, by* William Albert Robinson, 1972, published by John de Graff, Inc., p.206)

Acknowledgements

This is the first book I have written. I have learned much through the process of writing and editing my manuscript. I now have a better understanding of using hyphenated words and active voice. However, comma usage remains an enigma. I am indebted to those who have assisted me in the process.

I thank my wife Laurie, Lei Ann Marshall, and Ellen Skolnik for their helpful editing suggestions, Beth Shadur for creating the hand-drawn maps, and Euan Monaghan for designing the interior layout. I am also grateful to Anna Etlinger, Liz Clark, and my sister Anne for encouraging me to complete this book (which I began writing decades ago). Of course, the story could not have been written without my partners in the adventure, Louis Gordon and Clark Pellett.

Glossary

Note: These definitions represent my intended meanings of terms, as used within this book. There may be other definitions of these terms when used elsewhere.

Abeam- on a line at right angles to a boat's length.

Aft- at, near, or toward the stern (rear part) of a vessel.

Afterguy- a line used to stabilize a whisker pole or spinnaker pole to prevent it from swinging forward and upward.

Airplane dope- (see Dope)

Albacore- the name of a 15-foot, centerboard one-design sailboat class with a planing hull form. It was designed by Uffa Fox in 1954.

Aloft- up the mast or into the rigging.

Amidships- in or toward the center of a boat with respect to the bow and stern, or along the line of the keel

Aries wind vane- a type of self-steering wind vane for sailboats.

Astern- toward the stern (rear part) of a vessel or aft of (behind) a vessel.

Atoll- a ring-shaped reef, island, or chain of islands formed of coral.

Baggywrinkles- protective gear made from frayed out rope and used on a sailboat or ship's rigging to prevent chafing.

Bascule bridge- a type of opening bridge with a pivoting section that is raised and lowered using counterweights.

Beam- 1. a boat's breadth at her widest point; 2. a horizontal piece of squared timber or metal supporting the deck and joining the sides of a ship; 3. the direction of an object visible from the port or starboard side of a ship when it is perpendicular to the center line of the vessel.

Beam-ends- (onto her beam-ends) (of a boat) inclined so much on one side that the beams approach a vertical position.

Beam reach- a point of sail with the wind coming over a boat's beam (perpendicular to the center line of the vessel).

Bearing- the direction or position of something, or the direction of movement, relative to a fixed point. It is usually measured in degrees, typically with magnetic north as zero.

Beat- (v.) to sail into the wind as directly as a boat is able.

Bifid thumb- a congenitally duplicated thumb, sometimes appearing as a forked digit.

Bilge- the lowest internal portion of the hull of a boat.

Bimini- a lightweight cover over a boat's cockpit, usually made of cloth fabric stretched over a metal frame.

Block- the housing of a pulley, sometimes simply used to refer to a pulley.

Bollard- a short, thick post on the deck of a ship or on a wharf, to which a vessel's rope may be secured.

Bolt rope- a rope sewn around the edge of a sail to prevent tearing.

Boom- a spar pivoting on the after side of the mast and to which the foot of a vessel's sail is attached, allowing the angle of the sail to be changed.

Boom vang- a line or system on a sailboat used to exert downward force on the boom and thus control the shape of the sail.

Boulanger- (French) baker

Bow- the forward end of a boat.

Brigantine- (in modern terminology) a vessel with the foremast square-rigged and the main mast fore-and-aft rigged.

Broach- a sudden or hazardous veering or pitching of a boat.

Broad reach- a point of sail with the wind coming from the aft quarter of the boat (between a beam reach and a run.)

Burgee- a triangular flag bearing the colors or emblem of a sailing club.

C Class Catamaran- a particular class of high-speed catamarans of open design within a specific rule of limiting parameters.

Cabin trunk- the deck structure on a sailboat rising above deck level that covers the cabin.

Cal 2-30- a 30-foot-long production fiberglass sailboat model built in the 1960s by Jensen Marine (see Appendix 3).

Cal 40- a 40-foot-long production fiberglass sailboat model built in the 1960s by Jensen Marine known as a popular racing sailboat and legendary for her performance in Transpac races.

Cal Cruising 46- a 46-foot-long sailboat model built by Jensen Marine in the 1960s specifically for cruising.

Capsize- (v.) to overturn in the water (used to describe the action of a boat).

Careen- (v.) to tilt a ship or boat on her side for cleaning, caulking, or repair (usually performed during a low tide).

Cat's paws- irregular patches of small ripples on smooth water indicative of scattered areas of light wind.

Catamaran- a boat with two parallel hulls of the same length joined by a rigid structure.

Celestial navigation- the action of finding one's way by observing celestial bodies (the sun, moon, stars, and planets).

Centerboard- a pivoted board that can be lowered through the keel or midline of a sailboat, used to prevent sideward motion (leeway).

Chamber- the enclosed space within the lock of a canal.

Chart- a map used aboard a boat for navigation.

Chronometer- an accurate timepiece, suitable for use aboard a vessel at sea in conjunction with celestial navigation.

Chute- an informal name for a spinnaker.

Class- a grouping of sailboats conforming to the same design or design rule to facilitate races between similar boats.

Clearing-in- the process of obtaining official permission for a vessel to have dealings with a port or for her crew to go ashore.

Clevis pin- a type of fastener that allows rotation of the connected parts about the axis of the pin. A clevis pin consists of a head, shank, and hole. The hole passes through the shank at the opposite end of the pin from the head. A cotter pin through the hole keeps the clevis pin in place.

Clew- the lower or after corner of a sail to which a sheet is attached.

Close hauled- a point of sail with the boat directed to make optimal progress into the wind (beating).

Coachroof- a raised part of the cabin roof of a yacht

Coaming- a raised border around the cockpit or hatch of a boat to keep out water.

Cockpit- a sunken area in the after deck or mid deck of a boat providing space for crew members.

Companionway- a set of steps or ladder leading from a ship's deck down to a cabin.

Con- (v.) to direct the steering of a vessel.

Convergence zone- a location where differing airflows meet, characteristically marked by upwelling of air (e.g., a sea breeze meeting a land breeze, or two trade wind belts meeting)

Copra- the dried coconut meat from which coconut oil is extracted.

Course- the direction in which a vessel is traveling relative to the earth.

Courtesy flag- the flag of a host nation flown by a foreign vessel within the host nation's waters. A sailboat typically flies this flag just beneath the starboard lower spreader of the mainmast.

CQ- a radio call used at the beginning of messages of general information or safety notices.

CQR- one type of plow anchor with a pivoting shank commonly used on sailboats.

Cumbia- a kind of dance music of Colombian origin, similar to salsa.

Cumulonimbus- a rain cloud with a flat base forming a towering mass, often seen in a thunderstorm.

Cutter- a boat normally sailed with a mainsail and two foresails.

Cyclone- a system of winds rotating inward to an area of low atmospheric pressure, with a counterclockwise (northern hemisphere) or clockwise (southern hemisphere) circulation; a depression.

Danforth anchor- one type of anchor designed with two triangular flukes. This is best known for its holding power in hard sand bottoms.

Daysail- a sailboat outing completed on a single day.

Dead reckoning- the process of calculating one's position by estimating the direction and distance traveled from a known position rather than by using landmarks, celestial observations, or electronic navigation methods. This is usually accomplished by drawing a line upon a chart accounting for the estimated direction and distance traveled from a previous fix.

Deck house- the deck structure on a sailboat rising above deck level that covers the cabin.

Depth sounder- a device for determining the depth of the seabed by measuring the time taken for sound echoes to return to the surface.

Deviation- the deflection of a vessel's compass needle from the vessel's actual magnetic heading, caused by iron in the vessel. Deviation varies with the vessel's heading.

Deviation table- a list of the amount of deviation of a particular compass at specified headings.

Dinghy- a small boat (often a rowboat, an inflatable tender or small sailboat).

Dismast- v. the action of a sailboat losing her mast.

Displacement- the weight of water displaced by a vessel (i.e., the weight of a boat)

Dock line- a rope securing a boat to a dock.

Doldrums- 1. an equatorial region of the ocean with calms, sudden storms, and light unpredictable winds often found within the inter-tropical convergence zone; 2. a state or period of inactivity, stagnation, or depression.

Dope- a thick varnish applied to the fabric surface of aircraft to strengthen them and make them airtight. This was commonly used in early airplane construction.

Double reef- (v.) to reduce the working area of a sail by furling a portion of the sail to the second available position (less sail area remains than with a single reef, more than with a triple reef).

Double-ended- a boat having a stern that resembles her bow.

Downwind- a direction generally away from the wind.

Drag anchor- (v.) to drift due to an anchor's loss of holding power.

Drift- movement in the water along with the current.

El Niño- an irregularly occurring and complex series of climatic changes affecting the equatorial Pacific region and beyond every few years, characterized by the appearance of unusually warm, nutrient-poor water off northern Peru and Ecuador, typically in late December.

Elephantiasis- a condition in which a limb or other part of the body becomes grossly enlarged due to obstruction of the lymphatic vessels, typically by the nematode parasites which cause filariasis.

EPIRB- (Emergency Position Indicating Radio Beacon) a transmitter used to broadcast a localizing distress signal from a vessel in an emergency.

Fall off- (v.) (of a sailboat) to alter course away from the wind.

Fantail- the rounded overhanging part of the stern of a vessel.

Fin keel- a boat's keel shaped like the inverted dorsal fin of a fish or cetacean.

Fix- an exact location obtained by visual bearings, celestial observations, or electronic navigational devices.

Foot- the lower edge of a sail.

Fore-and-aft rigged- (used to describe a sailing vessel) that mainly has sails that are set along the line of the keel instead of perpendicular to it.

Foredeck- the portion of the boat's deck forward of the mast.

Foreguy- a line used to stabilize a whisker pole or spinnaker pole to prevent it from swinging aft and upward.

Forehatch- the most forward opening from a boat's cabin leading up to the deck.

Forepeak- the forwardmost compartment of a boat's hull.

Foresail- a general term for sails carried forward of the mast or the principal sail on the foremast of a vessel with multiple masts.

Forestay- the most forward part of the standing rigging of a sailboat leading from the mast to the bow. The forestay helps to support the mast.

Forward- toward the front (bow) of the boat.

Full keel- a boat's keel that extends along most of the underwater length of the hull, as distinct from a fin keel.

Furl- (v.) to roll or fold up and secure neatly.

Gaff- 1. A spar to which the head of a for-and-aft sail is attached. 2. A stick with a large hook for landing a big fish.

Gaff-rigged- (used to describe a sailboat) with a spar to which the head of a fore-and-aft sail is attached.

Gale- a wind of force 7 to 10 on the Beaufort scale (28-55 knots).

Galley- the kitchen or food preparation area aboard a boat.

Gendarmerie- (French) police station.

Genoa jib- a large jib or foresail whose foot extends aft of the mast.

Ghost- (v.) to sail slowly and quietly in a light wind.

Gibbous- (of the moon) having the observable illuminated part greater than a semicircle and less than a circle.

Gimbals- a mechanism for keeping an object such as a compass or a ship's stove horizontal in a moving vessel.

Gooseneck barnacles- stalked barnacles that live tenaciously attached to hard surfaces including boat bottoms.

Great circle- circle on the surface of a sphere which lies in a plane passing through the sphere's center. As it represents the shortest distance between any two points on a sphere, a great circle of the earth is the preferred route taken by a ship.

Grommet- an eyelet placed in a hole in cloth or a panel to protect or insulate a rope or cable passed through it in order to prevent the cloth or panel from being torn.

Gybe- (v.) The action of turning a sailboat's stern through the wind from port to starboard tack or vice versa.

Gyre- a circular pattern of currents in an ocean basin.

H.O. 249- one of several specific published books of tables, used to determine the position of celestial bodies when performing celestial navigation calculations.

Halyard- a rope or wire used to hoist a sail, flag, or other object up a mast.

Hank- a small clip, shackle, or similar device used to secure a sail (usually a jib) along the length of a stay.

Head- 1. The toilet aboard a boat; 2. The upper corner of a triangular sail; 3. The top of a mast (masthead).

Head rig- the configuration of a sailboat's rigging including a forestay leading to the masthead; or if a fractional head rig (e.g. 7/8 head rig), with a forestay attached to a point at that fraction of the total mast height from the deck.

Heading- the direction toward which the bow of a vessel is pointed.

Head up - (v.) (of a sailboat) to alter course toward the wind.

Headsail- a jib or sail attached to the forestay.

Heave- (v.) 1. Rise and fall (movement of a vessel along the vertical axis); 2. To pull, move, or raise by hauling on a rope; 3. To throw.

Heave to- (v.) to bring a sailboat to a slowly drifting "stop" usually by turning across the wind leaving the headsail backed.

Heaving line- a small line with an added weight used to throw a larger line such as a messenger line.

Heel- (v.) (describes the action of a sailboat) to be tilted toward one side temporarily by the pressure of wind or by an uneven distribution of weight on board.

Helm- a tiller, wheel, or any associated equipment for steering a boat or ship.

Hook- an informal word meaning "anchor".

Hove to- (v.) past tense of "heave to"

Hull- the main body of a ship or other vessel, including the bottom, sides, and deck but not the masts, superstructure, rigging, engines, and other fittings.

Hurricane- a named tropical cyclone that occurs in the Atlantic Ocean and northeastern Pacific Ocean with sustained winds greater than 64 knots.

Hurricane hole- a protected location where boats may find shelter from a major storm.

Hydrofoil- hydrodynamically shaped vanes or appendages (foils) that can lift a vessel clear of the water, permitting increased speed due to decreased drag.

Hydrofoil sailboat- a wind driven vessel with a hull that may be lifted above the surface of the water by hydrofoils.

Îles Sous le Vent- the Leeward islands in the Society Islands of French Polynesia.

Islander 44- a 44-foot-long production fiberglass sloop built by Islander Yachts

in the 1960s and 1970s with a good reputation as a live aboard cruiser.

Islas Encantadas- (Spanish meaning "enchanted islands"), a name for the Galapagos Islands long used by sailors and whalers.

Jib- a triangular staysail set forward of the mast.

Jib sheet- a control line on a sailboat used to trim (adjust the set of) a jib.

Katabatic wind- a *wind* that carries high-density air from a higher elevation down a slope under the force of gravity.

Kedge- 1.a small anchor used to reposition a boat by having the anchor's rode hauled in; 2. (v.) To haul in the rode of an anchor specifically to reposition a boat (often performed to free a grounded vessel).

Keel boat- a sailboat with a fixed, immovable keel.

Keel- the longitudinal structure along the centerline at the bottom of a vessel's hull. In some vessels the keel extends downward as a ridge or fin to increase stability and prevent sideways motion (leeway).

Ketch- a two-masted sailboat with a mizzenmast stepped forward of the rudder. The mizzenmast on a ketch is shorter than the more forward located mainmast.

Knot- a velocity of one nautical mile per hour.

La Niña- a cooling of the water in the equatorial Pacific, which occurs at irregular intervals, and is associated with widespread changes in weather patterns complementary to those of El Niño, but less extensive and damaging in their effects.

Lash- (v.) to fasten (something) securely with a cord or rope

Latitude- the angular distance measured in degrees, minutes, and seconds, of a place north or south of the earth's equator.

Launch- a motorboat used especially for short trips.

Lazarette- a small compartment below the deck in the after end of a boat, usually used for storage.

Leadline- a sounding line used to manually measure water depth, usually consisting of a lead weight on a rope that is marked to indicate depths. Soft wax or grease may be inserted in the bottom of the lead weight in order to pick up a sample of the sea floor to determine its composition.

Leeway- sideways motion or slipping of a sailboat.

Lifelines- a rope or cable strung between stanchions to help prevent people from falling overboard.

Lift- a line supporting a whisker pole, spinnaker pole or boom to prevent the outboard end from dropping down.

Lighter- a flat-bottomed barge or other unpowered boat used to transfer cargo to and from ships in harbor.

Line- a length of cord, rope, wire, or other material serving a particular purpose.

Lock- a short confined section of a canal or other waterway in which the water level can be changed using gates and sluices. A lock is used for raising and lowering vessels between two gates.

Longboat- an open boat carried aboard old-time sailing ships, to be rowed by eight or ten oarsmen seated two abreast.

Longitude- the angular distance of a place east or west of the meridian at Greenwich, England usually expressed in degrees, minutes, and seconds.

Low aspect- a low height to width ratio.

Luff- 1. the leading edge of sail; 2. (v.) (for a sail) to flutter or spill the wind 3. (v.) to turn a boat toward head to wind.

Main halyard- a rope or wire used to hoist the mainsail.

Main- the mainsail.

Mainsail- 1. the principal sail of a sailing vessel; 2. the sail set on the after side of the mainmast in a fore-and-aft-rigged vessel.

Mainsail slide- a small fitting used to secure the luff (leading edge) of the mainsail to a track running along the after side of the main mast.

Mainsheet- a control line on a sailboat used to trim (adjust the set of) a mainsail.

Mast- a tall upright spar on a sailboat used for carrying sails.

Mast step- the structure upon which the foot of a sailboat mast is mounted.

Med mooring- (Mediterranean mooring) a hybrid of anchoring and docking in which boats tie up stern-to or bow-to a pier, wall, or quay with an anchor or fixed mooring secured to the opposite end of the boat in order to hold the vessel off the dock.

Messenger line- a lightweight rope often used along with a heaving line to pull a larger rope or hawser between vessels or between a vessel and shore.

Mizzen mast- the after mast of a sailboat having two masts where the second one is shorter, such as on a ketch or yawl.

Monkey's fist- a type of knot, so named because it looks somewhat like a small bunched *fist*. It is tied at the end of a rope to serve as a weight, making it easier to throw.

Moonbow- (also known as a lunar rainbow or white rainbow) is a rainbow produced by moonlight rather than direct sunlight.

Mooring- a place where a boat is made fast by attaching it by cable or rope to the shore, to an anchor, or to a fixed object.

Morgan 41- a 41-foot-long sailboat model designed by Charley Morgan, built by Morgan Yachts in the 1960s and 1970s.

Morgan Out-Island 41- a 41-foot-long center cockpit sailboat model designed by Charley Morgan, built by Morgan Yachts intended for cruising or charter.

Moth- a small development class of racing dinghy of open design within specific rules limiting the design parameters (known as International Moth Class).

Motorsailer- a hybrid yacht designed with nearly equal consideration to use under sail and under power.

Motu- (Tahitian) an islet on a reef, usually with vegetation.

Nautical almanac- an annual publication describing the positions of a selection of celestial bodies for use in celestial navigation.

Nautical mile (NM)- a unit used in measuring distances at sea, equal to one minute

(1/60 degree) of latitude, approximately 6076 feet, 1852 meters, and 1.1508 statute miles.

Navigation protractor triangles- plastic triangles with small handles, often used in pairs, to assist in navigational plotting upon a nautical chart.

Navigation- the process or activity of accurately ascertaining one's position and planning and following a route.

Offshore- at sea beyond sight of land.

Off the wind- in a direction away from the wind or across the wind (in contrast to beating upwind which is sometimes termed "on the wind.")

On the hard- an informal expression referring to a boat that is in dry-dock or hauled out on dry land.

Outrigger- 1. a float or secondary hull fixed parallel to a canoe or other boat to stabilize it. 2. a canoe or small boat fitted with an outrigger.

Painter- a rope or cord used to secure or tow a dinghy.

Palapa- a traditional Mexican shelter roofed with palm leaves or branches.

Pandanus- a genus of monocot, palm-like plant (unrelated to palms). Leaves are frequently woven or used in other handicrafts.

Parachute flare- a flare that is fired into the air by a rocket to float suspended from a small parachute.

Pelorus- a sighting device on a ship for taking the relative bearings of a distant object.

Pennant- a cable or rope attached to the head or tack of a sail.

Pilot- a guide who boards a vessel to direct it through a canal, harbor, or waterway.

Pilot chart- a chart depicting averages in prevailing winds, currents, gales, and other environmental parameters for each sector of an ocean for each month of the year.

Pirogue- (French) a long, narrow canoe made from a single tree trunk. In the south Pacific these are often outriggers.

Pitch- oscillation or movement of a vessel around a horizontal axis perpendicular to the direction of motion.

Plotting sheet- a Universal Plotting sheet is a preprinted page with a graduated circle printed at the center allowing meridians of longitude to be constructed for any latitude. It allows you to create a custom-made chart for any geographical position.

Point higher or Point up- (v.) to direct the boat closer to head to wind.

Poisson cru- (French) literally meaning "raw fish," (*ia-ota* in Tahitian) generally considered the national dish of French Polynesia.

Poop- (v.) (of a wave) to break over the stern of a vessel.

Port- 1. On a boat, the left side as one faces forward; 2. A harbor or city associated with a harbor.

Port of convenience- (also called "flag of convenience") a business practice whereby a ship's owners register a merchant ship in a ship registry of a country other than that of the ship's owners for regulatory or financial reasons (e.g. more favorable taxation).

Port tack- A sailboat is said to be "on port tack" whenever the wind is coming from her port side. (In right of way rules this is when the main boom is carried on the starboard side.)

Pratique- permission granted to a vessel to have dealings with a port or for her crew to go ashore, given after quarantine or on showing a clean bill of health.

Preventer- a line used to restrain the boom from inadvertently swinging as during a gybe.

Project boat- a boat requiring much work to attain a usable, seaworthy condition.

Pulpit- a guard rail enclosing a small area at the bow of a boat.

Quarter berth- a sleeping bunk tucked under the cockpit of a sailboat.

Radio direction finder (RDF)- a device for finding the direction or bearing to a radio source.

Ratlines- a series of small ropes fastened across a sailing vessel's shrouds like the rungs of a ladder, used for climbing the rigging.

Reach- a point of sail with the wind coming from the side of the boat distinguished from a beat (close hauled) or a run. A reach may be a close reach, beam reach, or broad reach.

Reduce- (v.) (in celestial navigation) to derive from a sextant observation the information needed to establish a line of position

Reef- 1. (v.) to shorten (reduce) the sail area of a sail by furling a portion of the sail; 2. a ridge of jagged rock, coral, or sand just above or below the surface of the sea.

Regatta- an organized event including a series of boat races.

Reverse transom- a transom that is angled from the waterline forward toward the deck.

Roadstead- a sheltered stretch of water near the shore in which ships can ride at anchor.

Rode- a rope for securing an anchor.

Roll- rotation of a vessel from side to side along her longitudinal axis.

Rounding up- (v.) the action of a sailboat turning up into the wind.

Rudder- a flat or streamlined appendage near the stern of a boat hinged vertically for steering.

Running- sailing directly or nearly directly downwind.

RVG wind vane- a type of self-steering wind vane for sailboats.

Safety harness- a body harness worn by a crew member that can be attached securely to the boat using a tether.

Sailplane- a glider used in the sport of soaring.

Schooner- a sailing ship with two or more masts, typically with the foremast smaller than the mainmast.

Scope- the length of rope and chain extended when a boat rides at anchor.

Scurvy- a disease caused by a deficiency of vitamin C, characterized by swollen bleeding gums and the opening of previously healed wounds, which particularly affected poorly nourished sailors until the end of the 18th century.

Self-steering wind vane- a wind driven mechanism used to automatically maintain the course of a sailboat.

Set- 1. the direction or course of a tide or current in a body of water; 2. (v.) to deploy (used for sails, as in "to set the sails").

Sextant- an instrument with a graduated arc of 60° and a sighting mechanism, used for measuring the angular distances between objects and especially for taking altitudes in celestial navigation.

Shackle- a metal link, typically U-shaped, closed by a bolt or pin, used to secure a chain, rope, or fitting to something.

Sheave- a wheel with a groove for a rope to run on, as in a pulley block.

Sheet- a control line on a sailboat used to trim (adjust the set) of a sail.

Shorten sail- (v.) to reduce sail area by reefing, using smaller sails, or deploying fewer sails.

Shrouds- a set of ropes, cables, or rods forming part of the standing rigging of a sailboat and supporting the mast from the sides.

Signal flags- International Signal Code Flags are 39 different flags used to communicate between vessels or between a vessel and shore according to a standard published code.

Skeg- a tapering or projecting stern section of a vessel's keel, which protects the propeller and/or supports the rudder.

Skookum 47- a model of very heavy displacement full-keeled cutter, popular in the Pacific Northwest and Alaska.

Sloop- a one-masted sailboat with a fore-and-aft mainsail and a jib.

Snub- (v.) to check the movement of boat, especially by a rope wound around a cleat or post.

Sole- the sailor's term for floor (of the cabin or cockpit).

Solent- the strait that separates the Isle of Wight from the mainland of England It is an important recreational area for water sports, particularly yachting.

Soundings- measurements of the depth of a body of water.

Spade rudder- a rudder suspended beneath a sailboat that is not attached to the keel, the transom, or a skeg.

Spar- a thick, strong pole such as is used for a mast, boom, or yard on a sailing vessel.

Spinnaker- a large three-cornered sail, typically bulging when full, set when sailing downwind.

Spinnaker hourglass- a twisted spinnaker that can become fouled on the forestay.

Spring tide- a tide just after a new or full moon, when there is the greatest difference between high and low water.

Squall- a localized storm, especially one bringing rain and often sudden violent gusty wind.

Square-rigged- (of a sailing ship) having the principal sails at right angles to the length of the ship, supported by horizontal spars (called yards) attached to the mast or masts.

St. Elmo's fire- a phenomenon in which a luminous electrical discharge appears on a ship during a storm (St. Elmo is the patron saint of sailors).

Stanchion- an upright post supporting the lifelines on a boat.

Standing rigging- the fixed lines, wires, or rods, which support each mast or bowsprit on a sailing vessel and reinforce those spars against wind loads transferred from the sails.

Starboard- on a boat, the right side as one faces forward.

Starboard tack- a sailboat is said to be "on starboard tack" whenever the wind is coming from her starboard side. (In right of way rules this is when the main boom is carried on the port side).

Stern- the rearmost part of a boat or ship.

Storm jib- a small sturdily constructed jib designed to be flown in a gale.

Sumlog- a navigational instrument that records distance travelled through the water (analagous to an odometer in a car).

Surf- 1. (v.) to use the forces of gravity and buoyancy to be propelled forward upon the face of a wave; 2. Breaking waves approaching a shoreline or shoal.

Surge- 1. a sudden powerful force created by waves or a back-and-forth movement of water in a harbor created by swell; 2. (v.) to suddenly increase speed or power.

Swan 65- a 65 foot long production fiberglass sailboat model built in the 1970s by Nautor of Finland and known as a luxurious sailboat, legendary for its performance in the early Whitbread Round the World sailing races in the 1970s and 1980s.

Swing ship- the action of turning a vessel slowly in a circle to compensate compass error or create a deviation table.

Taboo- (of a place or person) prohibited or restricted based on social or religious tradition.

Tack- 1. (v.) The action of turning a sailboat through head-to-wind from port to starboard tack or vice versa (also called "coming about"); 2. (v.) to sail a zigzag course in order to make progress into the wind; 3. the lower forward corner of a sail.

Taffrail log- a traditional type of sumlog trailed astern utilizing a spinner dragged through the water.

Tamure- popularized in many 1960s recordings, it is a dance from Tahiti and the Cook Islands (and although denied by the local purists, for the rest of the world it is the most popular dance of Tahiti).

Tapa cloth- a traditional decorated bark cloth made on many islands of the South Pacific.

Tender- a boat used to ferry people and supplies to and from a larger vessel.

Tiller- a horizontal bar fitted to the head of a boat's rudder post and used as a lever for steering.

Toggle- a small fitting that permits rotation about two orthogonal axes and used in rigging as a universal joint.

Topsail schooner- a sailing vessel fore-and-aft rigged on all of two or more masts with square sails above the foresail.

Topsides- the upper part of a boat's side, above the waterline.

Transom- the flat surface forming the stern of a boat.

Traveler- a track permitting the deck attachment of a mainsheet to move athwart ship.

Travelift- a vehicle used in boatyards and marinas to lift boats from the water with straps and to move them through the boatyard.

Trim- (v.) to adjust the shape of a sail using sheets and other control lines.

Trimaran- a vessel with three hulls in parallel, typically with a larger central hull and two outer hulls called "amas."

Triple reef- (v.) to reduce the working area of a sail by furling a portion of the sail to the third available position (less working sail area remains than with a double reef).

Troll- (v.) to fish by trailing a baited line along behind a boat.

Tropical Storm- a *tropical* cyclone that has maximum sustained surface winds ranging from 34 to 63 knots.

Trough- the low point on the water's surface between adjacent waves.

Tumlaren- a type of one-design racer/cruiser keelboat designed in Scandinavia in the 1930s. (A fleet of these boats raced for many years in Chicago.)

Turnbuckle- a screw coupling used to connect lengths of boat rigging lengthwise and to regulate their length or tension.

ULDB- ultra-light displacement boat. A long narrow light displacement type of racing keelboat designed to plane and surf quickly when sailing downwind. These were first developed and popularized on the US west coast for competition in the Transpac races.

Undercanvassed- sailing with too little sail area for the available wind.

Veer- (v.) 1. (for wind) to change direction clockwise around the points of the compass; 2. (v.) (for a vessel) to change direction suddenly.

VHF/FM- (Very High Frequency/Frequency Modulation) a line-of-sight radio system commonly found aboard commercial and private vessels used for routine and emergency communication.

Wake- a trail of disturbed water left by the passage of a vessel.

Waterline- the level normally reached by the water on the side of a boat.

Waterspout- a rotating column of water and spray formed by a whirlwind occurring over a body of water.

Weather helm- a tendency for a sailboat to turn toward the wind due to an imbalance of forces caused by the wind and water.

Whisker pole- a pole used to hold out a jib when sailing downwind.

Williwaw- a sudden violent gust or squall blowing offshore from a mountainous coast; a gust of katabatic wind.

Winch- a device consisting of a drum turned by a crank (winch handle) through internal gears, used to gain mechanical advantage when hauling on a rope line.

Wind vane- (See self-steering windvane.)

Windlass- a device consisting of a drum or capstan powered by a motor or manual lever used to gain mechanical advantage when raising an anchor to the deck of a boat.

Wing-on-wing- a configuration of sails used for running downwind in which the jib and the mainsail are carried on opposite sides of the boat.

Working jib- a moderate sized all-purpose jib. (On *Rhiannon* this filled 100% of the triangle formed by the mast, the forestay and the foredeck.)

Yacht- 1.a medium sized sailing vessel used for racing or cruising. 2. a powered boat or ship equipped for cruising, usually for private or official use.

How Cruising Has Changed in the 21st Century

Since my voyage of 1976-1977, I have continued to sail. I have owned several boats and cruised regularly on Lake Michigan. I have also chartered bareboats in the Caribbean, the Aegean, and the Great Lakes. In 2015, I had the opportunity to crew aboard a 44-foot sailboat for a 3-week passage between Mexico and the Marquesas. Over the past 45 years, much has changed.

The biggest transformations are secondary to the evolution of technology. The significant developments in sail handling systems, on board electronics, worldwide weather forecasting, long distance communication, and rapid dissemination of information have contributed to a proliferation of cruising sailboats around the world. With the new technology, a long passage at sea is now much more routine than it was in 1976. In short, far more people can cross oceans under sail today.

From my perspective, the most striking advancements affecting the comfort, safety, and simplicity of voyaging under sail include the following items, which were unavailable or inaccessible in 1976:

- **The Internet**- Shared information and the wealth of resources readily available to the sailor both before departure and while at sea, have completely altered the nature of cruising. Encyclopedic advice and guidance from experienced cruisers are quickly accessible.
- **Satellite weather and world-wide weather forecast models**- Planning routes, choosing departure "windows", and knowing what conditions to expect each day are invaluable to people spending time at anchor or at sea.
- **Global Navigation Satellite Systems (GNSS)**- GPS, GLONASS and other similar navigation systems are by far the biggest game changers in encouraging orders of magnitude more people to venture offshore than when celestial navigation was essential. The ability to instantaneously know one's position, in any weather, anywhere on earth at the push of a button, facilitates navigation to previously inaccessible destinations.
- **Satellite and aerial cartography**- A bird's eye view of an anchorage,

an island, a channel, or a coastline, correlated with precise geographic localization, facilitates navigation that previously relied upon paper charts drawn from archaic surveys.

- **Worldwide satellite communication**- Satellite telephones and emergency beacons are small, portable, self-contained, waterproof, and relatively affordable compared to SSB radios, which were once the only option for long range communication. Cruisers can now call anywhere in the world from mid-ocean or remote locations ashore. This affords the possibility of rescue and the ability to obtain information readily. It allows people to conduct business and to retain important links to others while at sea.
- **Advanced marine electronics**- This is a broad category of equipment commonly found upon cruising sailboats in the 21st century. Many sailors would not even consider venturing offshore without several of these items: electronic chartplotters, AIS, digital radar, forward looking depth sounders, electronic wind instruments, anchor alarms, selective calling VHF radios, digitally tuned SSB radios, night vision scopes, cellphones, and onboard computers. Many current systems integrate multiple components using microprocessors.
- **Advanced sail handling gear**- Roller furling headsails, top down furlers for downwind sails, in mast furling, high-tech marine cordage, self-tailing winches, powered winches, and rope clutches, all facilitate sail handling.
- **Processor controlled autopilots**- Efficient direct drive automated hydraulic steering systems are now available for cruising sailboats.
- **Reverse osmosis watermakers**- Most long-distance cruisers now have these systems that were unavailable in 1976.
- **Solar panels, wind generators, and hydro-generators**- These devices now recharge storage batteries using available natural sources, without burning fuel.
- **Advanced storage batteries**- These include various types of sealed lead-acid batteries and lithium ion systems.
- **Efficient marine refrigeration**- Small boat refrigeration units are more reliable, quieter, and energy efficient than in the past facilitating food preservation on board.
- **Clothing**- High tech foul-weather gear, wearable self-inflating PFDs, and safety harnesses have all advanced.
- **Sunblock**- Early suntan lotions and sunscreens did not afford the protection of current products.
- **Cruising rallies**- World cruising rallies, pioneered by Jimmy Cornell have enabled many to cruise the world in the company of others. Rally

participation has involved many sailors who otherwise would not venture offshore.

- **Yacht friendly marinas and boatyards**- As a byproduct of the increased number of cruising sailors, many new facilities cater to sailboats for moorings, repairs, parts, and provisioning in formerly isolated regions.

APPENDIX 2

Ignorance is Bliss (or The Importance of Good Luck)

Ocean cruising in small sailboats is a risky undertaking even for the best equipped, most experienced navigator. It is impossible to fully mitigate against inaccurate weather forecasts, unforeseen illness at sea, collision with submerged flotsam, or an adverse sequence of critical gear failures. The current trend toward reliance upon electronics in the harsh marine environment poses new risks for the sailor without non-electrical contingencies as back-up. Even renowned, expert world cruisers have met disaster, unrelated to negligence or carelessness. Good fortune often marks the difference between success and failure in any endeavor.

Louis, Clark, and I survived an epic adventure, completing our intended voyage unscathed. For a myriad of reasons, over the years, I have said to myself and to Louis that we were lucky. A sailing journey is always a compromise. For us, limiting factors included our lack of ocean sailing experience, the general absence of available instructional references for cruising, a limited budget, poor weather forecasting, our lack of a long range radio transmitter, and a boat not designed for ocean voyaging. Despite our belief that we had prepared thoroughly for this trip, with experience we discovered that we had made mistakes.

We could easily have been killed, shipwrecked, imprisoned, or otherwise punished for our audacity and neglect.

- In my opinion, our biggest mistake, which we overcame purely by chance, was crossing the Gulf of Mexico, the Caribbean, French Polynesia, the Cook Islands, and the Eastern Pacific, **all** during the heights of their respective tropical cyclone seasons. During every year on record, since 1976 and 1977 at least one major storm developed somewhere along our path of over 45 years ago, on approximately the same dates as our passages.
- Another error was having a gasoline engine and carrying jerry cans of gasoline on deck through many lightning storms. The risk of fire or explosion was significant. The containers of cooking alcohol on board *Rhiannon* only compounded the fire hazard.
- Though more common in 1976 than today, our inability to communicate over long distances also posed a significant risk. In the case of a

life-threatening medical emergency or boat accident, we would have had little recourse. We did carry a life raft and a short-range, line-of-sight EPIRB. But those would have been useless in many emergency situations.

- Some of our omissions, for expediency, such as occasionally entering countries without proper documentation and sailing at night without running lights could have been extremely problematic.

I realize that not everyone can have a fully equipped ocean-going vessel and do everything strictly by the books. In truth, nobody can. There have always been and there will always be great unknowns at sea. Perhaps that is why sailors tend to be superstitious. The *Titanic* teaches us that no ship is immune to the hazards of the ocean. It is important to be lucky as well as good.

The Cal 2-30

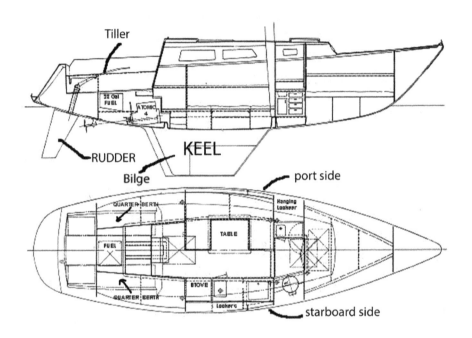

Cal 2-30 Data

Hull type: Fin with spade rudder
Rigging type: Fractional Sloop
LOA: 30.20 ft / 9.20 m
Beam: 9 ft / 2.74 m
Sail Area: 464 sq. ft. / 43.11 sq. m
Draft: 5 ft.
Displacement: 10,300 lb. / 4,672 kg
Auxiliary Power: Universal Atomic 4 (gasoline)
Construction: Fiberglass
Builder: Jensen Marine (U.S.A.)
Designer: C. William Lapworth

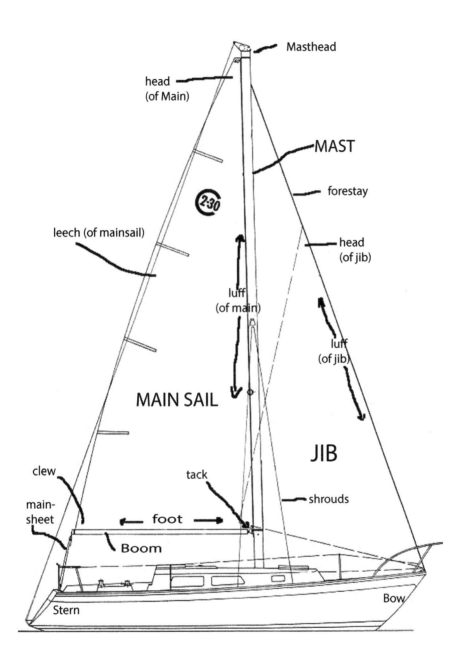

Masthead

head
(of Main)

MAST

forestay

head
(of jib)

leech (of mainsail)

luff
(of main)

luff
(of jib)

MAIN SAIL

JIB

clew

tack

main-
sheet

foot

shrouds

Boom

Stern

Bow

Checklists

<u>DAILY WATCH DUTIES</u>

CHECK CHAFE: sails, lines, fittings, etc.

CHECK SAILS: wear,bolt ropes,batten pockets,seams, hanks,slides,etc.

CHECK HALIARDS: tension, fraying,shackles

MAINTAIN COURSE AND SAIL TRIM

UPDATE LOG:1)enter course,speed,and time at every change
2)enter findings on maintenance check into maintenance
    log with time and corrective action taken or to be taken
3)at the end of the watch, enter complete weather
    conditions--temp.,wind,clouds,pressure,etc.
4)report any sightings--time,bearings(M),remarks (shore
    landmarks,ships,islands,unusual animals,or strange
    phenomena)

TAKE SEXTANT SIGHTS: when convenient or necessary

FISH

IF IN DOUBT AS TO A SAIL CHANGE WAKE UP OTHERS

FOR ANY BIG ADJUSTMENT (SAIL CHANGE,REEFING,ETC.) GET HELP ON DECK

EXAMINE MAINTENANCE CHECKLIST TO BE SURE DUTIES ARE CARRIED OUT

USE CHANNEL 16 OVER RADIOTELEPHONE.STATE: POSITION,NAME OF VESSEL,
                                        NATURE OF EMERGENCY, MAYDAY·
                                        MAYDAY (REPEAT MESSAGE)

EMERGENCY

EMERGENCY

SET UP AND TURN ON NARCO EPIRB & PLACE NEAR RAFT, <u>DISTRESS</u> <u>CALL</u> <u>CH.16</u>

*ABANDON SHIP PROCEDURE:

READY LIFERAFT BUT DO NOT LAUNCH UNTIL LAST MINUTE

GRAB: 1. 5 GALLON WATER CONTAINER

2. BOOKS: <u>SEA SURVIVAL</u> & <u>PARTICULARIZED NAVIGATION</u>

3. FIRST AID CHEST

4. SWEATER AND FOUL WEATHER GEAR FOR EVERYBODY

5. VITAMIN PILLS

6. DINGHY AND BELLOWS PUMP

7. LOCAL LARGE AREA CHART

8. ANY REMAINING FLARES AND LAUNCHER

9. PENCIL

10.FLASHLIGHT

11.MORE WATER

12.FOOD (CANS IN PREPARED BAG)

13.NAVIGATIONAL EQUIPMENT: sextant,chronometer,compass,almanac,
                          reduction tables H.O.249,pencil

14.SECOND DINGHY

15.SONY RADIO

16.DOCKLINE

17.FISHING GEAR

18.MORE FOOD

* BEFORE ABANDONNING SHIP, SEND OUT <u>DISTRESS MESSAGES</u>,<u>USE FLARES</u> IF
  POSSIBLY HELPFUL, MAKE EVERY EFFORT TO SAVE THE SAILBOAT USING
  FIRE EXTINGUISHERS,PUMP,SEA WATER FOR FIRES,SAILS TO PATCH HULL.
  ONLY GIVE ABANDON SHIP ORDER AND INFLATE RAFT IF SAILBOAT IS CLEARLY
  LOST AND UNSAFE TO REMAIN ABOARD.

MAINTENANCE

1. chafe-daily watch duty

2. mast check:condition of everything attached to the mast (i.e. antenna,wind indicator,lights,spreaders,haliards,clevis pins, cotter pins & rings,turnbuckles,winches)- every week

3. condition of sails-daily watch duty

4. check all bulbs-once a week and before entering port

5. check stanchions: anchor brackets,lifelines,pins,bases-once a week

6. check all bolts and screws-constantly (thoroughly once a week)

7. check attachment of liferaft-once a day late afternoon watch

8. look at forehatch: hinges,latch,gasket-once a week

9. check all rigging attachments at deck level: turnbuckles,pins,etc.- once a day late afternoon watch

10. check screws around windows-once a week

11. check handrails-once a day at least

12. check operation of winches, lubrication, and attachment-once a week

13. grease winches-as needed perhaps every three weeks

14. check tiller and post- once a day first daylight watch

15. check all tracks- once a week

16. check all blocks,clean and lubricate-once a week

17. check man overboard pole and horseshoe ring-once a day first daylight watch

18. check flashlights-once a day late afternoon watch

19. check watertanks for leakage,contamination- once a day after noon sight reduction

20. clean head-every other day

21. check water in bilge-once a day,early morning first daylight watch note in log any unusual accumulation of water

22. check stove:clogged burners,gimballing,knobs,leaks in alcohol line-by cook after every use of the stove or oven

23. engine:start ,check battery(levels and charge level),check oil,gas, water and exhaust outflow-every other day after noon sights

24. underwater:check sumlog & speedometers,scrape growth,examine and unclog through hulls,propeller,shaft,rudder-every calm day possible

<u>PORT ENTERING CHECKLIST</u>

CLEAN THE BOAT

STOW ALL UNNECESSARY ITEMS AND FISHING GEAR

GET OUT THE FOLLOWING:
1. DOCKLINES
2. DINGHIES
3. OARS
4. FENDERS
5. ANCHOR
6. ANCHORLINE
7. SIGNAL FLAGS
8. DOCUMENTS

TEST ENGINE

BE FAMILIAR WITH LOCAL NAVIGATIONAL AIDS AND CHARTS INCLUDING SAILING
DIRECTIONS

CHECK RUNNING LIGHTS

PUT ON CLOTHES AND WASH

STORM PREPARATIONS

DO A COMPLETE MAINTENANCE CHECK

BATTEN DOWN COMPANIONWAY HATCH

SECURE EVERYTHING BELOW

RUN STORM LIFELINES FORE AND AFT AND ACROSS THE COCKPIT

CLEAR THE DECK:POLES,LINES ANCHORS,SUPERFLUOUS GEAR

HOIST RADAR REFLECTOR

CLOSE ALL THROUGH HULL COCKS EXCEPT COCKPIT DRAINS

PLACE EMERGENCY TOOLS IN READY POSITION (CABLE CUTTERS,WINDOW COVERS)

PLACE LIFE VESTS IN READILY ACCESSIBLE POSITION

CLOSE OFF EXHAUST PIPE

GET STORM JIB READY

SECURE LIFERAFT (CONSIDER MOVING IT TO THE COCKPIT)

SCREW ON THE VENTILATOR CAP

TAKE SEASICKNESS PILLS IN ADVANCE

CHECK OPERATION OF THE BILGE PUMP AND PUMP OUT THE BILGE

GET WARPS AND SEA ANCHORS READY

PREPARE HOT FOODS AND PUT IN THERMOS BOTTLE

DISCUSS STRATEGY FOR SAILING THROUGH THE STORM

A Unique Celestial Fix

THIS IS AN interesting detail for those familiar with the theory of celestial navigation. One day in the mid-Pacific I used a method that I had never seen described. While studying the nautical almanac, I noticed that, by coincidence on that day, the sun would pass nearly directly overhead, within a degree of our zenith. I took two sun sights approximately an hour apart, around local noon. I simply used a compass to draw circles of position upon our large-area Mercator chart for both sextant readings. The radius of each circle in nautical miles was equal to the angular distance in minutes of arc, between the sun and our zenith point, determined by the sextant. The center of each circle was simply the position of the sun as obtained from the nautical almanac. The intersection of the two circles created a position fix without requiring complicated reduction. (The first circle was advanced to account for the distance sailed between the two fixes and one of the intersection points was disregarded based upon our assumed position.)

Stowage Key

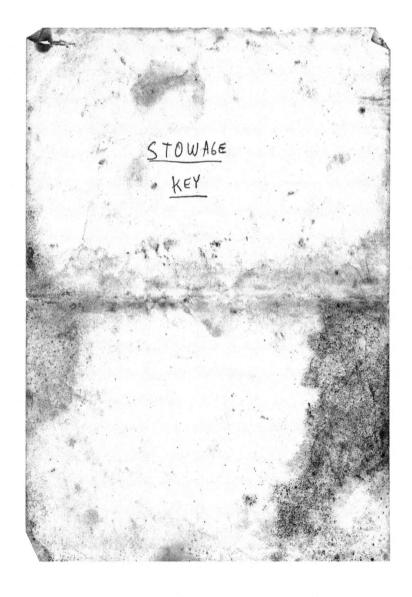

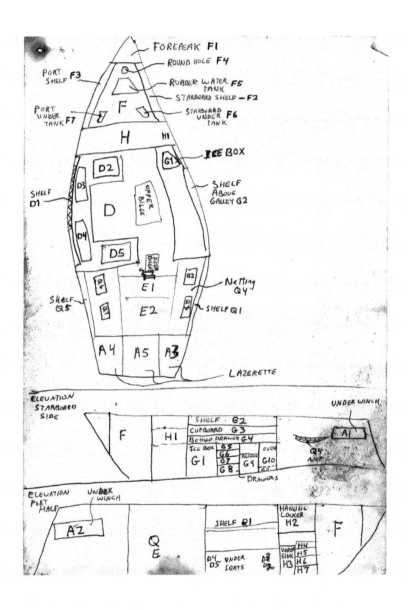

```
2Air horn ------------------------------------------- Q03
Air pump - hand (2) -------------------------------- D3 and G9
               bellows -------------------------------- F3
               extra foot pump and needles --------- F3
Alcohol, 6 one gallon cans (in box) ------------ A5
Alcohol, 5 gallon gas can -------------------- E2
Alcohol, 3 one gallon cans -------------------- D3
Alcohol tank -------------------------------------G9
Alcohol funnel ----------------------------------G9
Allen wrench set.--------------------------------D5
Aluminum foil -----------------------------------G6
Aluminum bar (cased)----------------------------#2
Awning ------------------------------------------ M4
Battens
```

```
BANK BAGS ---------------------------------- G2
Battens- 4 in main, 8' above handrail, 2' in Q2
Batteries 2 storage batteries --- starboard side engine
          D and C cell ---------------------- D3
Barometer -------------------------------- main bulkhead
Bellows ------------------------------------------ F 3
Binoculars --------------------------------------- Q5
Bits -------------------------------------------D5
Blocks - snatch --------------------------------G7
         spare ------------------------------------D5 (greenbag)
Bolts -------------------------------------------D5
Bolt Cutter -------------------------------------Q2
Books -------------------------------------------Q1
      H.O. 111 B
      H.O. 117 A
      H.O. 117B
      1977 Almanac
      Dutton's
8-6 Ship's log
      Royce's Sailing Illustrated
      Deep Water and Shoal
      Slocum
      Return to the Sea
      Sea Witch
      Review of Standard French
      Shogun
      The Bastard
      The Titans
      Homer's Odyssey
      Centennial
      Fletch
      Book of Card Games
      KON TIKI
      CATCH 22
      CONSTELLATIONS (STARS)
      EXODUS
      FRENCH DICTIONARY
      COASTAL PILOT
      Knots
      Clark's Courses
```

(2)

Books--- (continued)
    Louis' journal
    Celestial Navigation'
8   Code f Signal Flags
    Mike's Journal =------------------------------- Q4
    Navigation Course book ----------------------- Q4
    Nautical Almanac -------------------- magazine rack
    H. O. 249● Vol II ------------------- magazine rack
    H. O. 249 Vol I ------------------------------ Q4
    Joy of Cooking =-------------------------------G3
    Fish cookbook --------------------------------G3
Boom Vang ---F3
Bosun's chair ----------------------------------D5 G11 (under oven)
Buckets 3 small --------------------------------H3
         1 large --------------------------------A3
Bulbs Flashlights, navigation lights, compass ---D3
Bumpers ---A3
Burgee -----v-------- with signal flags --------A4
Bushing ---Q2
4Bowls ----- · · · · · · · ·   under cups main bulkhead A3 in plastic
Blankets -
6 LO A O %, 1603 ----------------------------- H1
crescent wrenches 6", 10", 12" · _ — ——— D5
Cable Clamps - _ _ _ _ _ _ _ — — —   D3
C-clamps - _ _ _ _ _ _ _ _ _ _   D5
Camera - 35 mm case in Q6   D + Q6
Cable - 50' galvanized ------------------------ Q2
Can Openers (2) ------------------------------- G5
Cars -- G7
Chess Set ------------------------------------Q4
Chronometer ----------------------------------Q1
Claw (boom vang) -----------------------------F3
Compass(2) -----------------------------------D1
Compass, magnetic (3)------- Cockpit, Q1, Q3
Copper tubing --------------------------------Q2
Cotter pin● ----------------------------------D5
Cups (4) ----------------- hanging above galley
Cups (3) -------------------- on main bulkhead (S)
Charts - _ _ —   above (P) quarterberth   F2
    Chafe Sleeves - - - _ _ _ _ _ _   D5
3 wood Chisels - _ _ _ _ _ _ _   G5
    Corkscrew
Deck Plate for Vent --------------------------- H5
Depth Sounder --see-also-head-line-Pl-------- Companionway
Dividers (2) =-------------------------------- D1
Drill ---------------------------------------D5
Dip stick for gasoline - · · · · · · · · ·   Q2

#3)

```
Engine controls ------------------------------------- G6
Engine crank --------------------------------------- under steps
Engine parts --------------------------------------- under steps
Ensign ------------------- with signal flags ----- A4
EPIRB ----------------------------------------------Q5
Eraser ---------------------------------------------D1
Etch a Scotch --------------------------------------Q4
```

Face Mask ---- . . . —— — — — — — — —— F1
3 Files - - - - - - - - - - - - - - - D5
Fibreglass - - - - - - - - - - - - - - - - - E1
~~Flyswatter~~ -------------------------------------- H1
Film --1 ~~rapid mailers~~ -----------------------------Q 3
```
Fishing Gear ---------------------------------------D1
Fish Scaler ----------------------------------------G5
Fire Extinguisher  B.C. ----------------------------Q (S)
                   A.B.C. --------------------------Q (P)
Flags, Signal --------------------------------------A4
Flares ---------------------------------------------G2
Flare Gun ------------------------------------------G2
Flashlights (6) Q1,Q5, ██, H5, Emergency Pack, 62
Flints ---------------------------------------------D2
Flyswatter------------------------------------------H1
Fog Horn  black ----------------------- next to speedometer
          air---------------------------------------Q4
Footpump -------------------------------------------F3
Frying Pan -----------------------------------------G10
Funnel, alcohol ------------------------------------G9
```
Fuses^{Balavlse} food (2) --------------------- drinking glasses
                       D3 - H3
Flippers - - - - - - - - - - - - - - - - F1
Funnel, gasoline - - - - - - - - - - E1
  kerosene - (w/ - Kerosene) - - - - - - - E1
```
Galley Strap --------------------------------------- D5
Gas Cap wrench ------------------------------------- H5
Glasses (eye) -------------------------------------- H5
Gloves --------------------------------------------- D5
GraPh Paper -------------------------- magazine rack
Grease- camera ------------------------------------- G8
         Barlow ----------------------------------- G8
         can greASE -------------------------------G8
Gunk ----------------------------------------------G8
```
Glue - - -   - G8

(4)

HAND LOTION ———————————————————————————— H3
Hacksaw + spare Blades ——————————————————— D5
Hanks ——————————————————————————————————— D3
Hammer --- D5
Handles (winch) -------------------------------------A2
Hose Clamp 1½", 3/4"; ------------------------------ D5
Claw Hammer ———————————————————————————————— D5

Inflatable Dinghies ------------------------------- F
Inflatable Cushions (2) --------------------------- F
Insect Repellant ---------------------------------- H6 & H4
Instruction Folder (blue) ------------------------ D3
     VFH
     Cal 2--30   SONY RADIO
     Depth Sounder
     RDF
   Kno Knotmeter
     underwater
     wind indicater
     Atomic - 4
Ivory Liquid -------------------------------------- H3
Ivory Soap -- H4

Kerosene ——————————————————————————— E1 AND A5
Kerosene lamp spare ------------------------------- D3
Kerosene wicks ------------------------------------ D3
Knife, curved ------------------------------------- D5

Leadline -- A1
Lens , 100mm -------------------------------------- Q4
     35mm ---------------------------------- on camera
Life Jackets (3)----------------------------------- A4
Line   3/8", 100ft. ------------------------------ F1
     5/32" -------------------------------------F
     5/16" ----------------------------------- F4
     ½" -------------------------------------- F
     3/4" ------------------------------------ D1
     5/8 ------------------------------------- F

(5)

Magnet - D5

Magnifying glass ------------------------------------- ~~HG~~ H5

Man Overboard - horse shoe, strobe, pole --- stern pulpit

Matches (6 boxes waxed) ---------------------- G8

measuring cup ------------------------------- G5

Mop Head ------------------------------------- H3

Mosquito Netting ---------------------------- D3 ; D4

Noodle Nose - D5

Nails -- D5

Narco -- Q5

Needle Nose Pliers -------------------------- D5

Netting (Mosquito) --------------------------D3 ; D4

Nuts, 1"# ------------ on tie rod ------------- Q2

Nuts (6?) ---------------- on various members of the crew)

tacked under

Oak ----------------------------- ~~over~~ Galley

Oil can - - - - - - - - - - - - - - - - D5

Paint, Bottom and Boot topm ---------- ------- E1

Parallel Rule ------------------------- magazine rack

Pawls -- D3

Pencils -------------------------------------- D1

Pencil Sharpener ---------------------------- D1

Phillips Screw Driver ----------------------- D5

Plain Paper --------------------------------- Q6

Plane --------------------------------------- D5

Plastic Freezer containers -----------------G2

Plates (4) ---------------------------------G2

Plate for Ventilater -----------------------H5

2 Pliers -------------------------------------D5

Plotting Sheets ----------------------------Q6

Prell (2 tubes) ----------------------------H4

Protracter ---------------------------------D1

Protractor (one arm) ----------------------D1

Pump, bilge, 2 foot, 2 hand, (see cross reference) under AIR

Pins for alcohol tauk - - - - - - - - - - - - - D3

Pointed Pliers - - - - - - - - - - - D5

2 Pipe Wrenches - - - - - - - - - - - D5

Radar reflector -----------------------------------A1

Radio, VHF --Q5

Radio, Sony and adapter --------------------- Q5

RDF -- F2

Reduction Sheets ------------------------- magazine racks

Resin Glue - - - - - - - - - - - - - E1

(6)

Rigging parts ------------------------------------D5
Rivits --- D5
Rivit Gun -- D5
Rubber Bands -------------------------------------D5
Rudder Post Head ---------------------------------D3
Rugs   A9

SkiM   D3
SheARS (scissors) [Thinning scissors in B4]   G5
Sheets (bedding) -   A5 in plastic
SAUce PAN   G10
Saw   Q2
Safety Harness   D1, (2) Q1
Sails :
    Main-- Boom
    Working Jib-------------------------------- Forward
    Storm Jib---------------------------------- H1
    Staysl ------------------------------------ F5
    175% light Jib ---------------------------- Forward
    175% heavy Jib ---------------------------- Forward
    150% jib ---------------------------------- Forward
    .75 Spinnaker ----------------------------- F5
    1.5 Spinnaker ----------------------------- Forward
Sail Cloth ----------------------------------- Q2
Sail Repair kit ------------------------------ D3
Sealer --------------------------------------- G5 — G5
Screens for portholes (2) -------------------- H5
Screen for bilge pump ------------------------ H5
Scouring Pads -------------------------------- H5 G9 : G5
Scrapers ------------------------------------- D5
screws --------------------------------------- D5
7 screw Drivers ------------------------------ D5
scrub brush ---------------------------------- D5
Sea Anchor ----------------------------------- F1
Sextents, Heath ------------------------------ Q5
          EBBCO ------------------------------ F2
Shampoo -------------------------------------- H4
Shock Cord stop ------------------------------ G7 : A2
Silicone (9tubes) ---------------------------- G8
Snatch blocks -------------------------------- G7
Soap --- H4
Soup Pot ------------------------------------- G10
Spark Lighter (Strike) ----------------------- G5
Spark Plug wrench ---------------------------- D5
Spatula -------------------------------------- H3
Sponges, large ------------------------------- G9
        small -------------------------------- F3
Sail Sheets   D5
Sledge hamer
Sea Sickness (Rec.)   G2

(7)

```
Spoon - non mixing-------------------------------- G5
Springs ------------------------------------------ D3
Strainer ----------------------------------------- G5
Strap- stinless steel ---------------------------- D3  +2 extras
Sumlog ------------------------------------------- Q5  S H7(full)
Suntan loion ------------------------------------- H4
swages ------------------------------------------- D3
Swage tool heads ( 2 ) --------------------------- D5
Syphon Tub --------------------------------------- G9
Surgical tube,                                       A2
Silverware                                           G5

Towels  ----                    ----  ---  ---  -  -  A3
Triangular bandages  --   --   -   -   -             D1
Tennis Balls                                         H1 (F1)
Tape Measure  --                                     D5
Tape, scotch --                                      B1
       grey,masking, electrical -----------------   G7 +Spares
Thermos ------------------------------------------  G9
Through Hull tube and valve ----------------------  D3
Tie Rods (2) -------------------------------------  Q2
Tiller Extension ---------------------------------  Q2
Toothpaste ---------------------------------------  H4
dish Towel ---------------------------------------  G6
Thimbles ---                                         D5
Turnbuckle ½" ------                                 D1
Velcro cement                                        G8
Varnish ------------------------------------------  E1
Vasoline -----------------------------------------  H4
Velcro -------------------------------------------  D3
Vise ---------------------------------------------  D5
Wet Suit -----------------------------------------  H2
Whipping Twine -----------------------------------  F3
Wicks --------------------------------------------  D3
Winch Handle (2) ---------------------------------  A1/A2
Wire Brush ---------------------------------------  D5
Wood Spare--------------------         over Galley; 1A
wrench -------------------------------------------  D5
Wrench, head, water tank, sparkplugs, -----------   G5
Wet Stone  -                                         D3
Wrench for gasoline line (handle for valve) -- ---  D5
Vise grip pliers  -                                  D5
Wirecutter  ---                                      H1
Wisk, 16 oz                                          Q2
wire (electric)                                      H7
Whisk brown                                         
Zinc Oxide                                 -  -     Q7
```